Television Histories in Asia

This book presents an analysis of television histories across India, China, Taiwan, Singapore, Indonesia, Japan, Hong Kong, the Philippines, Malaysia and Bhutan. It offers a set of standard data on the history of television's cultural, industrial and political structures in each specific national context, allowing for cross-regional comparative analysis. Each chapter presents a case study on a salient aspect of the contemporary television culture of the nation in question, such as analyses of ideology in television content in Japan and Singapore, and transformations of industry structure vis-à-vis state versus market control in China and Taiwan. The book provides a comprehensive overview of television histories in Asia as well as a survey of current issues and concerns in Asian television cultures and their social and political impact.

Jinna Tay is a Lecturer in the School of Media, Film and Journalism at Monash University, Australia.

Graeme Turner is Professor of Cultural Studies in the Centre for Critical and Cultural Studies at the University of Queensland, Australia.

Media, Culture and Social Change in Asia

Series Editor

Stephanie Hemelryk Donald, *University of Liverpool*

Editorial Board

Gregory N. Evon, *University of New South Wales*
Devleena Ghosh, *University of Technology, Sydney*
Peter Horsfield, *RMIT University, Melbourne*
Chris Hudson, *RMIT University, Melbourne*
K.P. Jayasankar, *Unit for Media and Communications,*
Tata Institute of Social Sciences, Bombay
Michael Keane, *Queensland University of Technology*
Tania Lewis, *RMIT University, Melbourne*
Vera Mackie, *University of Melbourne*
Kama Maclean, *University of New South Wales*
Jane Mills, *University of New South Wales*
Anjali Monteiro, *Unit for Media and Communications,*
Tata Institute of Social Sciences, Bombay
Laikwan Pang, *Chinese University of Hong Kong*
Gary Rawnsley, *Aberystwyth University*
Ming-yeh Rawnsley, *University of Leeds*
Jo Tacchi, *RMIT University, Melbourne*
Adrian Vickers, *University of Sydney*
Jing Wang, *MIT*
Ying Zhu, *City University of New York*

The aim of this series is to publish original, high-quality work by both new and established scholars in the West and the East, on all aspects of media, culture and social change in Asia.

1 Television Across Asia
Television industries, programme formats and globalisation
Edited by Albert Moran and Michael Keane

2 Journalism and Democracy in Asia
Edited by Angela Romano and Michael Bromley

3 Cultural Control and Globalization in Asia
Copyright, piracy and cinema
Laikwan Pang

4 Conflict, Terrorism and the Media in Asia
Edited by Benjamin Cole

5 **Media and the Chinese Diaspora**
Community, communications and commerce
Edited by Wanning Sun

6 **Hong Kong Film, Hollywood and the New Global Cinema**
No film is an island
Edited by Gina Marchetti and Tan See Kam

7 **Media in Hong Kong**
Press freedom and political change 1967–2005
Carol P. Lai

8 **Chinese Documentaries**
From dogma to polyphony
Yingchi Chu

9 **Japanese Popular Music**
Culture, authenticity and power
Carolyn S. Stevens

10 **The Origins of the Modern Chinese Press**
The influence of the Protestant missionary press in late Qing China
Xiantao Zhang

11 **Created in China**
The great new leap forward
Michael Keane

12 **Political Regimes and the Media in Asia**
Edited by Krishna Sen and Terence Lee

13 **Television in Post-Reform China**
Serial dramas, Confucian leadership and the global television market
Ying Zhu

14 **Tamil Cinema**
The cultural politics of India's other film industry
Edited by Selvaraj Velayutham

15 **Popular Culture in Indonesia**
Fluid identities in post-authoritarian politics
Edited by Ariel Heryanto

16 **Television in India**
Satellites, politics and cultural change
Edited by Nalin Mehta

17 **Media and Cultural Transformation in China**
Haiqing Yu

18 **Global Chinese Cinema**
The culture and politics of 'Hero'
Edited by Gary D. Rawnsley and Ming-Yeh T. Rawnsley

19 **Youth, Society and Mobile Media in Asia**
Edited by Stephanie Hemelryk Donald, Theresa Dirndorfer Anderson and Damien Spry

20 **The Media, Cultural Control and Government in Singapore**
Terence Lee

21 **Politics and the Media in Twenty-First Century Indonesia**
Edited by Krishna Sen and David T. Hill

22 **Media, Social Mobilization and Mass Protests in Post-colonial Hong Kong**
The power of a critical event
Francis L. F. Lee and Joseph M. Chan

23 **HIV/AIDS, Health and the Media in China**
Imagined immunity through racialized disease
Johanna Hood

24 **Islam and Popular Culture in Indonesia and Malaysia**
Edited by Andrew N. Weintraub

25 **Online Society in China**
Creating, celebrating, and instrumentalising the online carnival
Edited by David Kurt Herold and Peter Marolt

26 **Rethinking Transnational Chinese Cinemas**
The Amoy-dialect film industry in Cold War Asia
Jeremy E. Taylor

27 **Film in Contemporary Southeast Asia**
Cultural interpretation and social intervention
Edited by David C. L. Lim and Hiroyuki Yamamoto

28 **China's New Creative Clusters**
Governance, human capital, and investment
Michael Keane

29 **Media and Democratic Transition in South Korea**
Ki-Sung Kwak

30 **The Asian Cinema Experience**
Styles, spaces, theory
Stephen Teo

31 **Asian Popular Culture**
Edited by Anthony Y. H. Fung

32 **Rumor and Communication in Asia in the Internet Age**
Edited by Greg Dalziel

33 **Genders and Sexualities in Indonesian Cinema**
Constructing gay, lesbi and waria identities on screen
Ben Murtagh

34 **Contemporary Chinese Print Media**
Cultivating middle class taste
Yi Zheng

35 **Culture, Aesthetics and Affect in Ubiquitous Media**
The prosaic image
Helen Grace

36 **Democracy, Media and Law in Malaysia and Singapore**
A space for speech
Edited by Andrew T. Kenyon, Tim Marjoribanks and Amanda Whiting

37 **Indonesia-Malaysia Relations**
Cultural heritage, politics and labour migration
Marshall Clark and Juliet Pietsch

38 **Chinese and Japanese Films on the Second World War**
Edited by King-fai Tam, Timothy Y. Tsu and Sandra Wilson

39 **New Chinese-Language Documentaries**
Ethics, subject and place
Kuei-fen Chiu and Yingjin Zhang

40 **K-pop – The International Rise of the Korean Music Industry**
Edited by JungBong Choi and Roald Maliangkay

41 China Online
Locating society in online spaces
*Edited by Peter Marolt and
David Kurt Herold*

42 Multimedia Stardom in Hong Kong
Image, performance and identity
Leung Wing-Fai

43 Television Histories in Asia
Issues and contexts
*Edited by Jinna Tay and
Graeme Turner*

44 Media and Communication in the Chinese Diaspora
Rethinking transnationalism
*Edited by Wanning Sun and
John Sinclair*

Television Histories in Asia
Issues and contexts

Edited by Jinna Tay and Graeme Turner

LONDON AND NEW YORK

First published 2015
by Routledge
2 Park Square, Milton Park, Abingdon, Oxon OX14 4RN

and by Routledge
711 Third Avenue, New York, NY 10017

First issued in paperback 2017

Routledge is an imprint of the Taylor & Francis Group, an informa business

© 2015 Jinna Tay and Graeme Turner

The right of the editors to be identified as the authors of the editorial material, and of the authors for their individual chapters, has been asserted in accordance with sections 77 and 78 of the Copyright, Designs and Patents Act 1988.

All rights reserved. No part of this book may be reprinted or reproduced or utilized in any form or by any electronic, mechanical, or other means, now known or hereafter invented, including photocopying and recording, or in any information storage or retrieval system, without permission in writing from the publishers.

Trademark notice: Product or corporate names may be trademarks or registered trademarks, and are used only for identification and explanation without intent to infringe.

British Library Cataloguing in Publication Data
A catalogue record for this book is available from the British Library

Library of Congress Cataloguing in Publication data
Television histories in Asia : issues and contexts / edited by Jinna Tay and Graeme Turner.
    pages   cm. – (Media, culture and social change in asia series ; 43)
Includes bibliographical references and index.
1. Television broadcasting–Asia–History.   2. Television–Asia–History.
3. Television broadcasting–Asia–Case studies.   4. Television–Asia–
Case studies.   I. Tay, Jinna.   II. Turner, Graeme.
HE8700.9.A78T447 2015
384.55095–dc23
2014044548

ISBN 13: 978-0-8153-5520-5 (pbk)
ISBN 13: 978-0-415-85536-5 (hbk)

Typeset in Times New Roman
by Out of House Publishing

Contents

List of figures	xi
List of tables	xii
Notes on contributors	xiii
Acknowledgements	xvi

1 Introduction: television histories in Asia:
   nation-building, modernization and marketization   1
   JINNA TAY AND GRAEME TURNER

2 Television, scale and place-identity in the
   PRC: provincial, national and global influences
   from 1958 to 2013   19
   WANNING SUN AND LAUREN GORFINKEL

3 Trust and television in globalizing India   38
   DIVYA MCMILLIN

4 Watching television in Bhutan   58
   BUNTY AVIESON

5 Battling angels and golden orange blossoms: Thai
   television and/as the popular public sphere   74
   BRETT FARMER

6 Dramatizing the nation: television, history and the
   construction of Singaporean identity   92
   JINNA TAY

7 Working women and romance on Japanese television
   dramas: changes since *Tokyo Love Story*   112
   ALISA FREEDMAN

x *Contents*

8 Unpacking multiculturalism and Islam in
   Malaysia: state–corporate television celebrations of
   Bangsa Malaysia   127
   UMI KHATTAB

9 The television of intervention: mediating
   patron–client ties in the Philippines   144
   JONATHAN CORPUS ONG

10 Taiyu serial dramas in Taiwan: a history of
   problem-making   164
   FANG-CHIH IRENE YANG

11 Shifts in Korean television music
   programmes: democratization, transnationalization,
   digitalization   182
   SUN JUNG

12 Cultural polysemy and vernacular cosmopolitanism in
   the theme songs of Hong Kong television dramas   198
   LIEW KAI KHIUN

   Appendix: television data across countries   216
   Index   227

Figures

4.1	Popularity of different media	61
4.2	Bhutanese perception of the cultures they watch on cable television	66
4.3	People's perception of television's impact on Bhutanese society	68
4.4	A Twitter link sent on 24 February 2013 directed followers to the 2003 *Guardian* story	70
9.1	Fisherfolk on Bantayan Island received livelihood assistance from GMA Network following Typhoon Haiyan	145
12.1	Televisual rhythmic spectrum of TVB's drama theme songs	202

Tables

6.1	Nationalization and Singapore drama	97
11.1	Five periods in Korean television broadcasting	184
11.2	Major music programmes in KBS, 1961–4	185
11.3	Broadcasting programming ratio of each station, 1970–1	186
11.4	2011 audience behaviour in viewing methods	193
12.1	'Heroic' and 'happy': characteristics of historical drama and contemporary 'harmonious' family drama theme songs	206
12.2	Classification of TVB dramas and theme songs	209
A.1	List of television stations in Thailand	225
A.2	Structure of television provision in Thailand	226

Contributors

Bunty Avieson is a Lecturer in the media department of the University of Sydney. She went to Bhutan in 2008/9 as a UN-funded media consultant, training journalists and advising management on the *Bhutan Observer* newspaper, as well as consulting to Reporters Without Borders (Asia Desk). Her PhD investigated the emerging mediascape in the new democracy of Bhutan, winning a Vice Chancellor's Commendation for Excellence from Macquarie University. She has a Masters of Philosophy and an Associate Diploma of Journalism. She worked as a journalist for 25 years in Britain and Australia, has authored three crime novels, a novella, and a travel memoir and has written extensively on Bhutan. Her books have been translated variously into German, Japanese and Thai.

Brett Farmer is an independent scholar and Research Fellow of Chulalongkorn University. The author of numerous publications in cultural, media and sexuality studies, his current research focuses on Thai cinema and cultural modernity.

Alisa Freedman is Associate Professor of Japanese Literature and Film at the University of Oregon. Her books include *Tokyo in Transit: Japanese Culture on the Rails and Road* (Stanford University Press), an annotated translation of Kawabata Yasunari's *The Scarlet Gang of Asakusa* (University of California Press), and a co-edited volume, *Modern Girls on the Go: Gender, Mobility, and Labor in Japan* (Stanford University Press). She has authored articles and edited collections on Japanese modernism, urban studies, youth culture, gender discourses, television history and intersections of literature and digital media, along with publishing translations of Japanese novels and short stories.

Lauren Gorfinkel is a Lecturer in International Communication at Macquarie University. Her research interests include the cultural politics of Chinese media in China and the world, the media's constructions of national and ethnic identity, music television and intercultural/interlingual approaches to media education. Recent articles appeared in *Media Information Australia* (2014), *Critical Multimodal Studies of Popular Discourse* (2013), xiv *Contributors*

China's Rise to Power: Conceptions of State Governance (2012) and *Music as Intangible Cultural Heritage: Policy, Ideology, and Practice in the Preservation of East Asian Traditions* (2012).

Sun Jung is a Research Fellow at the Asia Research Institute. She has published broadly on South Korean popular cultures, lifestyles and transnational media flows, including the monograph *Korean Masculinities and Transcultural Consumption* (Hong Kong University Press, 2011) and the forthcoming monograph tentatively titled *K-pop and Korean Popular Culture* (Ashgate). Her current projects include social media and cross-border cultural transmissions; K-pop: art of cultural capital; neoliberal capitalism, sustainable lifestyles and media representations; participatory public space; and women and creative activism in neoliberal Asian cultural industries.

Umi Khattab is Senior Lecturer in the School of Communication, University of the Sunshine Coast. Prior to joining USC she taught and researched at the University of Melbourne and at Malaysian universities. Khattab freelanced and wrote as a columnist while teaching in Malaysia.

Liew Kai Khiun is an Assistant Professor with the Wee Kim Wee School of Communication and Information at the Nanyang Technological University

Divya McMillin is Professor of Global Media Studies and Director of the Institute for Global Engagement at the University of Washington Tacoma. She is author of *International Media Studies* (Blackwell Publishing, 2007) and *Mediated Identities: Youth, Agency, and Globalization* (Peter Lang Publishing, 2009), which draw from postcolonial theory to critique international scholarship and to empirically examine youth cultures within globalizing economies, respectively. McMillin's fieldwork and critical analyses of how globalization is experienced in various parts of the world, particularly India, have been published in the *Journal of Communication*, *Popular Communication Journal*, *International Journal of Cultural Studies*, *Economic and Political Weekly*, *Continuum: Journal of Media and Cultural Studies*, *Indian Journal of Gender Studies*, and the *International Communication Bulletin*, to name a few. Her book chapters have been published in such anthologies as *TV's Betty Goes Global* (I.B. Tauris, 2013), *Re-Orienting Global Communication* (University of Illinois Press, 2010), *South Asian Technospaces* (Peter Lang, 2008), *Girl Wide Web* (Peter Lang, 2006) and *Planet TV* (New York University Press, 2003). Currently she is developing new research on soft power and the global format industry.

Jonathan Corpus Ong is Lecturer in Media and Communications at the University of Leicester. Ong is a PhD in Sociology from Corpus Christi College, University of Cambridge, where he was also Bill Gates Trust Scholar. His first book is to be published by Anthem Press as *The Poverty of Television: Suffering, Ethics and the Media*. He is currently Co-Investigator to the 'Humanitarian Technologies Project: Communications in the Wake of Typhoon Haiyan', funded by the UK's Economic and Social Research Council.

Wanning Sun is Professor of Chinese Media and Cultural Studies in the China Research Centre at University of Technology, Sydney. She was Visiting Professor in the Asian and Asian American Studies programme at State University of New York from 2005 to 2006. Wanning is the author of two single-author monographs: *Leaving China: Media, Migration, and Transnational Imagination* (Rowman and Littlefield, 2002), and *Maid in China: Media, Morality and the Cultural Politics of Boundaries* (Routledge, 2009). She is the co-editor (with Michael Keane) of the four-volume *Media in China: Key Concepts and Critical Analyses* (Routledge, 2013). Currently she is completing a manuscript on the media practices of working-class rural migrants in China as well as co-authoring a manuscript on lifestyle television in Asia.

Jinna Tay is a Lecturer with the School of Media, Film, and Journalism in Monash University, Melbourne. Prior to that she completed her post-doctoral fellowship at the Centre for Critical and Cultural Studies at the University of Queensland. She co-edited *Television Studies After TV* with Graeme Turner and has published on *Asian Idol*, television systems, celebrity activism, and fashion magazines in Asia. Her research interests are: Asian cities and cultures, dance and sociality, community building, social media, cultural history, national identities and all manner of weird and wonderful television programmes.

Graeme Turner is Emeritus Professor in the Centre for Critical and Cultural Studies at the University of Queensland, Brisbane. Among the leaders in Australian cultural and media studies, he has published 23 books and his work has been translated into ten languages. His most recent books include a revised edition of his influential *Understanding Celebrity* (2014), *Locating Television: Zones of Consumption* (with Anna Cristina Pertierra, 2013), *What's Become of Cultural Studies?* (2012) and *Ordinary People and the Media: The Demotic Turn* (2010).

Fang-Chih Irene Yang is a Professor teaching Cultural Studies in the Department of Taiwanese Literature in National Cheng Kung University, Taiwan. Her publications focus on US and Asian influences on Taiwanese TV dramas and women's magazines and how these influences open up or close down gender, class and ethnic politics.

Acknowledgements

For reasons that were largely beyond our control, this volume has taken us a little longer to pull together than expected. So we would like to thank all our contributors for their patience and forbearance; hopefully they will feel it was worth the wait! We also wish to thank Fran Martin, who helped in planning the original framework for the book, and Koichi Iwabuchi, who provided valuable expertise, comment and advice as we developed the collection. And a big thank you to our families for their constant support of our work. Finally, we are grateful to our editor at Routledge, Peter Sowden, for his commitment to the project and staying with us along the way to completion. It has been a project of belief and passion: belief in the importance of pulling together all these scholars from Asia, and passion for the idea of retelling our television histories. We also wish to thank the Ministry of Information and The Arts Collection, courtesy of National Archives of Singapore for the permission to use the cover image.

1 Introduction

Television histories in Asia: nation-building, modernization and marketization

Jinna Tay and Graeme Turner

In Asia, as in so many other locations outside the US, television was global before it became local. Commencing as it did in the West, and in the Global North, the period of technological advancement that continued with ever-accelerating pace from the mid-1950s onwards often ran slightly ahead of the emergence of politically independent nation-states in Asia. That is especially true for postcolonial countries such as Hong Kong, Singapore, Malaysia and the Philippines – even, as Divya McMillin argues in this collection, for India – as well as for a nation-state such as Taiwan as it has struggled to construct a distinctly Taiwanese national identity. In Singapore, Jinna Tay watched the same programmes as she was growing up as did her contemporaries in Australia where she now works: *Little House on the Prairie* and *Hawaii Five-O*. The generation before her watched *Doctor Who, I Dream of Jeannie*, and so on. These Western texts would have made their rounds across many Asian television screens as national television systems began the cultural, political and industrial process of establishing their relation to their national audiences. As Umi Khattab's chapter on Malaysia in this volume argues, even the definition of these audiences as 'national' has often proven to be a long, highly contested and difficult process. This is evident at the most fundamental levels: for instance, before the creation of an independent nation-state, or in some cases before the establishment of an official 'national language' in multiethnic societies such Singapore, local dialects were often used in early broadcasting – and in some cases now (India, for example), they still are. As we shall see time and again in the national case studies collected in this book, the particular relation between the local and the national, the regional and the global, the indigenous and the imported, is the highly specific product of particular historical conditions and contingencies. The investigation of these conditions and contingencies in each of our locations is what this book sets out to provide – a nuanced and complicated understanding of the histories of television in Asia, across localities, states and the region.

As we have argued elsewhere (Turner and Tay, 2009) to speak of television now without recognition of the specificities of its operation across geographic, linguistic, social, cultural and political differences is to work against the grain of contemporary directions in television studies. The project of de-Westernizing media studies, and television studies in particular, has been in train since at least the early 2000s (Curran and Park 2000). As a consequence, even in the mainstream of Anglo-American television studies, the default normatization of the British or US context is much less common now than would have been the case 20 years ago. There is now a substantial body of work that turns its attention towards the specificities of the locations of television beyond the Anglo-American centre (for example Keane et al. 2007; Kraidy 2010; Pertierra and Turner 2013) and that is concerned with understanding the roots and provenance of such specificities. Even though much of the discussion about the industrial and technological changes that have swept through television industries in what is so often described as the post-broadcast era has tended to emphasize the common elements linking the various national systems, there is an increasing recognition of the scale and the importance of the differences between these systems, their functions and their histories. Among the shifts such a recognition entails has been the problematization of the longstanding tendency towards a national focus for television studies, with the exploration of other possibilities for conceptualizing what Pertierra and Turner (2013) describe as 'zones of consumption'. Asian television, however, remains an underexamined area. While there has been much written about certain aspects of the media's development in the region – the role of the Korean wave in the formation of a transnational East Asian popular culture, the rise of new regional and local production hubs establishing alternative new trading patterns for Asian media content, the marketizing transformation of the Chinese media as political conditions change, and so on – there is still room for many more attempts to enquire into, and to understand, what has gone into making up these distinctive histories.

This book, then, addresses a gap in the international literature on television: first, by focusing solely on Asia, rather than reducing it to the status of one more regional component within a larger international survey; and, second, by directing its attention to the histories of television in that region. The reason for the focus on history reflects the exceptionally close connection between the specific industrial formations and the politico-cultural function of television systems in Asia and their local, national and regional histories. In a region that has been particularly engaged, each state in its own way, in an historic, vigorous and highly diverse programme of modernization over precisely the period during which television established itself as the primary medium of mass communication for the nation-state, Asian television has played an exceptionally prominent role in expressing, managing and representing the cultures of modernity as they have been shaped by political and historical forces.

Among the outcomes of the modernizing and industrializing process of development within the Asia region, and its more recent alignment with a shift away from the manufacture of material commodities towards the development of services and cultural industries, has been the growth of the local/national audience for television and, relatedly, the capacity for local production. In Asia, as elsewhere, the strong preference for local or national programming has proven significant in generating markets of sufficient size to support local production industries. In the past few years, some of this localized programming has capitalized on the existence of strong regional demand that is driven by linguistic and cultural factors; the circulation of Tamil programming across Sri Lanka, India and Singapore is an instance of this (Sankaran and Pillai, 2011). Regional markets for Asian television content have developed, structurally as well as geographically separated from the Western content providers. Western content providers continue to sell their wares in the region, highly successfully, but there are now some important contrasts to the simple colonialist model referred to at the beginning of this chapter. The expanding trade in global formats over the past decade or so has benefited these emerging industries in a new way: global brands that are identified with the modern and fashionable West have become more accessible to Asian audiences through adaptation and franchising. Where the manner in which Western fashions are taken up often carries negative political consequences – in those countries suspicious of cultural Westernization, for instance – the flexibility of formats such as *Idol* has allowed the tailoring of particular local or national versions to the tastes and values of the targeted market. As numerous studies have demonstrated in relation to China in particular (Keane et al. 2007; Sun and Zhao 2009) such tailoring is not only able to accommodate the local value systems but can also adjust to current political priorities.

While it has been relatively common (but not uncontested) within Anglo-American discussions of the post-digital and post-broadcast environment to downplay the continuing relevance of the nation-state, the situation in Asia certainly demands revision of these assumptions. Not only has the nation-state persisted, with more or less the same levels of authority and power it has always enjoyed, but it continues to play a highly interventionist and fundamental role in many of the locations we examine in this book. The chapters on Thailand, Taiwan, Singapore, China, Bhutan and Malaysia all provide examples of this. In general, although the specifics can get quite complicated, it would be true to say that television in Asia remains more closely tied to the construction of national identity than is currently the case in Western Europe, for instance. Indeed, as this collection will demonstrate, there are numerous countries in Asia where this relationship is directly and openly managed by the state. Given the circumstances, this is not surprising. Many Asian states are currently engaged in a significant historical process of transition towards a variety of political, economic or developmental ends: towards a more democratic polity, towards a market economy, towards a postcolonial or modernized and unified national identity, or towards new forms of governance and political control. Television, particularly in states where the levels of literacy and educational access vary widely, is a crucial instrument for those charged with managing such transitions. In fact, it has always played such a role, as Jinna Tay's contribution to this collection argues, television, and in particular television's representation of national histories, has been crucial to the construction of an independent postcolonial national identity in Singapore, and the chapters on Malaysia, Taiwan and Thailand also have their stories to tell about the way such a role has been managed in each location. In the case of the Philippines, where the media is strong but the state is weak, as Jonathan Corpus Ong argues in his chapter, television has actually appropriated some of the nation- and community-building roles more customarily performed by the state.

As so many accounts of television over the past decade or so have been preoccupied with technological change and, perhaps as a consequence of an informal Western tendency to regard American television as the eventual evolutionary destination for systems around the world, much of our sense of the particularity of the functions television performs for its audiences has been dominated by an American perspective. Such a perspective does not help us to understand television histories in Asia. Asian nations have had a diverse and varied relationship to the West, and television has emerged out of equally diverse policy configurations, philosophies and agendas within different Asian countries. While it has had to borrow and adapt from the West, the region has also generated its own more compatible models for production and exchange, as demonstrated by the manner in which Hong Kong, Korea and Japan have developed their own local industries. As we shall see throughout this book, while the project of modernization is in train everywhere, it is not always executed the same way. This is demonstrated in Sun Jung's chapter on the rise of K-pop music and the development of the South Korean media industries.

Television histories are not just about the production of institutional and structural accounts of the history of television; they are also about capturing how television programming has participated in generating and circulating particular understandings of national identities. In their respective chapters, Alisa Freedman (Japan), Brett Farmer (Thailand), Fang-Chih Irene Yang (Taiwan) and Jinna Tay (Singapore) all examine the part played by particular forms of serial drama in the process of nation formation. The genres employed – historical drama and soap opera – may be familiar across cultures but, as these chapters demonstrate, the work they do in each instance is highly specific. It is a reminder to Western media studies that while television may not be always *qualitatively* different (that is, we may not always notice much variation in the kinds of texts produced), the *conditions* under which television is produced, distributed and consumed can vary markedly – and therefore so can the meanings it generates. Television can be both local and global all at once.

While there is a currently dominant tendency within media studies in general towards global accounts and global explanations, examining the histories of television within a region that is so linguistically, culturally, socially, ethnically and politically diverse as Asia unearths a wealth of countervailing stories. Among them are the more detailed accounts of the experience of television that come from the audiences – from their personal memories of their own reception of the programmes. In their *Remembering Television* (2012), Darian-Smith and Turnbull acknowledge that while the accounts produced by such memories are imperfect and informal accounts of personal practices, they are nonetheless important; they help us recover the popular culture experiences that are displaced by the privileging of the more formal accounts of national histories. The retrieval of these memories of television foregrounds the social role of television in interesting and useful ways: it links these broader historical formations to what is an intrinsically domestic experience of identity formation, where 'the theorisation of memory and its engagement with politics and questions of identity, belonging, affect and temporality position the media as both a repository and creator of memories' (Darian-Smith and Turnbull 2012: 2). The media is thus seen as a site of cultural production rather than merely a site of consumption. These memories also return us to the closer consideration of more specific arenas of consumption – such as television's participation in defining the domestic space of the home. Relevant here is the material culture surrounding the television set – the choice and arrangement of furniture, and accessories such as TV lamps, trays, chairs and so on. Frances Bonner (2012) has examined television product 'spin-offs' such as these material objects, seeing them as triggers for memories but also as 'technologies of attachment' that frame the individual's relationship with television through their imbrication within a larger network of everyday practices. In this collection, Liew Kai Khiun's chapter deals with the theme music for Hong Kong television drama as, in a sense, another 'technology of attachment', by highlighting the ways in which this music circulates as memory, both locally and globally. Such approaches locate television as extending beyond its most immediate categorizations as programmes, objects or a set of meanings; the cultural practices that gather around television also provide us with ways of accessing the past and retrieving the historicity of everyday life.

This collection of essays explores a wide range of the ways in which Asian television histories have played out, and it examines them from many perspectives and in many locations. Its coverage is not comprehensive, in that not every nation from the region is represented; we are particularly disappointed that a chapter on Indonesia has not eventuated, for instance. However, the collection does include chapters on China, India, Malaysia, Singapore, Hong Kong, the Philippines, Thailand, Taiwan, Bhutan and Japan; as such, it constitutes a substantial beginning to the process of helping media studies to pay closer attention to the histories of television in Asia. In the remainder of this introduction, we wish to briefly review some themes that run through all of the contributions to this collection and that may inform further studies in the future. Over the next three sections we will summarize three major

6 *Jinna Tay and Graeme Turner*

historical processes we wish to highlight in order to frame the project of this book: the processes are those of nation-building, modernization and marketization.

Nation-building

The history of broadcast television has its foundations in the project of nation-building. In his book on BBC programming in radio and television, Thomas Hajkowski (2010) charts the relations between one of the world's earliest broadcasters' programming and its participation in a process of nation-building; his research demonstrates that, from the beginning, state broadcasters have been recruited to the service of developing the nation. In Asia, the big institutional state broadcasters such as CCTV (China), NHK (Hong Kong), Doordarshan (India) and Mediacorp (Singapore) have functioned as central mass communication apparatuses for their nation-states even though they each serve different political agendas – ranging from the authoritarian to the liberal democratic. Their agendas are broader than the strictly political, of course; state broadcasters have an informational, cultural and, at times, a pedagogical function. Television has been particularly effective as a national informational infrastructure; as a technology it can cut across demographic lines to speak to a mass audience that includes not only the educated elites but also the illiterate segments of the population. As a result, broadcast state-funded television remains the most flexible and powerful medium for mass communication and national identity formation, circulating ideas, images, values and, at times, propaganda with sufficient success to embed it within the processes of government. Even dominant non-state commercial broadcasters, such as TVB in Hong Kong, have performed similar socio-cultural functions (Ma 1999), serving as the key communication, pedagogical and narrative platform for its national audience. As Eric Ma points out, television's critical importance to the historical process of identity formation in Hong Kong does not 'mean that other media are irrelevant to identity formation'; however, where television excels is through its capacity 'reach the public on a regular basis and in a domestic setting' (1999: 33).

In many of the countries we examine in this collection, the timing of the arrival of television in each location was often closely concurrent with the establishment or development of the nation-state itself; this is the case with Singapore, Malaysia and, in more complicated ways, China and India. The strategic and political value of television in such a context cannot be over-estimated; it had the unique capacity to mediate between the interests of the national audience, government, advertisers and other institutions. The national audience in the broadcasting era was, of course, a captive audience, choosing from the same limited menu of content and addressed as a homogenous citizenry with common concerns (Hartley 2004: 9). As a consequence, national viewing patterns supported the idea that this national audience was interested in the affairs of the state and identified with concerns about the nation's development. The creation of the modern audience/citizenry is built on such assumptions, transforming the domestic space into multiple components of a larger nationalized public sphere.

Yet as Sun and Gorfinkel point out in their chapter on the history of Chinese television, the role of the state, and the manner of its participation in nation-building via television, is becoming increasingly blurred and complex. As a general observation, this has some force: Divya McMillin's chapter for instance, demonstrates just how complex the dynamics between the local, the national and the global have become for the television landscape in India. The observation is, however, particularly apposite to the situation in China. The top-down scrutiny and central control that once marked the management of the media is no longer such a key feature of contemporary realities in China. To be sure, TV is still carefully managed as an instrument for propaganda, information and national development. However, there are significant changes related to the arrival of digital technologies, as well as to the marketization and liberalization of aspects of the economy, which means the operation of television as a tool for nation-building in China is much less straightforward than it used to be. Even though China remains one of the strongest authoritarian states in the world, commercial imperatives are now also playing a significant role. Shifting the television industry from a state-sponsored to a self-funded model has opened the way for programme ratings to become key priorities for the commercial provincial stations. The upsurge in the popularity of programmes screened by provincial players such as Hunan Satellite Television, Jiangsu Satellite Television, Anhui Satellite Television, Jiangxi Satellite Television and so on has challenged the supremacy of state-run China Central Television (CCTV) in the areas of drama, entertainment and lifestyle programming. Given the increasing political power now accruing to the local authorities and to the new economic elites, it is debateable how conscientiously the local and provincial stations actually observe central directives. To further complicate this situation, the growth of digital media and the development of IPTV has seen TV downloads and streaming become a widespread means of access; television content is accessed privately via laptop or PC, rather than consumed via the big screen as a 'mass media' activity. While one might deduce from these political, economic and technical shifts that the relation between television and nation-building has become much more attenuated, the spectre of the nation is always there. It remains in the background, as the context against which all these texts are structured and consumed through the key identifiers and formations of contemporary Chinese-ness – from heritage, food, entertainment, future projections and health to political and environmental concerns. The nation is still the platform from which television speaks to its audiences; however, perhaps television now engages more often with the *national individual* rather than only with the national community.

8   *Jinna Tay and Graeme Turner*

Nation-building through television is not merely a simple matter of top-down control or political manipulation. The processes of nation formation we are talking about are more varied and subtle, as well as more politically and historically contingent, than such a formulation would suggest. Furthermore, it is important to note that the range of programming implicated in these processes is wide; it is not just about news or informational programming, but also about entertainment programming such as drama or sport. Indeed, in his analysis of how debates about national politics in Thailand have been covertly embedded in drama programming such as soap operas, Brett Farmer argues that 'fictional entertainment television' plays the role of a 'competing or adjunct popular public sphere for varying forms of socio-political expression and exchange'. In the programmes in question, social and political themes that could not be directly canvassed are worked into thinly veiled narratives that, the author argues, bring the issue before the public. This chapter highlights another way of thinking about television's engagement with the nation through less explicit forms of nation-building; that is, as an ongoing process that involves continual negotiation across the television landscape – from 'hard' politics in news and information to more 'soft' everyday issues in drama, lifestyle and variety programmes. Similar approaches to television entertainment genres and nation-building inform the chapters by Tay, Ong and Freedman. Yang's chapter discusses how serial drama in Taiwan has become a highly contested political space for debates about competing claims on national identity – between a dominant Chinese and a resistant Taiwanese culture. Ong's chapter is interesting for slightly different reasons, however, because of what he describes as the way in which television proprietors have taken on the nation-building role normally played by the state. Not content with participating merely symbolically in the construction of national identities, as outlined in the chapters mentioned above, the history of television in the Philippines has media companies providing local communities with material support by way of what Ong describes as a 'TV of intervention'.

Television texts and programmes can be seen to reflect each country's historical progression through taste and audience interests, as it moves from addressing immediate political contingencies to stabilizing economic affluence and growth. What people want to watch can change according to its relevance to their everyday life. An example of such a process is outlined in Alisa Freedman's chapter, which lays out a history of the shifts in the media construction of the single working woman in Japanese television drama – dramas that, Freedman says, operate as 'a barometer of the emotional impact of historical change'. Such shifts are open to negotiation, of course, as among the ways we make sense of 'our national selves' within our particular social, cultural or historical conjuncture.

There are, of course, very different ways of proposing the formation of 'our national selves': centralized and top-down processes of nation-building that programmatically promulgate national identities, what is now commonly described as nation-branding (Anholt 2010), have been widely characterized as a self-serving public relations strategy for legitimating the prioritization of particular sets of interests. As Graeme Turner argued in *Making it National* (1994), the nation is vulnerable to the scrutiny of the manner of its building, and it is not at all uncommon for centralized campaigns aimed at constructing national identities to attract fierce criticism for the artificiality of the cultural formations they propose, or for their failure to appropriately accommodate diverse cultural or political interests. Umi Khattab's chapter focuses on the explicit programme of campaigns conducted on Malaysian television by the Mahathir regime in an attempt to create, virtually from whole cloth, a unified Malaysian national identity. Outlining the reaction to these campaigns from ethnic minority groups, resisting what they regarded as Islamic and Malay supremacy, Khattab notes the key points of resistance to the idea of a collective national identity as something that is arbitrarily 'manufactured' or 'mediatized'. In the light of the history she presents, Khattab argues that 'television in the case of Malaysia does not appear to be the key site for the enabling of collective imagination or collective membership' of the nation – or, at least, not in the way that the ruling elites had intended. Rather, Khattab suggests, when seen as part of the 'everyday life of its people, television appears to empower Malaysians to rethink their national identity and citizenship and generate oppositional readings for the remaking of a new democratic nation'.

The power of the experience of everyday life in this situation is not to be underestimated. Jinna Tay's chapter describes a situation where there does appear to have been a much greater degree of compatibility between the top-down construction of the nation and a more 'authentic' grassroots or popular experience of national identity. In her examination of the 1980s television dramas in Singapore, Tay argues that, while they were clearly produced with pedagogic and even propagandist intentions, the mood of the nation coincided with what was a celebratory and nostalgic revisiting of the past to embrace a history that had its kinks smoothed out and was freed from the insecurities of political interpretations. This candy-coated version of history seemed happily accepted by the audiences Tay interviewed. For them, the 1980s was the time when local television blossomed, generating a sense of pride in Singapore's regional and international achievements. The connection between television and a successful process of nation formation identified with national progress towards modernity, for this audience at that time, seemed to be virtually seamless. Far from being anomalous, this would seem to be an extremely common way, perhaps even one of the fundamental ways, in which audiences everywhere remember the function of national television systems in the context of a modernizing nation-state.

Modernization

As Pertierra and Turner have noted (2013), the relationship between television and the discourses of modernity has a long, ongoing history. The arrival of television in the nation-state is inevitably invoked as a pivotal point of progress for that society within its narratives of modernization. This is as true at the national level – where the introduction of the nation's television services always carries exactly that significance – as it is for the individual seeking to acquire for themselves that iconic material possession, their first television set. Eric Ma's (2012) research into the take-up of television in Hong Kong and China demonstrates the significance of the individual's possession of the television set in terms of the social status of the family – not just as a sign of personal affluence, but also in demonstrating an ideological positioning that signifies an implicit embrace of modernity. In recent times, such an embrace has often been interpreted as a welcoming response to globalization, as an indicator of a cultural and commercial openness to the rest of the world. That is certainly how the process of modernization is seen within the West these days. For our purposes here, however, it is important to qualify such an interpretation by emphasizing the specificities of the histories of modernity in Asia, and what the distinctive articulations of modernity within the region might actually mean. Pertierra and Turner remind us that 'when people seek to be modern, as they often seem to be when incorporating television into their lives, they can be seeking multiple or competing forms of modernity':

> Modernity needs to be understood as historically and geo-politically located even when it appears to be composed from a set repertoire of signs: industrialization, urbanization, secularization, globalization, marketization and, most recently, the rise of consumerism. In each historical or geo-political instance, some parts of such a repertoire may be more important than others; the precise manner in which societies have, in effect, selected and combined items from this repertoire is itself an important area for analysis.
>
> (Pertierra and Turner 2013: 109)

Television, of course, is one of the sites where this process of selection and combination is clearly visible; as we see in many of the contributions to this book, the construction of local and national histories, the construction and celebration of particular forms of cultural identity, and the precise modes of engagement with such indices of modernity as marketization or secularization, are all core territories for the role of television throughout Asia.

One of the threads that pull together the various contributions to this book is the historically determined, nuanced and instantiated relationship to modernity that is articulated through the nation's television – and by television here we mean the full range of formations and representations that involves: the structure and political economy of the television industry, the role of the state in relation to this structure as well as to television programming, the practices of commercialization in play at all levels (provision, regulation, programming) and the content of what is actually transmitted as programming. As a region, over the past two decades, Asia has been engaged in an historic, if

Introduction   11

highly contingent, phase of development, involving large-scale, transnational and regional trends towards industrialization, marketization, secularization and consumerization. These do not play out the same way in every location; the tight political management of the processes of marketization in China documented in Sun and Gorfinkel's chapter contrasts dramatically with the virtually untrammelled explosion of consumer markets (and in particular in television services) McMillin discusses in India. It should go without saying that such differences are the result of deeply embedded historical, economic, cultural and political factors – factors that are constraining as well as enabling. In Malaysia and Indonesia, the emergence of a modern industrialized state has led to a level of consumerism that raises serious socio-cultural and political concerns that have their roots in the complicated ethnic and religious composition of the citizenry; in both countries, many have expressed concern that value systems traditional to the culture are in danger of being undermined by those coming from elsewhere as a by-product of global trade flows in, for instance, television formats.

Furthermore, while it is often assumed in the West that cosmopolitanism goes happily hand-in-hand with modernization, it is as well to remember that cosmopolitanism is itself a product of a predominantly Western version of modernity that expresses Western middle-class levels of affluence as well as a classed desire for a particular context of consumption. Bunty Avieson's chapter, which shatters some of the Western media's mythologies around the history of the comparatively recent introduction of television into Bhutan, reminds us that we need to recognize that there are many communities and nations that do not necessarily covet such affluence and who do not necessarily share such a desire, and who therefore resist the naturalized coupling of modernization and cosmopolitanism as an unwarranted imposition of Western values onto the process of modernizing their economies and societies. In some locations, too, there is a history of Western colonization that gives added force to a principled political insistence on retaining local control over the socio-cultural, as well as the economic, processes involved in modernization.

Of particular significance in this region is the fact that television plays a crucial role in those emerging multi-ethnic nation-states where access to other forms of communication and information may be compromised by low levels of print literacy, or by the limited provision of print media services in a range of community languages. The visual requires no translation; nor does it require print literacy. In societies where the levels of development and progress are uneven, regionalized or otherwise compromised, television's capacity as a mode of communication with the citizenry is unparalleled. That capacity remains fundamental, even in the context of some forms of globalization. While television may seem to some as if it is the straightforward emissary of Western modernity, history tells us that it cannot prosper if it does not speak of, and to, its regional, national or local constituency. Television demands an audience and, even in this era of so-called globalization, that audience is just

12 *Jinna Tay and Graeme Turner*

as likely to think of itself as one of citizens rather than as one of consumers. In Asia, this is especially true.

As Avieson's case study of Bhutan so clearly demonstrates, television histories in Asia are very much histories of the region's and its nation-states' development of, and engagement with, the process of customizing modernity to local political, socio-cultural (including religious) conditions. Television is one of, if not *the*, most powerful tools available for such a task. As we shall see repeatedly through this book – and this is especially notable in the chapters dealing with India, China, and Japan – much of the history of television's function within Asian cultures and societies is tied up with the specific histories of modernization that have shaped each nation-state and region.

Marketization

In many of the locations we discuss in this book, the processes of modernization converge with (perhaps even at times are subsumed by) processes of marketization – that is, by the large-scale economic, political and social changes that go with the transformation of societies that had been hitherto structured around other economic logics and modes of governance, towards those of a market economy. The contexts in which this occurs of course vary dramatically. Consider how one might compare the situation that applies even within the one nation-state of the People's Republic of China – such as the very different formations of the market economy in play in contemporary Hong Kong and mainland China, where the former still retains elements of its longstanding identity as the hyper-capitalist hub for finance and commercial investment in Asia, and the latter carefully negotiates the contradictions implicit in operating an economy subject to significant authoritarian state intervention while nonetheless selectively opening itself up to market forces. Marketization, however, does not simply refer to what is going on within the economy or the polity of the individual nation-state; it also involves the external ambitions and influence of the nation-state through the establishment of a commercial presence within the region and beyond. The influence of changes in global trade flows and, more specifically, the post-digital climate for intra-state media regulation, has magnified the strategic importance of active participation in media markets external to the single nation-state, whatever the specifics of the relevant political or national context.

At the level of the individual consumer, the consequences of this process may well be experienced simply as a significant expansion in the range of consumer choice – as we have seen, itself one of the key markers of modernization. A key attribute of this expansion is the access greater choice provides to products that are desired because of their already established global reputations; television formats are high on the list of these and so the introduction of *Asian Idol*, for instance, is welcomed as a form of cultural enfranchisement for the region: that is, there is pleasure taken in the fact that the market has delivered a popular transnational platform upon which Asia's distinctive modernities might be performed (Tay 2012). Indeed, consumers' highly positive response to the benefits seen to flow from such opportunities may well be one of the reasons for the widespread currency of arguments that link consumer choice with the process of democratization – even in a region where there are a number of nation-states whose political regimes could only be described as authoritarian. The contradictions implicit in this should alert us to the regional relativities in play – what might be described as democratization in Singapore is not likely to be what would be regarded as democratization in Hong Kong. In more general terms, however, while it is certainly true that access to consumer goods, to entertainment and to customized personal services is on the increase throughout the region, it would be unwise to see this as an inherently democratic development; Yang's discussion of the commercialization of Taiwan television in this collection reinforces this point. Indeed, a number of scholars have been very persuasive in arguing that what has been called 'the Singapore model' has deployed consumer choice to precisely the opposite ends to those assumed within the democratization thesis (Chua 2001): that is, it is argued that the liberalization of consumer choice, delivered by way of, for instance, access to a wider range of choices in entertainment, has operated as a means of masking the lack of any significant equivalent liberalization of political control. The target for such strategies is the rising middle class, and for good reason: this is the sector with the capacity to take advantage of the new consumer marketplace, on the one hand, but also the sector that might well see their growing economic power as grounds for pursuing greater access to political power, on the other. This is widely noted in relation to the very different political contexts of India and China, as well as in Singapore, but across the region it would seem that this – the contradiction between enhanced consumer power and limited political power – is a growing tension for the nation-state to address.

The media has been a significant location for developments such as these; the increasing marketization of media provision and platforms has been transformative, generating social, cultural and economic consequences. Among these consequences has been the heightened competition between state-funded broadcast television and cable, satellite or other forms of subscription or pay TV; over the past decade in India, as McMillin's chapter explains, the virtual monopoly once enjoyed by the conservative state television broadcaster, Doordarshan, has been dramatically displaced by a veritable explosion of local commercial television with most consumers now able to access up to 100 channels in English, Hindi and several other regional languages (Athique 2009; Sen 2012: 205). Elsewhere, the expansion of choice has generated quite different results: in Hong Kong, for example, even though the penetration rate for cable or subscription television is among the highest in the region, the vast majority of viewers still use their subscription to watch the state broadcast channels. There is a similar pattern in Korea. In Taiwan, on the other hand, a market that was totally commercial from the start, we

14 *Jinna Tay and Graeme Turner*

have seen a brave attempt to develop a successful public broadcaster from scratch – although it requires cross-subsidization from a companion commercial channel to remain viable – that seems to have been motivated by discontent with what the commercial system has provided (Turner and Tay 2009).

Perhaps a more important, and widely noted, consequence of the processes of marketization is to do with the expansion of local production in the region, to the extent that Asia (especially Hong Kong and Shanghai) now figures large in recent accounts of the emergence of the new 'media capitals' (Curtin 2004). In the first instance, this reflects the growth of local production industries to meet the demand for local products; even in the post-broadcast environment it remains the case that audiences prefer the local product where they can access one, and this has proven to be particularly the case in Asia where the socio-cultural differences from the West are especially pronounced when represented on the screen. Japan is remarkable for the fact that it has been producing something like 95 per cent of its domestic television programming locally since 1980 – only the US has such a strong hold over its domestic market. This is a special case, of course, but the general point is worth making: as we noted at the beginning of this introduction, Asian television may have begun global, but it has become local as its industries have matured, as audiences have formed more elaborated preferences, and as the local industries have found ways of satisfying those preferences with varying levels of success and by way of varying formats.

In relation to the content and formats of the programming being produced locally, it is generally true that television has played an especially prominent role in the context of those nations that are responding to their achievement of independence or managing some form of major cultural transition through creating an audience for locally or nationally focused television drama – as the chapters by Tay, Freedman and Farmer argue, the role of national stories told in such contexts can be foundational. It is important, however, not to neglect the role played by modes of local programming where the connection to national cultural identities may seem less obvious. Many nations in the region have been extremely successful with their adaptations of global formats – from *Idol* to *Who Wants to be a Millionaire?* The indigenization of these formats is fundamental to their success (Oren and Shahaf, 2012); the programmes concerned are received as locally produced content rather than merely as imitations or translations of foreign models. The trade in formats goes both ways, as well – from the East to the West. A number of countries – including Indonesia, Japan, Korea and Hong Kong – have been very successful in selling their programming and their formats within East Asia, as well as carving out a space for themselves within the global media marketplace (albeit, at times in niches – such as in animation, in the case of Japan). Even though the Asian region is a major client for buying global television formats, many Asian television industries have also used the enhanced trade in formats as a way of selling television beyond their region (so, for instance, while many would think that it originated in the US, the format for *Funniest Home Videos* was developed in Japan back in the 1980s). Nonetheless, what is most notable about the transformation of the media markets in East Asia is the success of 'culturally proximate' (Iwabuchi 2004) programming within the region – that is, programming that has its origins within the region rather than within any one nation-state or culture –to the extent that there is now a significant media market that trades primarily in content that is produced from within Asia, especially East Asia. Certain trends do dominate these markets from time to time – the take-up of Korean soap opera, for instance, in Japan, Hong Kong and Taiwan – but this speaks to the dynamic nature of these markets and their close connection to shifts in the fashions of a popular culture that are understood as Asian rather than, say, cosmopolitan, in the sense in which that notion might be used in Europe.

Even though we might discern a common narrative across the region, to do with the rise of local production and regional media markets, one of the considerations that have influenced the organization of this book is our view of the importance of recognizing that the details of each story in each nation-state have their own particularities. So, to take one relatively familiar example, much has been written about the complicated negotiation between the political imperatives of the state and those of the commercial market as part of the process of determining how television functions in China. Such a negotiation, as the much quoted example of the *Supergirl* controversy (Fung 2009) demonstrates, has consequences right down to the level of the individual programme. As noted earlier, however, it is important to recognize that this is a more sophisticated matter than merely a straightforward process of direct state intervention; this local market has its own histories, and its preferences express these histories. Fung (2009), among others, has noted how the transformation of global formats based on Western concepts of individualism can be successfully tailored to the Chinese market (that is, successful in terms of audience ratings) by translating the format into a story about collectivism. Furthermore, this book's focus on the histories of television in Asia is also intended to remind us of the highly contingent character of the factors that have contributed to the successful development of the television industry in each market. In Japan, for instance, these would include the existence of a well-established film industry, and television's role in broadcasting a series of high profile national events at a crucial period in the industry's history – such as the wedding of the Empress in 1958 (the year television broadcasting began in Japan), the Tokyo Olympics in 1964 and the Seoul Olympics in 1988. Not only are each of the industrial histories distinctive, but the development of media in the region is related to broader and long-term historical patterns of economic and cultural development – with the pre-eminence of Hong Kong and Japan as the locations where processes of marketization and highly sophisticated forms of modernization most dramatically converged in the 1970s and 1980s, and the emergence of the so-called 'Asian Tigers' – Korean, Taiwan and Singapore – in the 1990s and beyond.

Comparing TV systems

Finally, a point that we should make before we conclude. While there is clearly a need for more comparative work across media systems – local, national and regional – those who attempt to explore this avenue find that it is often easier said than done. Even though there have been useful, if limited, attempts to create a typology of media systems that would assist comparison (Hallin and Mancini, 2004, for instance), the precise mix of determining conditions are so varied and diverse, and the politics driving them so specific, that one wonders whether such a goal is even worth pursuing. (Hallin and Mancini, for instance, have been widely criticized for their focus on the Global North, and the narrow range of political systems they consider.) As part of the material they provided to us, the contributors to this volume have collected information from which to construct a rudimentary map of the structure of the television industry in each of the nation-states with which we deal. From this data, it is clear that there are very few common elements. Even the date of the first transmission varies enormously; for Japan it is 1939, but for Bhutan is more than 60 years later, in 1999. We can note, however, that there is an increasing presence for cable and satellite providers – cable channels number over 100 in many locations, and in India are heading towards a total of 600. (This presents an interesting comparison with the US, where cable channels are now starting to lose market share to other platforms and would seem to be in decline.) While China has more than 1,000 FTA channels, in general it is clear that FTA services (and this is including as FTA services those that require a small licence fee to be paid, as in the UK system) have remained few in number. It is worth pointing out, however, that actual FTA consumption may well still be quite substantial, nonetheless. In Korea, Hong Kong and Thailand, the penetration of cable across the population is over 90 per cent, but in all of these cases the cable channels carry FTA access as well, according to government regulatory requirements. In both India and China, a process of modernization that is clearly politically driven has had a direct effect on television; there have been major changes in the structure and orientation of the television industry that are still generating shifts in the patterns of provision, regulation and consumption.

The system data is collected in an appendix at the end of this book, for the information of readers. We have done what we can to impose a common structure upon this information so that it may be more easily digested and compared, but even this has had its difficulties: some sorts of information are more easily obtained than others, some national industries collect their data in idiosyncratic ways that do not easily compare with others and some sources of data are simply unreliable. However, we have included this material in a relatively raw form as a resource for readers who wish to read the individual chapters against the background of the structure of the systems concerned.

References

Anholt, Simon (2010) *Places: Identity, Image and Reputation*, Basingstoke: Macmillan.

Athique, Adrian Mabbot (2009) 'From monopoly to polyphony: India in the era of television' in Graeme Turner and Jinna Tay (eds.) *Television Studies After TV: Understanding Television in the Post-Broadcast Era*, London and New York: Routledge.

Bonner, Frances (2012) 'My favourite things: spin-off products and television memories' in K. Darian-Smith and S. Turnbull (eds.) *Remembering Television: Histories, Technologies, Memories*, Newcastle upon Tyne: Cambridge Scholars Publishing.

Chua, Beng Huat (2001) 'Singapore as model: planning innovations, knowledge experts' in A. Roy and A. Ong (eds.) *Worlding Cities: Asian Experiment and the Art of Being Global*, London: Blackwell, pp. 29–53.

Curran, J. and Park, M. (eds.) (2000) *De-Westernizing Media Studies*, London: Routledge.

Curtin, Michael (2004) 'Media capitals: geographies of global TV' in Lynn Spigel and Jan Olsson (eds.) *Television after TV: Essays on a Medium in Transition*, Durham, NC: Duke University Press, pp. 270–302.

Darian-Smith, Kate and Turnbull, Susan (eds.) (2012) *Remembering Television: Histories, Technologies, Memories*, Newcastle upon Tyne: Cambridge Scholars Publishing.

Fung, Anthony Y.H. (2009) 'Globalizing television culture: the case of China' in Graeme Turner and Jinna Tay (eds.) *Television Studies After TV: Understanding Television in the Post-Broadcast Era*, London and New York: Routledge, pp. 178–88.

Hajkowski, T. (2010) *The BBC and National Identity in Britain 1922–53*, Manchester: Manchester University Press.

Hallin, D. and Mancini, P. (2004) *Comparing Media Systems: Three Models of Media and Politics*, New York: Cambridge University Press.

Hartley, John (2004) 'Television, nation, and indigenous media', *Television & New Media*, 5(1): 7–25.

Iwabuchi, Koichi (ed.) (2004) *Feeling Asian Modernities: Transnational Consumption of Japanese TV Dramas*, Hong Kong: Hong Kong University Press.

Keane, Michael, Fung, Anthony Y.H. and Moran, Albert (2007) *New Television, Globalisation, and the East Asian Cultural Imagination*, Hong Kong: Hong Kong University Press.

Kraidy, Marwan (2010) *Reality Television and Arab Politics: Contention in Public Life*, New York: Cambridge University Press.

Ma, Eric (1999) *Culture Politics and Television in Hong Kong*, London: Routledge.

Ma, Eric (2012) *Desiring Hong Kong, Consuming South China: Transborder Cultural Politics 1970–2010*, Hong Kong: Hong Kong University Press.

Oren, T. and Shahaf, S. (eds.) (2012) *Global Television Formats: Understanding Television Across Borders*, New York and London: Routledge.

Pertierra, Anna Cristina and Turner, Graeme (2013) *Locating Television: Zones of Consumption*, London and New York: Routledge.

Sankaran, Chitra and Pillai, Shanthini (2011) 'Transnational Tamil television and diasporic imaginings', *International Journal of Cultural Studies*, 3: 277–89.

Sen, Biswarup (2012) '*Idol* worship: ethnicity and difference in global television', in Tasha Oren and Sharon Shahaf (eds.) *Global Television Formats: Understanding Television Across Borders*, New York and London: Routledge, pp. 203–22.

Sun, W. and Zhao, Y. (2009) 'Television culture with "Chinese characteristics": the politics of compassion and education' in Graeme Turner and Jinna Tay (eds.) *Television Studies After TV: Understanding Television in the Post-Broadcast Era*, London and New York: Routledge, pp. 96–104.

Tay, Jinna (2012) 'The search for an Asian Idol: the performance of regional identity in reality television', in K. Zwaan and J. de Bruin (eds.) *Adapting Idols: Authenticity, Identity and Performance in a Global Television Format*, Leeds: Ashgate, pp. 55–68.

Turner, Graeme (1999) *Making It National*, Crows Nest: Allen & Unwin.

Turner, Graeme and Tay, Jinna (eds.) (2009) *Television Studies After TV: Understanding Television in the Post-Broadcast Era*, London and New York: Routledge.

2 Television, scale and place-identity in the PRC

Provincial, national and global influences from 1958 to 2013

Wanning Sun and Lauren Gorfinkel

One may argue that Chinese television has already received more than its fair share of attention in the study of Chinese media. As compared with radio and cinema, which developed in the socialist era (1949–78), television has been seen as the dominant medium in the decades of marketization and economic reforms since the late 1970s (Zhu and Berry 2008). Television has been studied as a metonym for the ongoing tension and complicity between the Chinese state and the market (e.g., Zhao 1998; 2008a) and as a metaphor for the contradictions between a legacy of socialist rhetoric and ethos and a neoliberal market agenda. It is precisely these contradictions that make up what is often referred to as the 'Chinese characteristics' (Zhao 2008a; Sun and Zhao 2009) of China's television culture.

China's complex and changing television landscape has been examined in terms of its funding, ownership, censorship, regulation and institutional restructuring (Chang 2002; Zhao 1998, 2008a, 2008b; Zhao and Guo 2005). The changes and development of Chinese television have been viewed through the prism of format innovation and industries (Keane 2002a, 2002b; Moran and Keane 2004; Keane et al. 2007; Donald et al. 2002), advertising (Wang 2008) and entertainment (Bai and Song 2015). The cultural economy of certain television dramas, one of China's most popular television genres, has also been a popular topic for analysis (Keane 2001; Zhu 2008; Zhu et al. 2008; Sun 2007; Zhong 2010). Other studies have focused on the progressive entrenchment of neoliberal subject positions (Lewis et al. 2012), nation-building through the staging of television events via satellite (Sun 2002, 2010) and televisual texts as public culture (Rofel 2007; Sun 2008, 2009). In the past few years, we have also witnessed growing attention to the role of television in extending the Chinese government's public diplomacy and soft power policy, especially in the context of Chinese television's attempts to internationalize (Curtin 2007; Zhang 2008; Sun 2010) and reach out to diasporic Chinese communities (Zhu and Berry 2008; Sun 2010).

While there has been an explosion of works dedicated to updating the dynamic and fast-changing landscape of Chinese television as it unfolds, it is important that analysis of current practices is situated in a historical framework. Earlier works that shed light on the material, infrastructural, institutional and discursive dimensions of Chinese television in its early stages of development (e.g., Chang 2002; Lull 1991; Lee 1994; Li 1991; Hong 1998; Zhao 1998) are vital for understanding Chinese television today, and are likely to continue to hold relevance in the context of the future development of the industry. Yet, useful as this literature on Chinese television's early development is, there are still gaps in our understanding of how Chinese television was configured in the earlier days, including how Chinese television facilitated a particular imagination of the various scale of places – be it the village, the city, the province, the nation or the geopolitical imagination of the world outside China – and how the early configurations of television and space have been maintained and shifted over time.

Taking a cultural-interpretative angle of space and place, and reconsidering the various geographic scales of production, this chapter concerns itself with the changing and contested notion of the nation, region, province and locality, as well as the idea of China in a global perspective, in the context of the management of Chinese television. By offering an account of the history and the political economy of the production and consumption of Chinese television, we argue that, while television arrived in China initially to assist the party-state's project of socialist modernity, political mobilization and nation-building, it has now also acquired an additional and equally important function of promoting neoliberalism with 'Chinese characteristics'. These narratives provide ample evidence of a transition from centralization to decentralization, and highlight how Chinese television was first introduced for the purpose of nation-building but now has to contend with a more diverse range of place-based identity politics. This chapter considers how local visions are articulated and negotiated in the context of a decentralized television system that still has to respond to the centre.

We start by considering the transition and transformation of Chinese television in the domains of technology, regulatory mechanisms and institutional practices. We then examine the production of local, provincial and regional identity and the contestation between the central, provincial and local (municipal and county) powers through the prism of programme content and strategies of place-making. As we will show, effective functioning is contingent on, and in turn further unleashes, an increasingly intense process of reordering a long-established spatial hierarchy. A number of crucial dimensions are integral to this history, including the desire of the Chinese state to control and regulate television at a national level as well as provincial and local levels for the purpose of maintaining legitimacy and stability, the rapacious ambition and capacity of capital to challenge the existing spatial hierarchy and provincial and local television industries' creative and innovative practice of impacting on and resisting central control.

Scale and technical reach

Television first came to China in 1958, less than a decade after the Chinese Communist Party took over and founded the People's Republic of China.

While this historical fact has been well-documented, the scale and purpose in television production and consumption at the time has often lacked emphasis. Significantly, even though Beijing was firmly established as the political centre of the nation in the political geography for two decades after its inception, Chinese television did not have a national dimension either in terms of reach or impact. Called Beijing Television, the earliest form of Chinese television was transmitted only in the Beijing area, in black and white, and broadcast for a couple of hours four times a week to a small number of people who had access to television sets. 'National events' were framed 'through the eyes of Beijing' (Li 1991: 343).

On an international level, the birth of the earliest form of television of China betrays a historically specific geopolitical and spatial imagination of the world and of China's understanding of itself in relation to others in the world. Beijing TV was launched during the height of the Cold War at a time when China allied itself with the Soviet Union and the Eastern European block, and saw the United States and its ally Taiwan as its enemies. The very project of establishing a television industry was framed as an act of political necessity. China felt that it needed to act more quickly than the US-backed Taiwan, which was on the verge of launching its own television station (Guo 1991; Chang 2002).

Furthermore, even though the technology meant that access to television was limited to relatively small areas, the early phase of Beijing TV neverthe-less embodied a centralized form of management, with a vision for targeting both national and global audiences. This pattern would dominate the Chinese media for two decades. In the early 1960s, well before it could reach most of the domestic population, it had already attempted to influence populations beyond its own borders by sending its programmes to a select number of foreign countries with whom China had signed exchange agreements, including television stations in East Germany, Brazil and Australia. At the same time, Beijing TV also sent out its own foreign correspondents to a few foreign countries, mainly in Vietnam and Africa, to bring news of the world to its own viewers through the lens of the central authority's foreign affairs activities (Chang 2002). Due to the perceived need for political control and the mechanism of centralization, only Beijing Television was authorized to import programmes and to distrib-ute programmes overseas. The other 16 (out of 29 provinces that had already set up their own stations between 1958 and 1960, including Shanghai TV and Guangzhou TV – which were comparable in audience size, programme variety and transmission capacity to Beijing TV – were restricted from broadcasting news and entertainment from other countries to their audiences (Chang 2002).

The television industry in China did not see consistent growth after its inception. In 1959, there were only around 30 television sets in Beijing; these were owned by households and organizations. Instead of growth, the incipi-ent Chinese television experienced a major setback in the 1960s due to a num-ber of factors. The withdrawal of economic aid from the Soviet Union was a heavy blow to the Chinese economy and forced some fledgling television stations to close down. This devastating economic downturn was followed by a progressively worsening decade of ideological and political chaos, now widely known as the Great Cultural Revolution. The impact of television on society in general in this period was minimal, and was limited to the ideological cause of class struggles (Li 1991; Chang 2002). There was virtually no growth in the Chinese television industry for almost two decades until the late 1970s. For this reason, in major scholarly works on China's communication and propaganda practices in the socialist era from the 1950s to the 1980s (e.g., Yu 1964; Schurmann 1966; Chu 1977), there is no mention of television in people's political and social lives. Newspapers, radio, posters and, to some extent, cinema were the main forms of mass media.

The development of Chinese television mirrors that of the administrative structure of the Chinese state bureaucracy. Consisting of four levels – central, provincial, municipal and counties – the relationship between the central and lower-level administrative bodies was, until the 1980s, that of submission. When this multi-level structure of Chinese television first took shape, it reflected a clear understanding of the supremacy of the national-level television channel and the unequal central–peripheral relationship. The model whereby the national-level media was most authoritative was reflected in all major mediums, including newspapers and radio.

The decade of the 1980s saw the most dramatic growth of Chinese television in terms of its transmission technologies, ownership of receivers and quantity of programme content. From the mid-1980s, improved living standards meant that ordinary Chinese people could afford to buy television sets. As more Chinese purchased television sets, the Chinese government sensed the potential of television to consolidate its control on a national scale by reaching out to its people in the most remote areas of its territory and connecting citizens across the country. The number of stations, including provincial and local stations, grew dramatically from 38 in the early 1980s to 202 in 1985 and 541 in 1991. The number of television stations has increased exponentially since then with around 1,000 stations currently operating across all levels in China (W.S. Sun 2012).

Access to television has also increased significantly. While as few as 1 per cent of the population could receive television in 1980, the figure rose to 16.2 per cent by 1990 (Lee 1994), and to more than 97 per cent in 2009, including almost 92 per cent of the population in rural areas (National Bureau of Statistics of China 2010). In terms of infrastructure, in the early 1980s there were 400 relay stations in China, which transmitted to more than 50 existing television stations. By the end of the 1980s, 22,000 relay stations were transmitting terrestrial signals to all parts of the country. By the mid-1990s, the number of relay stations had exceeded 40,000, due to the proliferation of municipal and county-level stations (Chang 2002). Studies of Chinese television made their debut at the beginning of the 1990s (e.g., Lull 1991; Li 1991) following the rapid proliferation of television activity and increase in access to television across the country.

Cable TV, which was mainly limited to work units in the 1980s, developed rapidly after the State Council issued a document in 1991 proclaiming cable TV as an important part of China's television industry. Cable TV was to be controlled by the central government, but subject to the supervision of provincial and local governments (Hong 1998; Chang 2002). China now has the world's largest number of cable users. In 1999, cable TV (also known as Community Access TV, CATV) was available to 60 million households and, by 2009, this number had grown to 163 million households, reaching around 500 million people (Zhuang and Fang 2009) and 189 million families in 2011 (*China Daily* 2011).[1] The core role of cable TV, as with terrestrial broadcasts and satellite, is to serve the political agenda of the CCP, which entails providing 'affordable and ubiquitous carriage of the country's exclusively state-owned broadcasters' (Zhuang and Fang 2009: 1). While cable fees are not particularly onerous (in 2010 households paid an average of RMB 18 per month – less than US$3 – for the service), by 2010 few people had taken up a *premium* pay TV option given the wide range of free-to-air analogue cable channels (Wang et al. 2010). Under political direction, cable operators are being encouraged to upgrade to digital, and analogue cable was due to be switched off by 2015. In 2010, there were 63 million digital cable TV subscribers (Wang et al. 2010). By 2009, 2.3 million households or individuals were testing out the Internet Protocol Television (IPTV) offered by China's telecom carriers (Zhuang and Fang 2009).

The adoption of satellite technologies has played a particularly crucial role in China's nation-building, particularly in terms of bringing audiences in remote and mountainous areas into the 'simultaneous' yet individuated act of 'imagining the nation' (Anderson 1983). China's first telecommunications satellite was launched in 1984, which enabled live transmissions of the central television network's programmes to remote and ethnic-autonomous regions across China, including Tibet and Xinjiang. By 1986, China had purchased two transponders on the fifth telecommunications satellite to transmit television regularly on two national channels (Li 1991). This marked the first phase of satellite transmission in China and enabled the central government to conquer the tyranny of distance to reach a national population. In 2008, China launched its first Direct Broadcast Satellite (DBS) for TV broadcasting, the Chinasat-9 satellite, which is able to transmit signals covering 98 per cent of China's territory, and can transmit up to 200 radio and TV channels to users in China, Hong Kong, Macau and Taiwan (Zhou 2008). On 5 September 2011, the *China Daily* reported that the special DBS service was due to replace wireless signals for about 200 million rural families in China by 2015, promising to dramatically improve the quality and quantity of reception.

China has also made use of satellite technologies to reach out to overseas viewers, including overseas Chinese and non-ethnic Chinese in a number of international languages, as part of its 'soft power' policy. CCTV International claims to transmit to 98 per cent of the world's landmass, with around 45 million subscribers, although it is unclear how many of these people actively subscribe to China's national broadcaster as opposed to packages that happen to include CCTV (Zhang 2011: 45).

Scale and content

With the tiered system of central, provincial, municipal and county-level television stations, it was taken for granted that the local and provincial media would submit to forces at the national level and would merely function as transmission services, relaying provincial and central programming with very little *programming* capacity themselves (W.S. Sun 2012). In the socialist era, television was considered an important mobilization tool in political campaigns and the 'mouthpiece' of the central government, and television was used to disseminate its policies and directives at all levels. Unlike public broadcasting in some liberal-democratic systems, which are funded by taxpayers but remain independent from government control and interference in content (or are funded by subscription fees and rely on the support of viewers and community), in socialist China all levels of television were financed by the central government with no regard for ratings and little consideration for content appeal.

At its extreme, during the politically charged era of the Cultural Revolution (1966–76), the few stations that the central authorities kept running (Beijing, Shanghai, Tianjin, Guangzhou, and Shenyang) were designed to drive the masses to fight against class enemies and glorify the thoughts of Mao Zedong. Entertainment television was largely reduced to eight model revolutionary operas, while newscasts were nothing but quotations of Mao's works and *People's Daily* reports (Chang 2002; Hong 1998). By the mid-1970s, more than 20 provincial television stations (including stations in autonomous regions and municipalities) were set up, all of which transmitted Beijing TV's content via microwave links (Li 1991). The only programmes produced by local and provincial stations were mainly news on the local and provincial implementation of political and economic policy directives from the central authorities.

In 1978, Chinese television started to have a truly national reach. It was at this time that Beijing Television changed its name to China Central Television (CCTV) and took on a clear new role as the national-level broadcaster. Since then, all provincial stations have still been required to relay important national events broadcast on CCTV. This has included the live transmission of television events such as the Hong Kong handover ceremony, the annual National Day celebrations and the commemoration of the victims of the Sichuan earthquake, as well as the evening news.

However, despite the requirement to carry certain national events and meet certain political obligations (Fung 2009; Yu 2001; Tay 2009; Curtin 2010), the theory of top-down national uniformity and strong control from the centre may no longer be an entirely accurate representation of the contemporary reality. Since 1983, the central government has dramatically reduced or terminated subsidies to all television stations, which has led to the decentralization of China's television structure. This process was originally driven by a desire for a greater level of efficiency and effectiveness of central control, rather than a genuine intention to devolve political power to provincial and local governments and the television stations they run. Yet, as a result of becoming financially self-reliant, television stations came to rely strongly on market forces and commercial interests to operate. Advertising, which did not exist on Chinese television until 1979 (the first advertisement was on Shanghai TV) (Zhao 1998), was by the 1980s the most aggressive, ubiquitous and stable source of revenue generation for Chinese television at all levels.

One of the outcomes of the delegation of financial control to the lower levels of the television system has been the increase of intense economic competition between CCTV and provincial television stations, as well as among different provincial and local stations. This has been particularly the case since 1998, by which time almost 30 provincial stations were granted direct access to a national audience via a satellite channel. This allowed provincial stations to expand their reach well beyond their traditional provincial jurisdiction, effectively 'challeng[ing] the monopoly of CCTV in the national television market' (Zhao 2008a: 96). Furthermore, while provincial stations were required to carry certain CCTV programmes, such as the evening news, it became increasingly difficult to enforce these rules (Zhao 2008a).

As noted earlier, prior to the 1980s, the media was centrally administered and 'bound by authoritarian, if not totalitarian, Communist ideological prerequisites with little regard to the market conditions' (Chang 2002: 33). Its tasks were to propagate state policies, educate the masses and mobilize them for national development and revolution (Hong 1998; Chang 2002). Television was firmly controlled by the Party-state and even today is not open to private ownership, whether by Chinese or foreign companies or via Sino–foreign joint ventures.[2] The state still fosters a strong belief in the power of television to propagate state policies. However, since the reforms there has been an important shift to a 'legal-rational mechanism' in which economic and technical development rather than class struggle or ideological motives have been of primary concern (Chang 2002: 32–8). In this period of decentralization, media professionals, who may or may not be officially connected to the Party, have been given the opportunity to manage television stations as long as they do not challenge the leadership and policies of the central government (Chang 2002).

Since 1982, the Ministry of Radio, Film and TV (MRFT), which became the State Administration of Radio, Film and Television (SARFT) in June 1998, has been the central authority in charge of broadcasting policymaking and regulation (Chin 2011; Chang 2002). It has implemented regulations that cover a wide range of areas, including advertising, training, educational television, drama production, overseas Chinese productions, foreign imports, ground reception devices and foreign satellite TV (Chang 2002). Yet, while the voice of the centre is still strong, and all levels – central, provincial, municipal, county and township – are expected to promote the policies and priorities set by the Propaganda Ministry of the Party's Central Committee (Hong 1998), the extent to which local and provincial authorities actually follow and enforce central directives is debatable. As Chin (2011) suggests, the process of management is often two-way, with some provincial stations, such as Guangdong Television, heavily involved in guiding policy changes at the national level. While the CCP still 'promotes' and desires strong leadership, it is critical to understand the increasing power of local authorities and economic elites and the role they play in determining the direction and content of the media.

At the same time as responding to lobbying by the provincial media, the central authorities have also responded to audience criticisms of provincial stations, with national directives issued at provincial stations on issues such as poor management. For instance, on 28 November 2011, SARFT announced that it would ban the interruption of popular television dramas with advertising, although it would continue to allow advertising before and after dramas as well as product placements within programming (Bandurski 2011). This move by SARFT was in reaction to huge levels of public discontent with provincial television stations' arbitrary insertion of advertising into television programmes, to the extent that some off-peak programmes were totally supplanted with commercials for the television station's own non-journalistic business endeavours, which included medicinal ventures, hotels and real estate (Chin 2011). There were so many grievances about the proliferation of advertising, including untruthful and illegal advertisements for medicine and food brought to the attention of CCP leaders via phone calls, letters, online forums and in-house surveys, that SARFT had to address the issue in order to preserve social harmony, a key tenet of the Hu Jintao–Wen Jiabao leadership (Chin 2011).

Also significant is that it is often the local media, rather than the central authorities, who are placing controls on the type of content that is broadcast on their channels. For instance Tong (2010) has found evidence of local authorities imposing bans on the negative coverage of local events, which are implemented in order to protect the reputation of local elites and maintain the good image of the local area upon which their promotion depends. With positive economic achievements receiving the bulk of attention, other issues such as social justice, the environment, employment, housing and social benefits receive little exposure from local media. In many cases, local censorship and framing goes against current central policies. This is made possible because local media now depend on the support of local governments and not the central government to guarantee their financial survival. To guarantee the smooth running of the television stations' businesses (such as through providing the right to the use of land), the local media owe favours to local authorities. Control may still *appear* to be central and monolithic, largely because local governments use the same Marxist mantras and concerns for ideological integrity and national stability as the central government, but the local media taps into this discourse in ways that suit their own purposes (Tong 2010).

The central authorities have, however, sought to maintain strict control over access to foreign content through control over satellite television. In 1990, for instance, the MRFT, the Ministry of Public Security and the Ministry of State Security promulgated a decree labelled 'Administrative Measures for Reception of Television Programmes Transmitted via Foreign Satellites by Ground Satellite Receiving Facilities'. The decree limited access to overseas satellite services to 'eligible viewers', who included foreigners staying in hostels or guesthouses, as well as workers involved in education, scientific research, journalism, finance, economic relations and trade, who required up-to-date information on 'international financial and marketing'. In 1993, the State Council promulgated another decree for the administration of ground receiving facilities for satellite television transmissions, which initiated a state licensing system for the production, importation, sale, installation and use of ground receiving facilities, and would require application to administrative departments of radio and television at a local county or municipal level, to be approved at the provincial level (or people's government of an autonomous region or municipality directly under the central government). It banned individual unauthorized import and installation of satellite dishes with the threat of confiscation and a fine of up to 5,000 yuan for an individual or 50,000 yuan for the unit.

On the other hand, since 1998 the state has offered subsidies for people in rural, remote and western regions to buy satellite dishes in order to access national and provincial television services where they are not serviced by cable or other networks (Zhou 2010).[3] However, while SARFT has banned the use and purchase of satellite dishes in urban areas, it has been unable to force local government branches to enforce the rules, and there is a 'black market' trade in satellite dishes in unauthorized areas. Some residents are purchasing satellite dishes to avoid paying cable fees for domestic television services, while others are doing so specifically to access foreign satellite channels such as CNN, ESPN, HBO, Bloomberg and MTV (Fletcher 2010). There were an estimated 10 million satellite dishes 'illegally' receiving foreign signals in 2008 (according to market researcher iSuppli, in Fletcher 2010). Recognizing the extent of unauthorized use of illegal dishes, on 7 April 2010, SARFT issued another decree – 'The Provisional Law Regarding Servicing/Installation of Satellite Broadcast Ground Receivers' – in an attempt to control the situation. There is little evidence that the decrees or fines have had any major effect on the illegal purchase and use of satellite equipment.

Locality and identity

One of the most significant challenges posed by provincial television stations as a result of competition for a national audience is the challenge to CCTV's monopoly over the production of the notion of Chineseness. In the past, whether communicated through the language and symbolism contained in popular documentaries like *River Elegy* (1988), television dramas like

Yearnings (1989) or national news and current affairs, CCTV was seen as the primary creator of a quintessential Chinese identity, spirit and sentiment. However, through access to the provincial networks' alternative programming, audiences have been able to shop around and reduce their reliance on the once agenda-setting CCTV. It has become increasingly difficult for the Party and government to reach China's increasingly fragmented audiences. Even traditionally high-rating, national televised events like the CCTV Spring Festival Gala, which has allowed the Party-state to unite the nation and spread propaganda in an entertaining fashion to millions of Chinese since 1983, is facing the prospect of a diminishing audience with six Chinese regional satellite television stations – including Anhui, Jiangsu and Hunan Satellite TV – deciding not to broadcast the show in 2012 (China Media Project 2011).

While CCTV is still restricted by its particularly strong requirement to present Party-state ideological messages in both news and entertainment programmes, competition with provincial channels has impacted on CCTV's own approaches to programming. CCTV staff are now sent to provincial stations like Hunan Television to learn from them. CCTV has also created niche channels to cater to audiences with interests in areas such as news, finance, arts and entertainment, sport, TV drama, movies, music and Peking opera. In an era where audiences have plenty of choice in what they watch, CCTV has to provide programming that is attractive or risk losing audiences altogether. CCTV's music entertainment programming, for instance, contains a mixture of styles, including a more overtly political style required of the central broadcaster, with popular cosmopolitan styles more commonly found on provincial stations (Gorfinkel 2012). It is also mixing up the focus on the politics of place, at times attempting to appeal to a sense of national cohesion alongside appeals to local and transnational identities. For instance, popular CCTV music entertainment shows like *Happy in China* (lit: *Happy China Roaming, Hunale Zhongguo xing*) carry a mix of messages about national unity as well as local identities based on showcasing the unique cultures of specific localities (now tourist destinations) around China to which the show travels each week. It also contains messages of regional unity and cosmopolitanism through performances by stars from Hong Kong and Taiwan and from overseas Chinese. Nonetheless, while CCTV may be offering more varied visions of China and Chineseness than before, the artistic style and content of CCTV productions tend to be more restricted and differentiated from provincial stations as a result of its mandate as the central, national-level network, which was set up to serve the nation.

With provincial stations now vying for a national audience, and indeed a transnational audience through beaming their programmes via international satellite alongside CCTV, the notion of how to best represent China and Chineseness has become increasingly contested. Provincial television is deliberately and consciously differentiating itself from the central television network's monopoly on symbolic 'China'. Since 2004, Hunan Satellite TV started to promote itself as a provincial station specializing in the production of 'fun', evidenced in the paraphernalia of shows and programmes which have a motif of happiness. Promoting itself with the slogan of 'fun-loving China', Hunan TV has captured the imagination of Chinese as well as transnational Chinese audiences with its innovative formats such as the 'Super Girl' singing contest (based on the *Idol* format), television dramas with a time-travel theme and a wide range of variety-type entertainment shows that are dedicated to little else than delivering fun. Hunan's success was an inspiration to other provincial television stations, so much so that we have now a plethora of place-based promotional slogans for provincial television stations, including Jilin TV as the 'humorous' China, Guangdong TV as the 'open-minded' China, Guangxi as the 'fashionable' China and Jiangsu TV as the 'Happy China' (Ding 2011: 61). This strategy of production differentiation has so far paid off. Instead of automatically turning to CCTV, Chinese viewers, especially those from the younger generations, go to Hunan Satellite TV for fun-loving entertainment, to Jiangsu Satellite TV for 'touchy, feely' programmes, Anhui Satellite TV for dramas, Jiangxi Satellite TV for legends and folktales, Hainan Satellite TV for tourism and Chongqing Satellite TV for history and culture (W. Sun 2012).

The provincial stations' main purpose in product differentiation is not aimed at directly challenging the centre's supremacy in political and ideological control, although from time to time it has incurred the ire of SARFT – SARFT's intervention into Jiangsu TV's dating show *You Are the One* is but one example (Sun and Chio 2012). Instead, they are more interested in promoting and maintaining provincial cultural identities, as well as reaping economic benefits from promoting local identities. In the process, they are actively engaging in 'reviving regionalism and reinventing "Chineseness"' (Oakes 2000: 667). For purposes of survival, provincial stations also form alliances in order to draw on comparative advantages. A number of provincial stations have grouped together to form strategic alliances under a singular regional identity, hence the 'hot and spicy' regional television cultures from Hunan and Hubei, and the 'earthy, rural, humourous' television cultures from north-eastern provinces such as Jilin, Liaoning and Heilongjiang.

Cut-throat competition has given rise to a plethora of innovations, which range from the substantive to the superficial. Starting in 2010, Hunan TV marketed its television content and its value-added products such as magazines and games as 'mango products', kick-starting another round of production differentiation, this time along the theme of fruit. Jiangsu TV, not to be left behind, soon adopted the lychee as its product logo, while Oriental TV of the Shanghai Media Group identified itself with the tomato. On a more abstract level, Zhejiang Province, on the east coast of China and boasting of being the most economically developed province, positioned itself in terms of colour, launching its programme content under the hue of China blue. In contrast, Chongqing Television, which, until the recent demise of Bo Xilai's leadership, had been positively described as the city that has revived socialist culture and was dedicated to the promotion of 'revolutionary classics', is unapologetically red (Ding 2011: 61).

The diverse content and 'branding' of stations by individual provincial and local stations in the current era contrasts dramatically with television production in the socialist era, when all television was tightly controlled by the central authorities and 'branded' with the single purpose of achieving not market share but mass education and political indoctrination (Chang 2002). The vision of China was not of a 'fun-loving', innovative society, with advertising suggesting to audiences that capital could buy pleasure, but of a productive, hardworking society, and one that emphasized belonging to a communist nation that was blessed by the leadership of Chairman Mao. The majority of 'entertainment' programmes in the early days were old films and live operas, supplemented with highly propagandistic content made up of revolutionary songs and folk songs, teleplays and dramas, often featuring school, factory and army units (Hong 1998: 50). Some shows like *Passionate Square* (*Jiqing Guangchang*) on CCTV (which are occasionally mirrored by local government-sponsored performances that are broadcast on local television), which feature the gathering of construction workers, farmers, nurses, teachers and students in small town squares singing together, often led by army and state performing arts troupes, continue to reflect this earlier focus.

As for foreign entertainment programmes, in the socialist era when there was a policy of self-reliance and a concern for the need to protect China's national identity and revolutionary spirit, there were few television programmes from overseas. Those that were aired were mainly from the Soviet Union and a few Eastern European nations (Hong 1998: 50–1). There was a period during the 1980s, however, when provincial stations broadcast an overabundance of foreign programmes, largely because it was cheaper to buy foreign programmes than to produce local ones, and stations needed to fill up air time and attract audiences. However, ongoing moral concerns over foreign content led to a change in regulations. The development of the Chinese drama and entertainment television industries was promoted to compete against foreign imports, eventually leading to concerns for the need to manage local production as well (Hong 1998; Chang 2002).

The impact of scale and capital on news and entertainment

While news used to be the province of the central broadcaster, competition between the central and provincial television stations has had an impact on the significance of news in the Chinese television landscape. As is the case elsewhere, news in the Chinese media is considered to be the most authoritative media genre. But unlike liberal-democratic media systems, news in the Chinese media is usually associated with propaganda, and is usually seen to communicate the official version of truth and reality. It is often centrally produced and locally transmitted, and is subject to the strictest form of regulation, control and censorship. By 1976 (the year Mao died), when television stations from 25 provinces, municipalities and autonomous regions were up and running and linked to the centre via microwave trunk lines, all the stations agreed to relay the Beijing Television network news (the forerunner to CCTV's *Xinwen Lianbo*) at 7pm each night (Chang 2002).

For the most part, news remains the remit of the national broadcaster. The practice of provincial television stations relaying the prime-time CCTV *Xinwen Lianbo* news bulletin continues today, and there is no sign that this is going to change in the near future. Foreign information and culture may no longer be imagined as a 'poison' to the Chinese nation, news may not be restricted to China's 'communist' allies, and 'capitalist' societies may no longer be merely constructed as places ravaged by riots, crime, poverty and natural disasters, as was the limit to international news during the Cultural Revolution (Chang 2002; Hong 1998). Yet there are still tight restrictions on the way in which centralized news production constructs a reality of China and the world for viewers.

While local and provincial level television stations are now able to produce some of their own news and current affairs programming, it is limited in scope and amount and, significantly, is often perceived by local audiences as having much less credibility than national news, which it sometimes contradicts. Politically, the production of news is always seen as a risky business, and the handling of politically sensitive topics and issues such as social inequality and social unrest, which may threaten stability, is always a delicate balancing act. Furthermore, news is much more expensive to produce and generally does not attract high ratings. Given the decentralization of provincial and local television industries in fiscal and administrative terms, it is understandable that local and provincial television does not want to make the production of news its core business. This is made all the more challenging by the fact that other media forms such as the Internet and social media are bringing about diverse sources of information, which makes production of news on TV onerous.

These days, however, news is transmitted in various formats, and we need to look beyond the traditional news programme for clues on how the media fulfils its core functions. In China, as in many other countries, we are witnessing the blending of news and commentary, and the emergence of commentators as media celebrities (e.g., Lang Xianping, Yang Yu, Ye Tan). This suggests that the long-guarded distinction between news and entertainment may be breaking down. News can now be entertaining, and entertainment may have information value. Television celebrities introduce news, provide background and offer their own interpretations and perspectives. They make complex and difficult issues (economics, politics, finances, law and order) easy and accessible to audiences.

From another perspective, however, one may argue that news is to a great extent being *replaced* by entertainment genres, including television dramas, dating shows, reality TV and lifestyle TV. The desire to avoid politically sensitive and financially expensive news genres leads to the embrace of entertainment programmes as the new 'mainstream', whose mission is to produce happiness and, in doing so, generate profit. The 2010 *China Statistical Yearbook* indicates that, for the first time, the audience for entertainment programmes from provincial television had exceeded that for news programmes, marking a significant shift in the overriding function of television (National Bureau of Statistics of China 2010).

But this does not mean that provincial television has finally gotten the better hand in the central–provincial contestation. The will, capacity and propensity of the central Party-state to enforce control is most clearly illustrated in its ongoing crackdowns on provincial television's entertainment programmes. In October 2011, SARFT issued a set of directives that set out to shake up the Chinese television industry in a number of profound ways. Among the changes stipulated in SARFT's 'Further Recommendations on the Regulation of Provincial Satellite Television Programs' ('Recommendations' hereafter), there was to be an increase in the quantity of news versus content, a reduction of the quantity of entertainment content, and improvement of the quality of remaining entertainment programmes. According to the 'Recommendations', as of 1 January 2012, all provincial satellite stations were to ensure the broadcast of at least two hours of locally produced news content from 6am to midnight each day, including at least two news programmes between 6pm and 11.30pm each day. Each of these two news programmes was not to be shorter than half an hour in duration.

According to SARFT's official spokesperson, these recommendations are intended to address a worrisome tendency towards 'excessive entertainization' (*yule guodu hua*). It is clear that 'excessive entertainization' refers to both the quantity and quality of entertainment programmes. A recent survey commissioned by SARFT of entertainment programmes on provincial satellite television found that there were 126 entertainment programmes on 34 provincial satellite television stations, mainly consisting of dating and friendship shows, talent contests, melodramas, games and quizzes, comprehensive variety shows and talk shows featuring celebrity hosts. In addition, the 'vulgar taste' of entertainment programmes, and 'widespread uniformity of entertainment formats' on Chinese television was said to lead to a waste of resources and the stifling of content innovation (*People's Daily* 2011).

Current trends: using the past to serve the present

This discussion has shown that television arrived in China initially to assist the Party-state's project of socialist modernity and political mobilization but, half a century since its initial arrival, it has now acquired an additional and equally important function of promoting capitalism with 'Chinese characteristics'. Initially thought to be a potentially powerful tool to pursue the national 'mass line' and raise the class consciousness of the peasants and workers, it has metamorphosed into an apparatus tasked with defusing class conflicts and producing stability and harmony. With the consolidation of China's status as a global economic and political powerhouse, Chinese television in the twenty-first century has also progressively extended its presence offshore, functioning as a key vehicle to promote China's soft power in the global mediasphere. An historical account of Chinese television is necessarily an account of the role that television plays in the various junctures of China's social transformations. In such an account, Chinese television can be configured simultaneously as a social practice, a cultural artefact and a market commodity where state control, commercial competition and the creative and innovative impulse of the television industry intertwine.

Most rural television viewers still watch television as their main source of daily entertainment, and spend more time watching television dramas (Zhao 2008a) compared with educated, urban youth who are increasingly taking to the Internet as their favourite pastime (Chen 2011). This does not mean, however, that television no longer has a place in the lives of urban youth; it simply means that we need to understand the shifting material, technological and social environments in which television content is consumed. There is a certain element of truth in a quip widely circulating among television industry people in China: television content is accessed these days anywhere but on television. With the growing access to broadband of individual households, and the maturity of video sharing sites such as Youku and Tudou, watching television content online has become widespread, and an increasing number of viewers are shifting from downloading programmes to online streaming. Television content producers and television stations have to increasingly reconsider strategies of production, format and presentation style to suit the new material environment in which television content is accessed. The central authorities have also jumped on the bandwagon, with (as of 2012) 24 CCTV channels, 35 provincial satellite channels, 74 city-level channels, five nationality channels and 3 digital channels accessible in an online format from one website, the China Television Network (www.cntv.com.cn).

In recent years, two major changes have taken place that have reshaped the landscape of Chinese television. The first is the shifting dynamics between the central, regional, provincial and local television industries as a result of the decentralization process in administrative and fiscal terms. The second is the adoption of satellite transmission of provincial television content in the second half of the 1990s. These changes have posed real challenges – both analytical and methodological – to studies of nation-building, place identity and the central-peripheral relationship (W. Sun 2012; Sun and Chio 2012). They have also brought about uncertainty on the continuous operation of the long-established four-level structure of Chinese television – national, provincial, municipal and county (W.S. Sun 2012). But although one can always be sure of constant change, one thing is certain: there will be an even greater level of disjuncture in scale between the production and consumption of television due to the impact of technological changes, competing economic pressures and shifting spatial and geographical boundaries in the future. Given ongoing

34 *Wanning Sun and Lauren Gorfinkel*

transformations, understanding how television was produced, transmitted and circulated in the past with a view to seeing how it has evolved due to technological, institutional and economic developments may be a good place to start.

Notes

1 Wang et al. (2010) say there were 174.6 million cable TV households in 2009.
2 See Article 10, Regulations on Broadcasting and Television Administration, adopted at the 61st Executive Meeting of the State Council and promulgated by Decree No. 228 of the State Council of the PRC in August 1997.
3 In 2009, the popularization rate of cable radio and TV in rural areas in 2009 was 27.77 per cent compared with 43.99 per cent across the nation as a whole. The overall penetration rate of television in rural areas in 2009 was 91.9 per cent, compared to a total penetration rate of 97.23 per cent (National Bureau of Statistics of China 2010). According to Wang et al. (2010), by the end of 2009, China had 388 million TV households and 174.6 million cable TV households.

References

Anderson, B. (1983) *Imagined Communities: Reflections on the Origin and Spread of Nationalism*, London: Verso.

Bai, R. and Song, G. (2015) 'Introduction' in Ruoyun Bai and Geng Song, Chinese Television in the Twenty-First Century: Entertaining the nation, Oxon, UK: Routledge. p. 1–14.

Bandurski, D. (2011) 'Who's paying for the public welfare on TV?' *China Media Project*, 29 November. Available at http://cmp.hku.hk/2011/11/29/17213/ (accessed 12 December 2011).

Chang, T.-K. (2002) *China's Window on the World: TV News, Social Knowledge and International Spectacles*, New Jersey: Hampton Press.

Chen, M. (2011) '2010 zhongguo dianshi hongpishu', *Xin Zhoukan*, 343: 45–8.

Chin, Y.C. (2011) 'Policy process, policy learning, and the role of the provincial media in China', *Media, Culture & Society*, 33(2):193–210.

China Daily (2011) 'Satellite TV service to cover 200m rural families', *China Daily*, 5 September. Available at www.chinadaily.com.cn/china/2011-09/05/content_13625096.htm (accessed 5 December 2011).

China Media Project (2011) 'Saying NO to the CCTV Gala', *China Media Project*, February. Available at http://cmp.hku.hk/2011/02/07/9891 (accessed 12 December 2011).

Chu, G.C. (1977) *Radical Change Through Communication in Mao's China*, Honolulu: The University of Hawaii Press.

Curtin, M. (2007) *Playing to the World's Biggest Audience: The Globalization of Chinese Film and TV*, Berkeley: University of California Press.

Curtin, M. (2010) 'Introduction', *Cinema Journal*, 49(3): 117–20.

Ding, X.J. (2011) '2010 nian weishi pingdao xin wan fa', *Xin Zhou Kan*, 15 March.

Donald, S.H., Keane, M. and Yin, H. (eds.) (2002) *Media in China: Consumption, Content and Crisis*, London: Routledge Curzon.

Fletcher, O. (2010) 'Illegal satellite TV in China brings CNN to the masses', *IDG News*, 22 April. Available at www.pcworld.com/businesscenter/article/194755/illegal_satellite_tv_in_china_brings_cnn_to_the_masses.html (accessed 25 November 2011).

Fung, A. (2009) 'Globalizing televised culture: the case of China' in G. Turner and J. Tay (eds.) *Television Studies After TV: Understanding Television in the Post-Broadcast Era*, London: Routledge, pp. 178–88.

Gorfinkel, L. (2012) *Performing the Chinese Nation: The Politics of Identity in China Central Television's Music-Entertainment Programs*, PhD thesis, University of Technology, Sydney.

Guo, Z. (1991) *History of Chinese Television [Zhongguo dianshi shi]*, Beijing: Chinese People's University Press.

Hong, J.H. (1998) *The Internationalization of Television in China: The Evolution of Ideology, Society, and Media Since the Reform*, Westport, CO, and London: Praeger.

Keane, M. (2001) 'Television drama in China: engineering souls for the market' in R. King and T. Craig (eds.) *Global Goes Local: Popular Culture in Asia*, Vancouver: University of British Columbia Press, pp. 176–202.

Keane, M. (2002a) 'Send in the clones: television formats and content creation in the People's Republic of China' in S.H. Donald, M. Keane and H. Yin (eds.) *Media in China: Consumption, Content and Crisis*, London: Routledge Curzon, pp. 80–90.

Keane, M. (2002b) 'As a hundred television formats bloom, a thousand television stations contend', *Journal of Contemporary China* 11(30): 5–16.

Keane, M., Fung, A. and Moran, A. (2007) *New Television, Globalization and the East Asian Imagination*, Hong Kong: Hong Kong University Press.

Lee, P. S. N. (1994) 'Mass communication and national development in China: media roles reconsidered', *Journal of Communication*, 44(3): 22–37.

Lewis, T., Martin, F., and Sun, W. (2012) 'Lifestyling Asia? Shaping modernity and selfhood on life advice programming', *International Journal of Cultural Studies*, 25(5).

Li, X.P. (1991) 'The Chinese television system and television news', *The China Quarterly*, 126: 340–55.

Lull, J. (1991) *China Turned On: TV Reform and Resistance*, London: Routledge.

Moran, A. and Keane, M. (eds.) (2004) *Television Across Asia: Television Industries, Programme Formats and Globalization*, New York: Routledge Curzon.

National Bureau of Statistics of China (2010) 'Basic statistics on radio and television industry', *China Statistical Yearbook*. Available at www.stats.gov.cn/tjsj/ndsj/2010/indexeh.htm (accessed 10 November 2011).

Oakes, T. (2000) 'China's provincial identities: reviving regionalism and reinventing "Chineseness"', *The Journal of Asian Studies*, 59(3): 667–92.

People's Daily (2011) 'Debates on new regulation on entertainment programs in various corners of the sector', *People's Daily*. Available at http://news.xinhuanet.com/ent/2011-10/28/c_122208016.htm (accessed 25 March 2014).

Rofel, L. (2007) *Desiring China: Experiments in Neoliberalism, Sexuality, and Public Culture*, Durham, NC: Duke University Press.

Schurmann, F. (1966) *Ideology and Organization in Communist China*, Berkeley: University of California Press.

Sun, W. (2002) *Leaving China: Media, Migration, and Transnational Imagination*, New York and Oxford: Rowman and Littlefield.

Sun, W. (2007) 'Dancing with chains: significant moments on China Central Television', *International Journal of Cultural Studies*, 10: 187–204.

Sun, W. (2008) 'The curse of the everyday: politics of representation and new social semiotics in post-socialist China' in K. Sen and T. Lee (eds.) *Politics, Media and Regime Change in Asia*, London: Routledge.

36 *Wanning Sun and Lauren Gorfinkel*

Sun, W. (2009) *Maid in China: Media, Morality, and the Cultural Politics of Boundaries*, London: Routledge.

Sun, W. (2010) 'Mission impossible? Soft power, communication capacity, and the globalization of Chinese media', *International Journal of Communication*, 4. Available at http://ijoc.org/ojs/index.php/ijoc/article/view/617 (accessed 6 March 2015).

Sun, W. (2012) 'Rescaling media in China: the formations of local, provincial, and regional media cultures', *Journal of Chinese Communication*, 5(1): 10–15.

Sun, W. and Chio, J. (2012) 'Introduction' in W. Sun and J. Chio (eds.) *Mapping Media in China: Region, Province and Locality*, London: Routledge.

Sun, W. and Zhao, Y. (2009) 'Television culture with "Chinese characteristics": the politics of compassion and education' in G. Turner and J. Tay (eds.) *Television Studies After TV: Understanding Television in the Post-Broadcast Era*, London: Routledge, pp. 96–104.

Sun, W.S. (2012) 'Top-down policies versus grassroots resistance: the management of illegal satellites in the Chinese village' in W. Sun and J. Chio (eds.) *Mapping Media in China: Region, Province and Locality*, London: Routledge.

Tay, J. (2009) 'Television in Chinese geo-linguistic markets: deregulation, reregulation and market forces in the post-broadcast era' in G. Turner and J. Tay (eds.) *Television Studies After TV: Understanding Television in the Post-Broadcast Era*, Routledge: London, pp. 105–14.

Tong, J.R. (2010) 'The crisis of the centralized media control theory: how local power controls media in China', *Media, Culture & Society*, 32(6): 925–42.

Wang, J. (2008) *Brand New China: Advertising, Media, and Commercial Culture*, Cambridge, MA: Harvard University Press.

Wang, L.Z. (ed.) (2010) *China TV Rating Yearbook 2010*, Beijing: Communication University of China Press.

Wang, W.B., Bisson, G. and Aguete, M.R. (2010) 'China cable television market assessment and forecast to 2014', 21 October. Available at www.screendigest.com/reports/2010920a/10_10_china_cable_television/view.html (accessed 25 November 2011).

Yu, F.T. (1964) *Mass Persuasion in Communist China*, New York: Praeger.

Yu, Y. (2001) 'Can the news media meet the challenges in China's post-Deng reform?' in X. Hu and G. Lin (eds.) *Transition Towards Post-Deng China*, Singapore: Singapore University Press, pp. 195–218.

Zhang, X.L. (2008) 'China's international broadcasting: a case study of CCTV international', in J. Wang (ed.) *Soft Power in China: Public Diplomacy through Communication*, New York: Palgrave Macmillan, pp. 57–72.

Zhang, X.L. (2011) *The Transformation of Political Communication in China: From Propaganda to Hegemony*, Singapore: World Scientific Publishing.

Zhao, B. (1999) 'Mouthpiece or money-spinner? The double life of Chinese television in the late 1990s', *International Journal of Cultural Studies*, 2(3): 291–305.

Zhao, Y.Z. (1998) *Media, Market, and Democracy in China: Between the Party Line and the Bottom Line*, Urbana: Illinois University Press.

Zhao, Y.Z. (2008a) *Communication in China: Political Economy, Power, and Conflict*, Lanham, MD: Rowman & Littlefield.

Zhao, Y.Z. (2008b) 'Neoliberal strategies, socialist legacies: communication and state transformation in China' in P. Chakravarty and Y.Z. Zhao (eds.)

Global Communications: Towards a Transcultural Political Economy, Lanham, MD: Rowman & Littlefield, pp. 23–50.

Zhao, Y.Z. and Guo, Z.Z. (2005) 'Television in China: history, political economy, and ideology' in J. Wasko (ed.) *A Companion to Television*, Malden, MA: Blackwell Publishing, pp. 521–39.

Zhong, X.P. (2010) *Mainstream Culture Refocused: Television Drama, Society, and the Production of Meaning in Reform-Era China*, Honolulu: University of Hawai'i Press.

Zhou, H. (2008) 'China's first direct broadcast satellite to enter service', *China Daily*, 20 May. Available at www.chinadaily.com.cn/bizchina/2008-05/20/content_6698467.htm (accessed 5 December 2011).

Zhou, Y. (2010) 'The positioning and current situation of China's digital TV', *International Journal of Digital Television*, 1(1): 95–104.

Zhu, Y. (2008) *Television in Post-Reform China: Serial Dramas, Confucian Leadership and the Global Television Market*, London: Routledge.

Zhu, Y. and Berry, C. (2008) 'Introduction' in Y. Zhu and C. Berry (eds.) *TV China*, Bloomington and Indianapolis: Indiana University Press, pp. 15–39.

Zhu, Y., Keane, M. and Bai, R. (2008) *TV Drama in China*, Hong Kong: Hong Kong University Press.

Zhuang, W.R. and Fang, M.Q. (2009) *Cable TV in China: Has Great Potential – and Always Will?* China Analyst Note, 18 June. Available at www.ftchinaconfidential. com/Industries/InformationTechnology/Research/WebOnly/article/20090723/ ff0b87e6-77ac-11de-bac6-0015171400aa/cmsassets/Assets/Pdf/Research/BDA%20 China%20Cable%20TV%201.pdf (accessed 28 November 2011).

3 Trust and television in globalizing India

Divya McMillin

A globally relevant history

Writing a history of Indian television immediately begs the question, how do we want it read? Exhaustive chronological treatments anchor the field (Kumar 2000), ideological examinations reveal a Hindu-centric nation with serious consequences for religious and gender minorities (Rajagopal 1996; Mitra 1993; Van der Veer 1997), development analyses demonstrate the failures of a socialist state (Fürisch and Shrikhande 2007), and audience studies reveal complex negotiations among multiple identity positions (Mankekar 1999). These critical approaches to the study of television in India rightly expose power differentials that facilitate, through the centuries, the inequities of interwoven structures of imperialism, colonialism, casteism, and capitalist patriarchy. Most importantly, they highlight the chronic condition of distrust in postcolonial societies, making it highly challenging to legitimize profitable connections to global circuits as they modernize under the very conditions that once constrained them.

In the global press, India is increasingly profiled as a progressive democracy, ripe with potential for its vast skilled labor and its growing middle class (Mullen and Ganguly 2012; Sukumar 2003; Zakaria 2006). Industry analyses such as Ernst and Young's 2014 Attractiveness Survey cast a highly positive glow on the country, noting that more than half the respondents were optimistic about investing in India for the long term. The thriving domestic market, rapidly increasing middle class, and ever-expanding pool of world-class talent are tempered only by what could be transient problems: unstable infrastructure and lack of transparency. Most likely to happen in the next decade is the increase of manufacturing, quite possibly propelling the nation to third place globally as a site for production.

India's hybrid television environment is representative of the nation's liberalized economy, urging a narrative that is relevant to the context of globalization, where we read not only of power structures that constrain expression and that may force out diversity, but of the opportunism inherent in encounters between local and global. This reading is prompted by a postcolonial *and* globalization framework where the first is a revisionist effort, demanding scrutiny of how the ground responds to Western constructions of modernity and development, while the second explores the possibilities of myriad relationships, some even positive, in local–global interactions (Krishnaswamy 2008).

Drawing from fieldwork spanning two decades (1993–2013) that included interviews with television executives, cable operators, and radio and newspaper journalists, this chapter reconstructs a history of television in India, weaving in the perspectives of these professionals for whom an understanding of global dynamics and local audiences is a matter of survival. Contrary to the trend in scholarship on Indian television that positions the state-sponsored network Doordarshan as a strongly protectionist national enterprise, this chapter argues, through archival research and field interviews, that television in India has also been driven by a global sensibility; Doordarshan was modeled after the BBC and its early function mirrored the imperatives of a Soviet-inspired socialist state.

Using postcolonial theory, particularly the concept of opportunism as developed by Ashcroft (2001), the chapter highlights the interdependencies of a globalizing television industry, which simultaneously reinstates hierarchies while opening up transformative possibilities. A postcolonial framework recognizes that current world relations are developments of Western imperialism; indeed it is obvious that current developments in infrastructure in India have emerged from British colonial blueprints. It also recognizes that communities across the world experience forces of globalization in patterns similar to those of colonized societies experiencing imperialism. Studies of globalization have to highlight the continuity of imperial, colonial and postcolonial (and now global) eras (Pieterse 1995). The chapter begins with the complex, contemporary globalized television environment in India that is both an opportunity for innovation and entrepreneurship *and* a moment of crisis where technological advancements and transnational mergers and acquisitions have far outpaced policy and regulation.

Globalization and the Indian television industry

If we could carve out a nation's industries into concentric circles with decreasing levels of modernity spanning from the innermost circle to the outermost, India's media and entertainment (M&E) industry would occupy the core, being the most lucrative and the quickest to connect to global circuits of production and distribution. Its agricultural sector would lie on the periphery, a topic worthy of a hefty chapter in itself. The Indian government's decision of November 25, 2011, to allow international retailers majority ownership in the Indian market, with foreign direct investment (FDI) of up to 100 percent in advertising and film, was a response to the incredible profitability of these industries. It was just the next step in the government's move to liberalization, most significantly established in its economic liberalization policy of 1991 (led by then economic minister Manmohan Singh), which is noted by India media watchers as a pivotal document that has led to India's status as an emerging market. The policy paved the way for foreign and local private cable and satellite television channels in the country. This latest privatization decision generated a conservative backlash, causing the government to shelve its move and India analysts to shake their heads. CNN's Fareed Zakaria wrote in a December 21, 2011, column that India could be the broken BRIC, referring to Goldman Sachs' Jim O'Neill's 2001 term to spotlight the rapid economic development of Brazil, Russia, India, and China. Zakaria noted that India's economic growth actually dropped 7 percent in 2011 because, as reform-minded as Manmohan Singh was, the government as a whole could not work through its own protectionism and lack of quick action on its highly inefficient agricultural industry. Around 70 percent of India's population lives in rural areas and almost 25 percent lives below the poverty line. Per capita GDP is only around US$700.

Decisions by the government based on its weakest sectors certainly hamper the progress that can be made by its strongest, a dynamic that is near impossible to balance in such a populous country. The casualty is trust both from citizens toward government and from foreign investors to the Indian government. Trust, then, becomes a valuable commodity among media and political players, who often join forces to gather and maintain as large a loyal following as possible. The 2014 national elections provided rich evidence of this dynamic, with various parties accusing each other of manipulating news coverage. It has also led to another phenomenon: increasing popular participation in political processes. A middle-class outcry over political corruption and gender discrimination, among other issues, led to the rise of the Aam Admi ("common man") Party headed by former Delhi chief minister Arvind Kejriwal. While the party fizzled out before it could become a serious contender with the top two parties—the Hindu fundamentalist Bharatiya Janata Party (BJP) and the Gandhi-family dominated Congress Party—it triggered anti-corruption demonstrations all across the country and on social media, primarily by middle- and upper-class urban Indians. Such waves of protest coupled with grounded efforts to take back the streets—whether through the Bangalore Rising or Pink Chaddi Campaigns, for example, which are primarily urban resident-driven efforts to clean up garbage in neighborhoods and stand up for women's rights, respectively—signal to other residents and to the world outside that the middle class is gaining strength both economically and politically. This certainly bodes well for foreign investors who still see the Indian government as the weakest link in the risky world of foreign investment. Nevertheless, analysts such as Hong (2011) emphasize that India's steady progress between 2004 and 2008, ahead of Brazil and Russia, and bolstered by its growing mergers and acquisitions (M&As), stabilizes its growth in the global economy, promoting trust among foreign investors in this growing market.

Indeed, despite a faltering government and widespread poverty, Indian industrialists are shoulder-to-shoulder with billionaires around the world, looking for opportunities to merge and acquire, most frequently in the television arena. Reliance MediaWorks (RMW) teamed up with Digital Domain, a visual effects company, positioning it to work on major Hollywood projects. Reliance will take over studios in Mumbai and London, with Digital Domain managing them. Cashing in on the government's move toward total openness, Discovery received permission in mid-2011 to launch four new channels: Discovery Kids, Military Channel, ID, and Discovery Home and Health. Also, infrastructural failures aside, the alarming slide of the Indian rupee against the US dollar in July 2013 prompted further mergers between foreign and private local media companies. A case in point is Disney's doubling of its equity holding up to 32 percent in UTV Software Communications and acquisition of 15 percent of UTV Global Broadcasting. Disney UTV has witnessed far more success than UTV alone, because of the money available to market movies that otherwise lacked the typical Bollywood formula appeal (Shashidhar 2013). Foreign investments in local companies and increased investments by Indian industrialists in media networks overseas significantly secure India's place in the global economy.

The government's huge shift from a socialist to capitalist patriarchy in the more than five decades since the first telecast in 1959 on the Doordarshan (named as such in 1976) television network has meant that the state-owned network is no longer a monopoly but one among many competitors in a rapidly expanding media market where the prize is the urban, middle-class consumer. Elites in the state-sponsored and private networks who have strong ties to the business community carry on the modernizing and, arguably, the civilizing mission of colonial projects, urging greater economic development for the industry as a whole precisely because their own profitability is tied to that of the industry. The deep and meaningful relationship between the part and the whole prompts an analysis that takes the application of the postcolonial framework several steps further to an examination of the process of *opportunism* and the nature of the *encounter* between local and global. We move now to significant moments in India's television history that forged ever stronger connections to the global economy.

Industry analysts identify two technological developments that caused major turns in television's trajectory in the country: the introduction of color television for the 1982 Asiad Games and the advent of satellite television across the Asia region through Star TV just a decade later. Both were bolstered by the Indian government's move to liberalization and privatization beginning in the early 1980s under the Rajiv Gandhi government, and the formalization of this process in the 1991 economic liberalization policy.

Television for unification

Throughout its history, the Indian government has created and employed various state apparatuses for the propagation of nationalist ideology to build trust in a populace long disillusioned by state power in the aftermath of colonial rule. After independence from the British in 1947, the Indian

42 Divya McMillin

government mobilized centralized television and radio systems for the promotion of national integrity and communal harmony (Doordarshan Audience Research Unit 1995). The overriding objective was to promote economic growth through family planning, development of industry and infrastructure, particularly for transport, water, and electricity, and to revise a national imaginary that situated the Indian people as subjects of a colonized state to one in which they were independent citizens of a free world (Kust 1964). Chakravarty (1993: 22) writes that the first prime minister, Jawaharlal Nehru's, text *The Discovery of India* undertook a 'hegemonic project of appeal to all sections of India's population, primarily Hindus and Muslims, to form one nation and not two.' While attempting to unify people divided by religion, caste, and class, Nehru also reinforced a dangerous hierarchy, upholding a chaste (female) Hindu nation as enduring and eternal despite invasions by first the Muslims and then the British (Prakash 1990).

Impressed by the Soviet Union's progress through central planning, Nehru implemented a centralized system of five-year planning in the nation. Emphasis was on the development of the core sector and of heavy industries through public sector units (PSUs). Early television broadcasts added weight to his vision; late 1950s and early 1960s film and television documentaries were crafted with great care to construct an India that was still Gandhi's India, a non-violent people, with the government benevolently and paternalistically initiating national development through a variety of state-run institutions. Depictions of mass political rallies, demonstrations of agricultural equipment, and a range of infrastructural elements such as hydroelectric power plants and railway lines highlighting Soviet and Israeli partnerships and technology, made their way in to these early television broadcasts, as did films depicting the long-suffering mother as metaphor for the life-giving nation.

In the mid-1970s, in the context of the New World Economic Order and the New World Information Order debates, the UN and UNESCO underwrote various development initiatives, prompting an in-depth study of the role of television for rural development in India. Most prominent is the SITE (Satellite Instructional Television Experiment) project, which was launched in 1976 through a collaboration of the Indian Space Research Centre (ISRO), NASA (USA), Doordarshan, and various state governments. Using the Application Technology Satellite (ATS-6), programs on agriculture, health, and sanitation were beamed to 2,400 villages in six states (Chatterji 1991). Also telecast were lessons for primary school students. In addition, various regional dance and music traditions were featured to foster national unity among various linguistic, religious, and political groups.

So it was from the 1960s to the 1980s; Doordarshan's primary function was to imitate that of the All India Radio: that is, to project a strong statist character with the Indian government as a benevolent deployer of development strategies to the mass of people as a whole. Unified conceptions of nation also meant that citizenship was a monolithic concept; audiences were likened to children with the patriarchal state constructing entertainment programs as antithetical and corrupting influences to its development objectives (Roy 2008). Reflecting on the early days of television, and hardly seeing much of a difference in post-liberalized India in the ways audiences were constructed, the director of the Bangalore Doordarshan, Kendra N.G. Srinivasa, emphasized his social commitment to audiences, who would 'quietly sit and watch' the films he screened after midday and evening mealtimes (see McMillin 2001).

The construction of the obedient and hardworking Indian rural character worked very well for Doordarshan's patriarchal leadership over the nation-family. All programming was developed with a national perspective, whether for the regional or central channels. The mission of unification, of 'holding India together', was reiterated at a 2014 public lecture by Jawarhar Sircar, chief executive officer of Prasar Bharathi, the National Public Service Broadcaster that oversees All India Radio and Doordarshan.[1]

A sophisticated body of work has been developed documenting the hegemonic role of the Indian government on national television in the 1980s. Doordarshan (translated as 'far image'), was dubbed *Rajiv Darshan* (translated as 'Rajiv image'), for its extensive coverage of then prime minister Rajiv Gandhi, who had already risen to star popularity status after a landslide victory for his Congress Party following the assassination of his mother, prime minister Indira Gandhi, in 1984. The vivid spectacle of Rajiv Gandhi performing funeral rites for his slain mother sealed in many voters' minds an unwavering loyalty for this lone, brave, Brahmin son. Sales of color TVs rose exponentially, as they had initially for the Asiad Games (telecast in color) in 1982. Out of this context arose the entertainment-education soap operas, *Hum Log* (1984–5) and *Buniyaad* (1985–6), modeled after Miguel Sabido's rags-to-riches telenovela, *Simplemente Maria*, not for its content, but for its format (Singhal and Rogers 1988). The commercial success of short-length, family-oriented soaps paved the way for the phenomenally successful Hindu epics *Ramayan* (1987–8) and *Mahabharat* (1989–90). Rajagopal (1996) and Mankekar (1999) examined the content and consumption of these complex, multilayered Hindu epics to demonstrate that the national hero who emerged in these narratives was a fundamentalist Hindu construction; Hindu mythology was conflated with national history. The lords of the small screen were Hindu male deities such as Krishna and Rama and their reincarnations as steadfast and all-knowing protagonists on prime-time dramas. The epics also primed a majority of the audience to elevate political families to the status of divine families.

News and information-oriented shows on Doordarshan during this decade invariably involved talking heads in roundtable discussions, panel presentations, and formal interviews. Interactive, phone-in programs such as *Sach ki Parichayiyan* (1986) and *Janvani* (1988–9), which primarily focused on rural development problems and political issues (Doordarshan Audience Research Unit, 1996), gradually expanded their scope to include broader medical, legal, and familial concerns. Whereas the 1980s witnessed some stirrings toward a more commercial model, with specific programming slots privatized,

44 *Divya McMillin*

Doordarshan was the central monopoly with a few regional stations. Perhaps the biggest lesson of the 1980s was the significant potential for prime-time dramas to not only draw in big-ticket advertisers but to spark widespread consumerism as well.

Local opportunism and the global encounter

With the increase in demand for diverse programming (Manchanda 1998), Doordarshan scrambled to contract with independent studios. The aggressive move to innovate across the industry began with the arrival of satellite television in 1991. The 1990s were a significant decade in Indian television history; it is here that we see the beginnings of format adaptation frenzy. While the dominant thrust of scholarship on television in India points to the sluggishness of Doordarshan in the face of cut-throat competition from local and foreign private channels, interviews with Doordarshan creative producers revealed not only a keen awareness of the new demands of the marketplace, but concrete strategies to meet these demands. An emphasis was on building trust, of keeping to established templates for news and documentaries, for example, to provide a sense of stability in the midst of programming chaos.

The unanticipated reception of CNN's telecast of the 1991 Gulf War through satellite dishes in high-rise apartments in urban locales such as Bombay, Delhi, and Bangalore triggered a confused and hypocritical state response, however. Manmohan Singh's 1991 policy coincided with Star TV's entry into the Asia region with headquarters in Hong Kong. Star TV commenced streaming into India legally in 1993 on ASIASAT-1. The government quickly projected foreign programming as an unwelcome and vulgar cultural influence, yet was lethargic in its disciplining of private satellite broadcasters because of their tremendous commercial potential (Shields and Muppidi 1996; Manchanda 1998).

Doordarshan executives immediately recognized they faced a significant challenge: they now had to fill 13 hours of programming a day when previously they had to plan for around two to three hours of prime-time programming. The success of the 1980s epics was still fresh, yet network executives recognized that Doordarshan could lose ground with the rampant imitation of programming by private vernacular language networks. The director of the Bangalore Doordarshan, Kendra N.G. Srinivasa, also commented that apart from programs that violated the networks ethics code—that is, incited violence, criticized national allies, hurt religious sentiment, or that were obscene—anything was fair game. With more than 800 transmitters, the network still led the ratings game through sheer reach, yet research was already underway to identify formats (call-in shows led the list) from other regional markets within the country that could be adapted for the Karnataka urban and rural market.

Speaking specifically to the development of formats, a program executive meticulously delineated the strategies undertaken by her team, every day, to produce programming that was relevant to local issues (her specialty was women's issues) and that met the approval of advertisers as well. A significant challenge, of course, was filling 13 hours of programming per day from the earlier two-hour requirement. Hardly any programs were turned away, as long as they did not violate the basic network code. Her job consisted of previewing story-based teleplays submitted by independent producers, a time-consuming and often fruitless endeavor since most were of poor quality and extremely amateurish in production. More relevant to the context of competition from private satellite channels such as Star TV were 'talk shows, quiz programs, magazine programs, documentaries, music, dance, so that there is a variety in the kind of programs telecast… it's kind of more or less open, apart from the feature films and apart from one or two slots which are already earmarked.'[2]

Marketing and creative personnel desired more commercially oriented programming to attract big-name sponsors. Their commitment to development objectives was stronger than ever, seeking newer formats to reinforce education and information priorities. Programming slots were filled by royalty-based programs, commissioned programs, and feature films. All primary languages of Karnataka (Kannada, Konkani, Tulu, and Kadua) had to be represented. Auditioned artists from All India Radio were siphoned off for Doordarshan's music programs, while dance and drama talent were auditioned by the network itself. Despite their awareness of an urban appetite for more entertainment, Doordarshan producers were committed to socially relevant programs that could match the production quality of commercially produced ones. The difficulty was in finding formally trained production assistants. Highly educated themselves from well-regarded private journalism programs across the country, these producers lamented they could not adequately implement their ideas because they were mired in trivial program operations instead of overseeing the quality productions that they were trained for. Altogether, rural audiences were still constructed as childlike, as needing and wanting guidance on every aspect of their development (see also Roy 2008). During field interviews, a couple of executives brought up the example of the Satellite Instructional Television Experiment (SITE) of 1976 as a model that could still work for rural development and literacy.

Similarly, news executives found themselves wearing multiple hats as scriptwriter, reporter, and sometimes even editor. Crime reporting had increased to match the content on the private news telecasts. The focus had shifted from voice-of-the-government to reluctant inclusion of other institutional activities that were development oriented, such as those conducted by the Lions Club or the Rotary Club. A news reporter discussed the inclusion of opposing points of view as a welcome innovation and significant departure from the earlier format of presenting primarily the government's point of view. The younger generation of news reporters combined with a possibly progressive government approach had resulted in more balanced news content and commentary.

Bangalore audiences had already demonstrated by the mid-1990s that a different approach by Doordarshan and AIR to its most lucrative clientele was necessary. Paternalistic, 'we know what's good for you' development programs would not be favorably received; the alternatives were easily accessible.

Rural audiences were highly responsive to news telecasts, prompting such telecasts on rural channels to be tailored to local needs. News vans travelled to remote areas, profiling regional writers and authors as well as local events to ensure such coverage in prime-time news and stem the flood of calls that would follow in case a rurally relevant issue was not covered. Most lower-level executives, however, were in agreement that, while the state monopoly still held its dominant position through its terrestrial broadcast and rural reach, times were changing more rapidly than they were prepared for and that, very soon, they would be in cut-throat competition with private networks for the urban consumer. Ultimately, education and entertainment slots were sacrificed to commercially sponsored prime-time serials. It should be noted, however, that this opportunist design was still crafted within a patriarchal structure with a great degree of control over the types of soap operas and films broadcast; market needs were still submerged under state goals. Executives all the way up Doordarshan's hierarchy were quite assured of the stability of their infrastructure and of government funding, which would, in their minds and in the mid-1990s moment, withstand all competition. As the Bangalore Doordarshan news executive Kendra N.G. Srinivasa commented,

> Basically we have a better infrastructure than (private networks). This organization has been running for the past 30 years, *more* than 30 years. So we have a well oiled machine that runs. So when Udaya TV (private Kannada-language cable network) did come up with its news bulletin, there was a fear that it might be taking away our audiences—but I don't think that has happened yet. I think our coverage is more extensive than theirs, and they try to dramatize quite a few of their stories, which, at that point of time, may sound good, but when *we* do a follow up on the story, we do a much more sensible story. They are [often] factually wrong, speculation is different from reporting, and they have been [doing] a lot of speculation.[3]

Audience research officers were ambivalent about the increasing presence of television in urban family lives. The trend in city homes, for children to spend much of their evening leisure time in front of the television, was quite a new one, as evidenced in both audience and network fieldwork at the time. One All India Radio audience research officer noted that, while his own fieldwork showed decreased interactions between parents and children, the latter's awareness of global issues had vastly increased. They could identify world figures of the time such as US president Bill Clinton, British prime minister John Major and tennis star Steffi Graf, as well as national heroes such as the Indian cricket captain Kapil Dev and the notorious Janata Dal leader Lalloo Prasad Yadav. The research officer said, 'Wimbledon, French Open, Australian Open, they follow these closely; they know there is a Swaziland, a Croatia, an Azerbaijan. With this exposure, comes a fear in us as parents and as broadcasters; everything has to be censored, everything is inappropriate.'[4] He mentioned MTV programming, broadcasts of communal riots in Northern India, and late night soft-porn films all in one comment, as endless programming that did little to promote values such as patriotism and peace. Private cable networks such as Sun TV and Eenadu seemed to have hit on the winning formula, according to this audience research officer, by offering the right variety of news and entertainment programming. His own efforts were to bring his favorite classically trained musicians to radio and television from the community stage.

These interviews from early fieldwork are useful as we move almost two decades later to examine, in the next section, the consequences of the material and philosophical positioning of Doordarshan. The views and values of middle- and upper-middle-class producers and audience research officers led to content that is constructed for this class of viewers. Embraced was the assumption that Doordarshan was and would continue to be a vehicle of modernization. Modernity as a desirable goal was deployed through the state behemoth, its subjects, both working for it and served by it, 'becoming' or realizing their potential because of it (see also Venn 2006). As we shall see, television professionals saw in themselves the need to develop further skills to keep up with and stay relevant within a multinational operating system. While the 'being' of the subject in modernity has been problematized by critical scholars, we remain ill-equipped in our analytical tools to address the 'being' in globalization, a topic we will return to at the end of this chapter.

The transnational moment

Doordarshan's biggest competitor for urban audiences in the 1990s was Star TV, octopus-like with arms extending into South and East Asia. Channels broadcast on the Rupert Murdoch-owned Star TV network, including MTV, Prime Time Sports, and BBC World Service, and those of Zee TV (initially co-owned by Murdoch and Bombay industrialist Subash Chandra in 1993 and completely acquired by Chandra in 1994), such as Zee TV, EL TV, Zee TV Cinema, and Music Asia, were standard urban offerings, much to the delight of cosmopolitan viewers.

India was, at the time, a model for Star TV's regional businesses, where the strategy was to operate local headquarters with decision-making and production executed locally. Executives at Star TV, interviewed during fieldwork in the mid-1990s, noted that the network relied on local management, technical, sales, creative, and performing talent. Field interviews with Star TV personnel revealed an overwhelming demand among urban audiences for sports telecasts. The vice-president for sales predicted in the mid-1990s that what would boost demand even higher for sports would be the privatization of cricket, as it now is in the 2000s (see Gupta 2009). Highly rated programs included regional-language movies and, to a smaller extent but nevertheless

48   Divya McMillin

reaching the target affluent audience, English-language serials. Format adaptation was just beginning to gather momentum, its potential yet to be realized. English-language serials were remade or dubbed in Hindi (such as Fox's *X Files*, remade as Sony TV's *Ahat*, and *Baywatch*, which was dubbed in Hindi respectively).

Only five out of the then 200 Star TV staff members were not Indian nationals. Sensitivity to Indian traditions and cultural nuances and responsiveness to audience needs were possible through this localized strategy. Speaking on this very topic, the vice-president of sales, Rajnath Kamat, remarked,

> I am [a] human being first, and next, I happen to be in India, and I'm an Indian. One of the reasons why I think P&G and Kellogg's are still finding it difficult to penetrate is because of they have to understand the Indian psyche first, the existing attitude. If you [want to] convert that [a native understanding] into a commercial proposition for yourself, you have to get the grassroots.[5]

At the same time, he discussed the case of elite brands like Cross and Parker pens that were priced exorbitantly yet were more sought after than the Indian versions of the same brands. For the very wealthy, localization of elite brands actually did *not* work; consumers considered it an insult to be offered an Indianized version when they had access to the markets where they were sold the original. As he put it: 'So *this* is the psyche of Indian audiences we need to work on. That is where Star TV comes into the picture, where we can use the water and gold analogy: water is life-giving, yet gold is much higher priced. In that way Star TV is gold, its perceived value is higher.'[6]

Zee TV, like Star TV, embarked on a bold and unabashed commercial strategy, positioning itself as a link between corporations and consumers. Education and information needs were the responsibility of Doordarshan, not the private networks. Widespread dubbing of English-language programs led to a proliferation of such programming across Star TV platforms leading to an overall decline in urban audiences. Advertisers, whether Indian or foreign, paid in US dollars. Star TV and Zee TV were responsible for many programming innovations such as 'mid-(program) breaks, break bumpers, opening and closing titles, and branding of programs, as well as "packaging" of [target] clients to advertisers. So I think to that effect, Star has really sort of been the harbinger of change that you are seeing right now.'[7] Kamat discussed Star TV as a window to the world, where young people could see through MTV exactly how Westerners dressed and behaved, and through Channel V could laugh at spoofs of Indians imitating Westerners. Audience ratings were a challenge; existing IMRB and MARG reports had different methodologies and sample sizes and were often at odds with one another, causing private networks to develop their own informal methods as we shall see in the case of the Kannada-language Udaya TV network. Difficulties in institutionalized ratings aside, Star TV executives noted that their target audiences were highly brand conscious, had disposable income, and were very discerning in their tastes. Advertisers also had to think globally because of Star TV's footprint across the Asia region.

By 1995, other vernacular-language private networks were established, most with funding provided by politicians. An example is the Sun TV network, established in 1993 and owned by the grandson of Tamil Nadu's Dravida Munetra Kazhagam (DMK) political party chief, Muthuvel Karunanidhi. Sun TV has since established networks in other regional languages such as the Kannada-language Udaya TV in Bengaluru and the Telugu-language Raj TV in Hyderabad. JJTV is another example of a politically backed network, established in 1993, and owned by former chief minister of Tamil Nadu, Jaylalitha (McMillin 2001). To fill hours of programming, the early strategy was to create call-in music and film shows that served the need for both content and audience feedback. Discussing its origins, Udaya TV's vice-president of programming, Srinath,[8] said the idea for the network grew out of the feedback he, as a Kannada film actor, received at social events and professional functions. Kannadigas kept pointing to the Hindi-language channels and the newly established Sun TV, and demanded one in their own language. His connection with the president of the Sun TV network led to the establishment of the branch Udaya TV in Bangalore in 1994. Call-in and viewer-response shows were an ingenious strategy where by the thousands of letters received per week also provided ideas for new formats and helped sales and marketing executives construct audience profiles for advertisers.

While Sun TV and its Telugu branch have an advantage in that they cater to urban and rural populations with strong language affinity and that are more conservative in attitudes and adherence to traditions, Udaya TV faced the challenge of catering to a highly cosmopolitan urban audience, many of whom were immigrants from other parts of India, most often the north. Programming in Kannada was appealing to middle- and lower-middle-class urban audiences and rural populations if they chose to pay for cable—a remote prospect in the latter 1990s with Doordarshan's free terrestrial telecasts. Adapting and cloning from other networks, Udaya TV struggled to find its niche, producing, more often than not, flops such as the cloned *Tic Tic Tic* and *Ek Minute* (early avatars of *A Minute to Win It*), even though these had been top-rated shows in their own markets. Audiences were just not ready for the harsh judging or even friendly sparring between host and guests; they preferred more serious programming where elders were respected and youth were given a serious chance to compete. The need for spontaneity or light-hearted banter was lost on middle-class audiences (see McMillin 2003).

Among the private networks, a marked difference between vernacular-language channels and Star TV was the high priority placed by the former on social responsibility. Personnel at Udaya TV discussed the creation of programs that would address legal, medical, and political problems; most discussed formats for these were, again, call-in shows and panel discussions. Entertainment program formats that quickly rose to the top were the game show, talk show, and call-in music show, all primarily film-based. Vernacular language and cultural context provided an edge over the English-language networks. A staff of around ten producers was devoted to watching programs on other channels to detect trends and develop ideas for new content based on best practices. The risks for new program production were huge, yet top executives recognized that in-house productions, no matter how lowly rated, were essential to establishing the network's identity. Creative producers were frustrated that, despite all the efforts that went into producing a show, the highest audiences were achieved for movie telecasts. The cost-efficient and highly popular movies, as well as reality-based shows taped outdoors, could only go so far in developing and maintaining a brand loyalty. With revenue coming in solely from advertisers, pressure was high for good quality, studio-produced, relevant programming. Despite the tremendous advantage Doordarshan had with its terrestrial reach and government funding, Udaya TV executives explained that they had the edge in terms of nimbleness and flexibility:

> There's no red tapism there, there is no bribery, there is absolutely nothing going on under the table. You wanted an interview with the top people and you've got it in five minutes, so that's the kind of openness and access we have, that an average person can have with the channel, and I think that has helped us to a very large extent. Secondly is the kind of diversity of programs which we are giving the people, which makes a *big* difference, you know.[9]

Ironically, Udaya TV struggled in its early days and even currently in the 2000s to compete with its own parent network, Sun TV. Despite the highly publicized conflict between Tamilians and Kannadigas, audience fieldwork also revealed that Kannada-speaking viewers often preferred Tamil-language programming on Sun TV because of the slick production quality. Doordarshan had at least 21 channels, reached around 87.2 percent of the population through a network of 1,090 terrestrial transmitters, and earned around US$15 million annually. Commercial sponsors accounted for at least 40 percent of its revenue with primary advertising for soaps, toothpaste, television sets, detergents, textiles, shampoos, corporate services (banking, legal, etc.), two-wheelers, detergent cakes, and cosmetic oils. Larger networks such as Zee moved to broadband in the mid-2000s and now offer high-speed Internet, video on demand, digital video recorder, voiceover Internet protocol (VOIP), and local and long-distance services as part of their subscriber packages.

In the early 2000s, Doordarshan continued its struggle to balance its information and education mission with entertainment, with a resurgence of documentaries and reality shows that emphasized the local in terms of settings, dialect, and content. Simultaneously, reality and game shows were gaining ground, pulling in B-grade and has-been actors from the big screen as hosts and drawing in vast audiences as a result of their residual celebrity status. Development programs suffered a further decline due to the high popularity of film-based programming such as movie song countdowns and film trivia game shows. During this time, mergers and fold-ups marked the Indian television environment, with many smaller networks finding themselves no match for the larger conglomerates. Notable mega-networks such as Sahara One, Zee TV, and Sun TV pushed aggressively for overseas markets and, in the past decade, have gained significant audiences among the Indian diaspora (McMillin 2010). Partnerships with movie studios and distribution networks have ensured their success overseas given the high demand for film-based programming.

A maturing global industry: the 2000s and beyond

By the mid-2000s, the Indian media and entertainment (M&E) industry was valued at around $10 billion, with the television industry, at $4.2 billion, accounting for the largest share of revenue. New distribution platforms such as digital cable, Direct to Home (DTH), and Internet protocol television (IPTV) accounted for growth as high as 19 percent between 2006 and 2007. In the latter part of the decade, even big networks that had acquired smaller ones in the early 2000s found themselves having to de-merge to combat government anti-monopoly regulations, to maintain efficient operations, and to respond to different technological requirements in each sector. Zee TV is a prime example, de-merging into four separate businesses: Content Creation and Broadcast, News Broadcast, Cable, and Direct-to-Home. From these emerged three units: Zee News Ltd. (News); Wire and Wireless India Ltd. (Cable) with ownership of Siticable, India's largest MSO; and Dish TV India Ltd. (DTH). Revenues at the company shot up, with consolidated revenues up 18 percent from 2006. In 2007, Zee acquired 50 percent of Ten Sports, a leading sports channel. By 2010–11, the leader of the Indian urban media market was Zee Entertainment Enterprises Limited (ZEEL) with a 36 percent growth in advertising revenues and 14 percent increase in subscription revenues. Zee's sports channels, particularly Ten Cricket, launched in time for the India–South Africa cricket series, drew in the most revenue. ZEEL's operating margin of 27–28 percent plateaued due to its revenue increase, despite its increase in content and carriage costs.

By contrast, news channels as a whole had very modest revenues, bolstered only by world cricket and high corruption stories. For example, TV Today Network Limited (which operates Aaj Tak, Headlines Today, Tez, and Dilli Aaj Tak) reported a revenue growth of only 3 percent. NDTV's growth was 0.3 percent, IBN18 Broadcast Limited's (which operates CNN IBN and IBN7) was 15 percent, TV 18's (which operates CNBC TV 18 and CNBC Awaaz) was 11 percent and Zee News Limited or ZNL (which operates Zee News, Zee Business, Zee 24 Taas, Zee 24 Ghantalu, Zee News Uttar Pradesh, Zee Punjabi, and 24 Ghanta) dropped dramatically by 48 percent. The primary reason for this was the demerger of all of its (general entertainment GEC) channels to ZEEL at the beginning of 2010. Its revenues were steadily climbing by the end of 2011.

52 *Divya McMillin*

Speaking to the decline in news audiences, the anchor and former partner of NewsX, a 24-hour private news channel rated the highest in 2008, noted that it was due to the trend toward sensational stories on corruption, rape, and Bollywood scandals. Journalistic objectivity was non-existent, profits were all-important, partisan politics were rampant. The constant need to respond to crises, whether real or manufactured, had produced any number of so-called journalists who lacked formal training and lacked an understanding of context.[10] Adding to this decline in quality of the news product was the open secret of 'paid news' (Sircar 2014, see footnote 1) where politicians and celebrities either had part ownership of news networks or were heavy sponsors to ensure favorable coverage, as demonstrated in recent accusations against BJP leader Narendra Modi by AAP leader Arvind Kejriwal (*Dna* 2014).

Batabyal (2010) offers a criticism of news professionals themselves in his assessment of declining news audiences. He attributes the low numbers to the construction of audiences for news as an elite, narrow group, by private networks. Even so, news reporting itself is a far cry from the state-oriented Doordarshan talking heads of television from the 1960s to the 1980s. Live outdoor broadcast is possible with hi-tech vans ready to pursue any and every story with drama potential. News as a genre has itself become diversified as has the technology through which media products are received. Fieldwork in July 2013, which included analysis of television news, showed that all channels had highly repetitious news stories with screens cluttered with scrolling content and advertising banners. News anchors and reporters conveyed bits of news in rapid-fire style with a great sense of urgency, while video clips looped seemingly endlessly, conveying only the most essential piece of the action. Political scandals, celebrity downfalls, accidents, and other such sensational items dominated content. Such a trend is perhaps a response to the declining priority of television as a news source itself.

With government mandates for digitization in metros, expanding broadband services, and multiplication of handheld technologies, the urban Indian consumer has a rich range of media choices. The small screen is only one avenue through which television programming reaches the consumer. Mobile phone gimmicks, computer games, and advertising campaigns are some of the many ways in which television celebrities and top-rated shows are intertextually woven into the pop culture landscape. Industry reports and television rating systems indicate that India continues to expand as an economy with television advertising as the fastest growing sector. The TAM (Television Audience Measurement) Annual Universe Update 2012 put total television households in India at 231 million, with cable and satellite households at 126 million and digital households at 42 million. In 2011, the Federation of Indian Chambers of Commerce and Industry (FICCI) reported that the Indian Media and Entertainment Industry (M&E) grew by 11 percent from the 2009–10 fiscal year (i.e., from US$12.9 billion to $14.4 billion). The industry is expected to grow to $28.1 billion by 2015.[11]

Batabyal (2010: 389) writes that the ratings industry itself is a highly profitable one. TAM 'has near complete monopoly over a lucrative market; television channels, advertising agencies, corporate clients and public relations firms all subscribe to TAM's ratings.' TAM's methods have been much criticized. First, it is able to track channels turned on but not whether people are actually watching them. Second, the sample size of tracked homes is miniscule (4,500 cable homes among 69 million). Third, the tracking pertains only to urban areas, specifically with a population of 100,000 or more. Finally, states that are most remote or among the poorest are entirely ignored. The sample therefore, is a subset of middle-class, urban India. With the method of tracking itself, problems have been identified. As stated earlier, tracking does not account for whether someone is actually watching or who exactly is watching. Each person who turns on the TV can be coded, but this does not mean the same person is the only one watching through the tracking period. The result of these inconsistencies is that TRPs are taken at face value, causing programs and advertisers to target the male, urban, middle-class viewer. Content that emerges as a consequence depicts urban affluence. This limited outlook packaged to viewers all over India is compatible with larger narratives of the nation being on the verge of becoming a serious global player where the focus is on those who are urban and mobile anyway, ignoring vast populations struggling with inequities exacerbated by globalization. It should be noted that dissatisfaction with TAM has led to pressure on the Broadcasting Audience Research Council to propose an alternative, to be launched in 2014 (Gopalan 2013).

Opportunism, mimicry, and new forms of representation

At the end of 2013, Indian television was estimated to be growing steadily at the rate of 12–15 percent per year, with an overall revenue of US$6.5 billion.[12] A close review of various industry reports revealed that advertising continues to be the primary form of revenue, accounting for at least 80 percent. The growth is mostly attributed to general entertainment channels (GECs) rather than news channels, which experienced a slower growth of 7 percent during the year. While cable subscriptions are on the rise, illegal connections and faulty data (with number of connections routinely underreported) make it difficult to evaluate just how extensive a contribution to overall revenue subscriptions make. On the other hand, the Ministry of Information and Broadcasting's (MIB) mandate that all four metros become fully digitized by May 2011 and the whole country digitized by December 2014, indicates that digitization will be a robust source of income for the industry. The number of direct-to-home subscribers (DTH) increased by 62 percent in 2010–11. During fieldwork in July 2013, fiber optic cables were laid throughout the city of Bengaluru, disrupting sidewalks and exacerbating traffic chaos. The trend to digitization is expected to increase exponentially as a result of the MIB's mandate with projections of digital homes at 64 percent by 2015 of a total of 155 million

54 *Divya McMillin*

cable households. To support innovations, venture capital funds emerged such as the India Innovation Fund (IIF) that, for example, with Accel Partners, invested approximately US$2.16 million in Bengaluru-based SureWaves MediaTech, a digital media company. InMobil, another Bengaluru-based company, acquired US-based Sprout.

India, as one of the BRICs countries, is still the one to watch and will remain so, due in part to technological and labor innovations, but more so because of its progressive and middle-class image mediated by members of this class. Transnational mergers predictably spawn low-risk, standardized television formats such as game shows, travel shows, talk shows, and cooking shows. The state-sponsored Doordarshan and private television networks in India strive toward brand-building and brand value management to attract and maintain advertisers and subscribers and, as a result, engage in frantic and large-scale program cloning, developing, collaging, and illegal copying or pirating of program formats. Foreign–local partnerships such as the Disney UTV deal hinge on the localization strategy where by Indians constitute the majority of executive teams and content is primarily local. Yet what exactly is 'local' is constantly shifting, resulting in programming that trends toward the Westernized Indian urban context.

Critical scholars warn that the framing of India as a hotspot for entrepreneurship also feeds into a Western-produced imperialist discourse that capitalism is a solution to terrorism. The racial coding of this argument is evident. The retraining of the spotlight on India from its infrastructural inadequacies, political conflicts, or treatment of women, to its growing middle-class consumerism and its skilled workforce, while perhaps promoting an imperialist discourse, also opens up complex opportunities for audience agency and meaningful consumer engagement with the global economy.

Throughout this chapter, we have seen how television networks in India, both state-sponsored and private, have watched carefully and consistently the moves and shifts of audience desires. The strong correspondence between audiences and producers, particularly in private, vernacular networks, demonstrates a jointly written narrative, no doubt fraught with power struggles, yet one that includes both producer and consumer. Such a collaboration demonstrates an interdependence and an opportunistic encounter that marks the difference between a globalized television environment and a nationalized one. Through a rewriting of television history in India that incorporates evidence from the professionals working within it, this chapter has offered perhaps a different view to the standard accounts by arguing that Doordarshan, while protected by state funding, was heavily engaged in innovation and format adaptation from the early days of liberalization and was not as complacent and sluggish as some histories have made it out to be.

In highlighting those strategies in networks in India that moved them forward to a globalized marketplace, this chapter responds to the criticisms of a postcolonial framework in three key ways. First, it critically engages with the global present instead of forcing a narrow analysis of the past as has been noted to be the trend in such analyses (see Loomba 1994). Second, it acknowledges the supremacy awarded to modernity in the pedagogical descriptions of network objectives, yet, contrary to the overt focus on Eurocentric constructions of the same (see Lazarus 2002), discusses an appropriated modernity where value is also placed on those television formats that can revive forgotten music and dance forms, and that can offer a stage for gender, caste, and class minorities. It historicizes capitalism in India as both an output of colonialism and socialism. Finally, it foregrounds the examination of the industry itself as a system of dynamic and fluid global, national, regional, and local elements and describes how these systems converge, compete, and are facilitated in various contexts (see Chowdhury 2006). In so doing, it has drawn out the opportunistic possibilities of all sides of such interdependent relationships upon which globalization thrives and through which it is even possible.

Notes

This chapter is dedicated to Jehangir Pocha (1969–2014), editor-in-chief of NewsX channel, former *Boston Globe* China correspondent and former editor of *Business World*, who, with generosity and thoroughness, kept the author informed of India's media industry over the years.

1 The author thanks Dr. Joost de Bruin, School of English, Film, Theatre and Media Studies, Victoria University, New Zealand, who summarized key points of the public lecture.
2 Usha Kini, program executive, Doordarshan. Personal communication, June 16, 1997.
3 Ibid.
4 S. Chandramoily, All India Radio Audience research officer. Personal communication, June 20, 1997.
5 Rajnath Kamat, vice-president of sales, Star TV. Personal communication, July 28, 1997.
6 Ibid.
7 Ibid.
8 Srinath, vice-president of Udaya TV. Personal communication, July 1, 1997.
9 Vijaykumar, general manager of Udaya TV. Personal communication, July 1, 1997.
10 Jehangir Pocha, editor-in-chief at NewsX, former *Boston Globe* China correspondent and former editor of *Business World*. Personal communication, January 21, 2013.
11 Retrieved September 5, 2013, from www.indiainbusiness.nic.in/industry-infrastructure/service-sectors/media-entertainment.htm.
12 *India Media and Entertainment Industry; Radio, Television and Broadcast* (2013). Retrieved February 14, 2013, from www.reportlinker.com/p01593383-summary/India-Media-and-Entertainment-Industry-Radio-Television-and-Broadcast.html.

References

Ashcroft, B. (2001) *Post-colonial Transformation*, London and New York: Routledge.
Batabyal, S. (2010) 'Constructing an audience: news television practices in India,' *Contemporary South Asia*, 18(4): 387–99.

56 Divya McMillin

Chakravarty, S. (1993) *National Identity in Indian Popular Cinema 1947–1987*, New Delhi: Oxford University Press.

Chatterji, P.C. (1991) *Broadcasting in India*, New Delhi: Sage.

Chowdhury, K. (2006) 'Interrogating "newness": globalization and postcolonial theory in the age of endless war,' *Cultural Critique*, 62: 126–60.

dna (2014) 'AAP chief Arvind Kejriwal threatens agitation if e-rickshaw issue not resolved,' October 8. Available at www.dnaindia.com/india/report-aap-chief-arvind-kejriwal-threatens-agitation-if-e-rickshaw-issue-not-resolved-2024443.

Doordarshan Audience Research Unit (1995) New Delhi: Nutech Pholithographers.

Doordarshan Audience Research Unit (1996) New Delhi: Nutech Pholithographers.

Economic Times (2014) 'AAP chief Arvind Kejriwal threatens to "jail" media; says TV channels have been "paid" by Modi,' March 14. Available at http://economictimes.indiatimes.com/news/politics-and-nation/aap-chief-arvind-kejriwalthreatens-to-jail-media-says-tv-channels-have-been-paid-by-modi/articleshow/31996511.cms.

Ernst and Young (2014) *India Attractiveness Survey 2014: Enabling the Prospects*. Available at www.ey.com/IN/en/Issues/Business-environment/EY-India-attractiveness-survey.

Fürsich, E. and Shrikhande, S. (2007) 'Development broadcasting in India and beyond: redefining an old mandate in an age of media globalization,' *Journal of Broadcasting & Electronic Media*, 51: 110–28.

Gopalan, K. (2013) 'The great TAMasha,' *Business Outlook*, 8(16): 30–2.

Gupta, A. (2009) 'India and the IPL: cricket's globalized empire,' *The Round Table*, 98(401): 201–11.

Hong, Z. (2011) 'The expansion of outward FDI: a comparative study of China and India,' *China: An International Journal*, 9(1): 1–25.

India in Business (2011) ITP Division, Ministry of External Affairs, Government of India. Available at www.indiainbusiness.nic.in/industry-infrastructure/servicesectors/media-entertainment.htm.

Krishnaswamy, R. (2008) 'Connections, conflicts, complicities' in R. Krishnaswamy and J.C. Hawley (eds.), *The Postcolonial and the Global*, Minneapolis: University of Minnesota Press, pp. 2–22.

Kumar, K.J. (2000) *Mass Communication in India*, New Delhi: Jaico House.

Kust, M.J. (1964) *Foreign Enterprise in India: Laws and Policies*, Chapel Hill: University of North Carolina Press.

Lazarus, N. (2002) 'The fetish of the "West" in postcolonial theory' in C. Bartolovich and N. Lazarus (eds.) *Marxism, Modernity, and Postcolonial Studies*, Cambridge: Cambridge University Press, pp. 43–64.

Loomba, A. (1994) 'Overworlding the "Third World"' in P. Williams and L. Chrisman (eds.), *Colonial Discourse and Post-colonial Theory: A Reader*, New York: Columbia University Press, pp. 305–24.

Manchanda, U. (1998) 'Invasion from the skies: the impact of foreign television on India,' *Australian Studies in Journalism*, 7: 136–61.

Mankekar, P. (1999) *Screening Culture, Viewing Politics: An Ethnography of Television, Womanhood, and Nation in Postcolonial India*, Durham, NC: Duke University Press.

McMillin, D.C. (2001) 'Localizing the global: television and hybrid programming in India,' *International Journal of Cultural Studies*, 4(1): 45–68.

McMillin, D.C. (2003) 'Television, gender, and labor in the global city,' *Journal of Communication*, 53(3): 496–511.

McMillin, D.C. (2010) 'The global face of Indian television' in H.G. Shah and M. Curtin (eds.) *Re-orienting Global Communication: Indian and Chinese Media Beyond Borders*, Chicago: University of Illinois Press, pp. 118–38.

Mitra, A. (1993) *Television and Popular Culture in India*, New Delhi: Sage.

Mullen, R.D. and Ganguly, S. (2012) 'The rise of India's soft power,' *Foreign Policy*. Available at www.foreignpolicy.com/articles/2012/05/08/the_rise_of_indian_soft_power.

Pieterse, J.N. (1995) 'Preface' in J.N. Pieterse and B. Parekh (eds.) *The Decolonization of Imagination: Culture, Knowledge and Power*, London and New Jersey: Zed Books, pp. ii–v.

Prakash, G. (1990) 'Writing post-orientalist histories of the Third World: perspectives from Indian historiography,' *Comparative Studies in Society and History*, 32(2): 383–408.

Rajagopal, A. (1996) 'Mediating modernity: theorizing reception on a non-Western society,' *The Communication Review*, 1(4): 441–69.

Roy, A. (2008) 'Bringing up TV: popular culture and the developmental modern in India,' *South Asian Popular Culture*, 6(1): 29–43.

Shashidhar, A. (2013) 'Waiting for the echo,' *Business Today*, 22(17): 44–60.

Shields, P. and Muppidi, S. (1996) *Integration, the Indian State and STAR TV: Policy and Theory Issues*, paper presented to the Annual Meeting of the International Communication Association, Chicago.

Singhal, A. and Rogers, E.M. (1988) 'Television soap operas for development in India,' *Gazette*, 41: 109–26.

Sukumar, R. (2003) 'The future of Indian cities is here,' *Business Today*, 17 August. Available at http://archives.digitaltoday.in/businesstoday/20030817/cover1.html.

Van der Veer, P. (1997) *Religious Nationalism: Hindus and Muslims in India*, Berkeley: University of California Press.

Venn, C. (2006) *The Postcolonial Challenge: Towards Alternative Worlds*, London and New Delhi: Sage.

Wan, C. (2011) 'Study: Indian TV industry losing $1.4bn due to piracy,' *Hindustan Times*, 1 November. Available at www.hindustantimes.com/world-news/RestOf Asia/Study-Indian-TV-industry-losing-1-4bn-due-to-piracy/Article1-763757.aspx.

Zakaria, F. (2006) 'India rising,' *Newsweek*, March 6, 34–42.

4 Watching television in Bhutan

Bunty Avieson

The kingdom of Bhutan drew the international spotlight in 1999 when it became the last nation on earth to introduce broadcast television. It was a deliberate and strategic move by a country that for centuries had chosen to isolate itself from the rest of the world, turning inward to nurture its own culture. The small Himalayan country, whose population in 2013 was estimated at just 733,000,[1] sits uneasily between two feisty behemoths – China and India – each with over a billion people and an ongoing history of border disputes. Bhutan has long been wary of being swamped, either politically or culturally, by these larger neighbours, as well as the world beyond (Penjore 2004).

As part of this endogenous focus, international broadcast television had been banned by royal decree.[2] The first outward indication that King Jigme Singye Wangchuck might be softening his stance came in July 1998, during the World Cup Final between Brazil and France. The royal government erected a large screen in the town square of the capital Thimphu to broadcast the match live to its soccer-mad citizens. Thousands turned out, sitting cross-legged on the ground, enjoying picnics and cheering France's resounding 3–0 victory.

At his silver jubilee celebrations the following year, King Jigme launched Bhutan Broadcasting Service TV, a free-to-air network. In his address to the nation he declared Bhutan was ready for the arrival of both television and the Internet, but warned that these new technologies should be approached with caution,

> The introduction of television and the Internet is a reflection of the level of progress that we have achieved. I would like to remind our youth that television and Internet provide a whole range of possibilities, which can be both beneficial as well as negative for the individual and the society. I trust that you will exercise your good sense and judgement in using the Internet and television. It is my sincere hope that the introduction of television will be beneficial to our people and country.
>
> His Majesty King Jigme Singye Wangchuck, 2 June 1999
> (Powdyel 2006)

Initially, BBS TV provided an hour of news each evening in Thimphu. The first 30 minutes was local news in Dzongkha, the national language, which was spoken naturally by about a third of the population, and then the same news was repeated in English. Both languages were taught in schools across the country. Three months later, cable television arrived from India, via newly established Bhutanese operators, providing packages of up to 45 channels. The cable operators were able to reach rural areas that free-to-air BBS TV couldn't, so the government required them also to provide the BBS news hour as part of their licence. Due to technological and business difficulties, this had mixed success. Media analyst Siok-San Pek, of the Bhutan Centre for Media and Democracy, described the introduction of international television as both 'sudden' and an 'explosion' (Media Impact Study 2003: 20).

Just over a decade later, in 2012, BBS TV was showing up to six hours of news, discussion panels and documentaries every evening, with a second channel, BBS TV2, offering 24 hours of varied local programming, which included cooking shows, *Bhutan Idol*, parenting advice, children's shows, cartoons and a youth travelogue about sites to visit within the country. As Bhutanese content increased, consumption of foreign television had decreased (*Kuensel*, 10 May 2010, editorial). In 2013, a government survey showed BBS TV was the most popular form of media for news and entertainment (BIMIS 2013: 41). Bhutanese voices and faces now dominated the airwaves, talking about things that mattered to Bhutanese citizens.

A short history

The king's decision to introduce television was part of an ongoing process of unification and modernization, which has been a long-term goal of the country's rulers, dating back to the seventeenth century and the arrival from Tibet of Shabdrung Rinpoche, considered the founder of modern Bhutan. The kingdom, known as Druk Yul, or Land of the Thunder Dragon, comprises multiple ethnicities, each with their own language, style of dress and traditions. Drawing together these ethnically and linguistically diverse tribes, scattered throughout a succession of mountain ridges and valleys, has been a 400-year process. An estimated 23 native languages are spoken and only one, Dzongkha, has a written form (Yeshi 2012).[3] The Shabdrung set about creating a distinctly Drukpa culture, establishing a style of architecture, dress codes, formal system of manners and religious festivals with distinctive lama dances (Fischer and Tashi 2009:21).

After Shabdrung Rinpoche's death in 1651, the country lost some of its cohesion, reverting to ancient tribal feuds. When the first king, Ugyen Wangchuck, was unanimously chosen as the first hereditary monarch in 1907, he resumed the process of reunification and modernization (Fischer and Tashi 2009:31–37). For the next century, while the rest of the world underwent seismic geopolitical upheavals, each successive king concentrated their resources inwards, on nation-building.

The first king (1907–26) improved transport and communication, and established education outside monasteries. The second king (1926–52) opened medical clinics and signed the first treaty with India. The third king (1952–72) took the first steps toward democratization, joining the Colombo Plan in 1962 and the United Nations in 1972, building a national highway that connected east to west and introducing telephone lines and Bhutan Post. When the fourth king assumed the throne in 1974, he invited foreign dignitaries to his coronation, marking the end of absolute isolation. His 34-year reign introduced democracy, the mass media and Gross National Happiness, as an alternate measure of progress to the economic focus of Gross Domestic Product used by other countries. In 2008 he devolved royal power to the first democratically elected government, signed the country's Constitution, and handed the titular crown to his son, the fifth king, King Khesar (Fischer and Tashi 2009).

Creating the king's media

As a first step in creating the conditions for democracy, King Jigme deemed a vibrant and diverse media space was necessary. In the late 1970s, he sent a bright graduate, Kinley Dorji, to Australia and America to study journalism. In 1986 Kinley was charged with turning the government newsletter into the country's first newspaper, *Kuensel*. The same year the royal government took over a youth radio station that broadcast on a short-wave transmitter for an hour on Sundays, and renamed it the Bhutanese Broadcasting Service. In 1999 BBS radio was extended to include BBS TV, cable operators set up business and the Internet arrived. In 2003 Bhutan got mobile phones. In 2006 the king granted two independent newspaper licences, then more followed. In 2011 the Internet, initially available only in the major cities, started to be rolled out across all 20 dzonkhags (regional government areas). BBS TV was able to stream live on its website such major events as the fifth king's wedding in 2011 for Bhutanese across the country as well as those studying abroad. In 2012 BBS TV2 was launched.

The Bhutanese joined the information age at a time when all modern media was available to them – print, electronic and digital. But the media matrix that is evolving is distinctly Bhutanese. They have approached this evolving media landscape with a crucial local specificity, befitting their cultural values. As an oral culture, with literacy at just 56 per cent and no history of print capitalism or culture of reading,[4] newspapers and magazines have achieved low penetration. Television is the dominant source of news.

In terms of good governance, the media, particularly TV, have helped in fostering public discourse and debates in a young democracy. For instance, during the first parliamentary and subsequent local government elections, public debates on TV drew people's attention across the country, which had impacts on the outcomes of the elections (BIMIS 2013: 78).

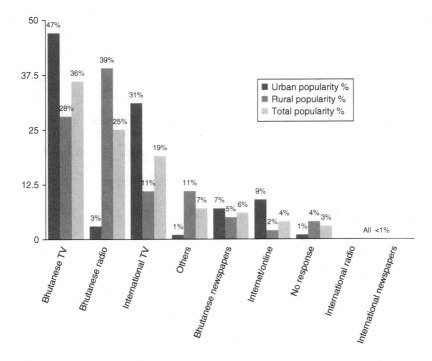

Figure 4.1 Popularity of different media
Source: Graph published in BIMIS 2013: 48.

In 2012, BBS TV was cited as the most preferred media source at 36 per cent, followed by Bhutanese radio at 25 per cent and then international TV at 19 per cent (BIMIS 2013: 41). In response to the question 'What country's culture do you view most on TV?', 50 per cent of respondents said they viewed Bhutanese culture the most, 22 per cent viewed Indian culture the most, 20 per cent viewed Western culture the most and 4 per cent viewed Korean (BIMIS 2013: 69). Most Bhutanese households owned a television set: 79 per cent of rural households and 68 per cent of urban households.

Television in Bhutan has been successful in showing Bhutan to itself. In this mountainous country, where 70 per cent of people live in rural areas, people often didn't travel beyond their own valleys. Just a decade ago, people in neighbouring villages, a few hours walk apart, would only have met each other at the annual *tsechu*.[5] Now they are seeing faces from nearby valleys and even further away, broadcast into their living rooms. Television has connected them to Benedict Anderson's (2006) 'imagined nation' that before they may not have considered. It expanded their world, not just in a global sense, but in showing them what is in their own 'neighbourhood'.

Bunty Avieson

Even though we live in Bumthang we never knew about some pilgrim sites in Bumthang and their significance until we saw programs about them on TV

(Media Impact Study 2008)

'We villagers cannot afford to go beyond Trashigang and Samdrup Jongkhar. Watching TV at home we could see what Thimphu looks like and how monasteries are. At the same time on BBS we could see what is happening around the country and National Assembly. Before I just heard about our politicians on radio but now I could see and recognize them,' said a shopkeeper

(Wangdi 2008)

The new media landscape is providing cultural reinforcement. As Graeme Turner (2010: 3) wrote: 'The media, and in particular television, have developed new capacities for constructing identities and these capacities are producing social effects.'

Fears for Bhutan

The power and influence of television has been debated since Marshall McLuhan and his contemporaries investigated its effects in American and Canadian societies in the 1950s. This continues today in academia and popular discourse. Following the launch of television in Bhutan many warned that cultural degradation would inevitably follow.

The recent, official introduction of television to Bhutan marks a decisive move – understandable, and yet not without marked risks for the erosion of Bhutanese cultural and contributory resources… Neither can it be assumed possible to stem what is likely to be a flood of global media products into Bhutan

(Hershock 2004: 74)

The recent arrival of commercial television in Bhutan represents more than the introduction of a merely benign technology. Global television brings with it a deeper process, one that systematically cultivates social isolation and the dissolution of all contrary cultural priorities

(McDonald 2004)

The more time we spend immersed in the corporate-controlled and packaged world of television, the less time we have for the direct human exchanges through which cultural identity and values were traditionally expressed, reinforced and updated

(D. Korten quoted in McDonald 2004)

Certainly television can be an attention-dominating medium. It simultaneously provides an audio and a visual experience, demanding capitulation of both senses. In any social space, a television, set at audible volume, can quickly render secondary any social interactions. Part of television's power is the moving pictures, which can be compelling.

South African novelist Doris Lessing observed the effect of television on the cultural life of a London community in the 1950s. In an evocative account she described its arrival as 'the end of an era, the death of a culture',

> Before, when the men came back from work, the tea was already on the table, a fire was roaring, the radio emitted words or music softly in a corner, they washed and sat down at their places, with the woman, the child, and whoever else could be inveigled downstairs. Food began emerging from the oven, dish after dish, tea was brewed, beer appeared, off went the jerseys or jackets, the men sat in their short-sleeves, glistening with well-being. They all talked, they sang, they told what had happened in their day, they talked dirty – a ritual; they quarreled, they shouted, they kissed and made up and went to bed at twelve or one, after six or so hours of energetic conviviality... And then from one day to the next – but literally from one evening to the next – came the end of the good times, for television had arrived and sat like a toad in the corner of the kitchen. Soon the big kitchen table had been pushed along the wall, chairs were installed in a semi-circle and, on the chair arms, the swivelling supper-trays. It was the end of an exuberant verbal culture
>
> (Lessing 1997)

In 1994, US researchers Paik and Comstock claimed to have found a link between violence on television and negative behaviour in children. They analysed more than 200 studies on television violence and concluded that there was 'a positive and significant correlation between television violence and aggressive behavior' (cited in Croteau and Hoynes 2000: 109). Similar concerns about television's influence, and its drug-like, addictive (Winn 1987) effects have continued to be raised. In 1982 Rosemary Kuptana, former president of the Inuit Broadcasting Corporation and Inuit Tapirisat of Canada (Canada's national Inuit political organization), in a speech to the Canadian Radio-television Telecommunications Commission famously characterized the social impact of American television on the Inuit as akin to the explosion of a 'neutron bomb', destroying the soul of her people while leaving everything else intact (Roth 2005: 146). As recently as 2000, Robert Putnam charted a dramatic decline in virtually every measurable dimension of civic participation by Americans and linked this decline to the arrival of television (Putnam 2000).

While many academic studies, particularly in the US, reflect these themes – television as propaganda; cultural thug; inciter of violence; responsible for dumbing down entire generations and destroyer of community (see also Bly 1996; Washburn and Thornton 1996) – many other media scholars have

64 *Bunty Avieson*

criticized such media effects theories as overly simplistic, and dismissive of a range of other social and economic factors (see Mackay 2002; McQuail 2005; Lumby and Fine 2006; Gauntlett 2008; Norris and Inglehart 2009). Lumby and Fine questioned US research conducted in collaboration with sponsors to establish cause-and-effect relationships between marketing and consumer behaviour; and they critiqued studies that purport to show a direct correlation between watching violence on television and the high violence experienced in the US. 'Sociological research into the causes of violence consistently puts media influences at the bottom and the availability of weapons, social inequality, drug abuse and dysfunctional parenting at the top' (Lumby and Fine 2006: 109). British television, they argued, showed just as much violence as the US, yet Britain has negligible gun ownership and one of the lowest murder rates in the world (Lumby and Fine 2006: 110). Anthropologist Levo-Henriksson (2007: 157) said: 'We cannot consider TV to be a uniform phenomenon cross-culturally: TV is a different thing to different people and its impact varies according to the cultural traditions that surround it.' Norris and Inglehart (2009: 2) adopted the concept of 'firewalls' to explain that a series of social constructions stand between the media consumer and a media message. They argue that cultures likely to be less affected by media content are those that are parochial by nature, containing many poor sectors, who lack the agency to access modern communications, as well as social and psychological barriers.

According to Siok-San Pek, some of the discourse inside Bhutan reflects various elements of these media effects myths, but not all.

> Discussions on the media in Bhutan tend to revolve around the traditional paradigm of the all-powerful effects of media. This views content in either a negative or occasionally a celebratory manner – for instance, the protectionist stance that sees most 'foreign' media products as dangerous and having negative effects on 'Bhutanese' ethics and culture. Or the view that the liberalising of the media economy has opened up a world of ideas to Bhutan and challenged negative attitudes and made Bhutanese less conservative. Most dominant, however, is the recognition of Bhutan's unique situation as a small country and culture in a globalised world
>
> (Media Impact Study 2008: 68)

Regardless of decades of studies that expose the myth of television as all-powerful and able to single-handedly wipe out cultures, the mainstream mass media continues to perpetuate that view. It is evident in some reportage of Bhutan, which embraced television after these fears had become entrenched in Western discourse.

A foreign view of Bhutan

In 2003 two journalists from Britain's respected *Guardian* flew in to report how this mountain idyll was coping with the introduction of television. In their story titled 'Fast forward into trouble', they presented the country as a crime-free paradise until television 'brought Bhutan's first crime wave – murder, fraud, drug offences' (Scott-Clark and Levy 2003). They claimed that half of Bhutan's children were watching television up to 12 hours a day and one third of Bhutanese girls wanted to 'look more American (whiter skin, blond hair) A similar proportion have new approaches to relationships (boyfriends not husbands, sex not marriage).' At the time covered by the story, only 35 per cent of the population had electricity to power a television and the total number of cable subscribers was an estimated 15,000 (Media Impact Study 2003). While viewers in the capital Thimphu and border town of Phuentsholing received up to 45 channels, some rural areas received less than eight (Media Impact Study 2003: 39).

It's not possible that half the country's children were watching up to 12 hours of television. They attended school five days a week, sometimes six. If they lived too remotely to get to a school, their families were unlikely to have electricity, much less a television. Nor did television alert the Bhutanese to the startling possibility of casual sex. Sex with or without a long-term relationship has been going on in Bhutan for... well, forever. The *Guardian* journalists imposed a paradigm of Western morality onto a culture that didn't see the world in those terms.

The writers presented as evidence of their crime wave a dozen or so recent incidents – including a man driving his in-laws off a cliff in a drunken rage, six bank employees jailed for fraud and a girl working as a prostitute in the border town of Phuentsholing. They wrote that there was a wealth of evidence that the 'impatient, selfish society promoted by television' was a critical factor in these crimes: 'The 700,000 inhabitants ... had never experienced serious law-breaking before.' This, too, is incorrect. Long before television arrived, Bhutan had serious crime. The country had suffered a prime ministerial assassination, bombings, murders, rapes, embezzlement and high-level corruption (Fischer and Tashi 2009). Bhutanese journalist Sonam Ongmo wrote on her blog:

> Juvenile delinquency problems in Bhutan are not new. They have existed even before the first reports appeared and before television came to Bhutan... This hopefully clarifies an article 'Fast Forward into trouble' in '*The Guardian*'... Broken families, alcoholism, gambling, murder, and abuse existed even before the road came into Bhutan, way before cable television invaded the privacy of our homes.
>
> (Ongmo 2009b)

The *Guardian* article contained many more unfounded assertions, including: 'There is something depressing about watching a society casting aside its unique character in favour of a Californian beach' (Scott-Clark and Levy 2003). This is an odd comment to make about a land-locked, mountain-loving, endogenous people. Rather than tuning in to *Baywatch*, which seems to be the implication, in fact, when Bhutanese viewers were watching non-Bhutanese television, it was most likely Indian.

66 *Bunty Avieson*

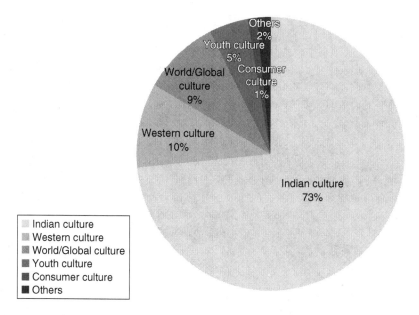

Figure 4.2 Bhutanese perception of the cultures they watch on cable television
Source: Media Impact Study 2003: 57.

The underlying assumptions of the *Guardian* story are both imperialistic and patronizing. They imply that Bhutanese culture is either so fragile that Western/American culture immediately overwhelmed it or that Bhutan is an empty vessel, waiting to be filled with whatever pours out of the television set. This overstates the appeal of Western culture, ignores the reality that they actually preferred Indian shows and disregards the strength and vitality of Bhutan's own culture. It also accords too much power to television.

Denis McQuail recognized these Western assumptions in his analyses of east–west relations. He said that, while theses on media imperialism or 'imbalanced flows' of communication argued against imposing Western paradigms on non-Western nations, it should be noted that the very assumptions underpinning such theses are imperialistic.

> Moreover, the imbalanced-flow critics tended to assume that the contents of global media, especially international news, fiction and entertainment, with their strong American imprint, would have powerful ideological and cultural effects on their audiences. This assumption implicitly overvalues the appeal, potency and persuasiveness of the 'message' of Western media. It also underestimates the vitality and flexibility of the receiving

Watching television in Bhutan   67

cultures and ignores the cultural and intellectual poverty, superficiality and ephemerality of much of the new global media culture

(McQuail 2005: 24)

During their visit, Scott-Clark and Levy interviewed a range of stakeholders, including the deputy communications minister, Leki Dorji. He categorically denied that television could be responsible for what the *Guardian* journalists had dubbed the 'April crime wave'. He told them: 'A culture as rich and sophisticated as ours can survive trash on TV and people are quite capable of turning off the rubbish.' Scott-Clark and Levy reported his comment but chose to disregard it.

Finally, the *Guardian* story ended with a sweeping, unjustified statement, which reveals the biases of the authors rather than anything objective about how television might be impacting on Bhutan.

Everyone is as yet too polite to say it, but, like all of us, the Dragon King underestimated the power of TV, perceiving it as a benign and controllable force, allowing it free rein, believing that his kingdom's culture was strong enough to resist its messages. But television is a portal, and in Bhutan it is systematically replacing one culture with another, skewing the notion of Gross National Happiness, persuading a nation of novice Buddhist consumers to become preoccupied with themselves, rather than searching for their self

(Scott-Clark and Levy 2003)

Gross National Happiness has not been 'skewed' by the portal of television. It is a measure to evaluate its impact. To say television is 'systematically replacing one culture with another' reflects outdated media effects theory, not what was happening in Bhutan in 2003, four years after television was introduced. In fact the society, traditionally suspicious of outside influences, was having a lively debate about television, in the letters pages of *Kuensel*, along with editorials and opinion pieces. Parents were concerned that their children were being distracted from their homework. Others expressed concern that people were watching television while doing their prayers. The Bhutanese were critically assessing this new medium in their midst.

The Media Impact Study 2003, which appeared the same year as the *Guardian* story, revealed what Bhutanese citizens thought about its influence on their society. It is the opposite of the views reported in the *Guardian* story.

The *Guardian* story was read inside Bhutan via the Internet.

A young government employee said that after reading the article, he has learnt not to believe everything that the media covers… exposure to international media has, therefore, made Bhutanese society more discerning about media, including local media

(Media Impact Study 2003: 60)

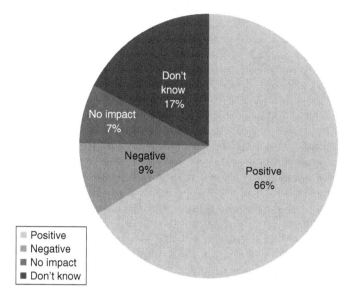

Figure 4.3 People's perception of television's impact on Bhutanese society
Source: Media Impact Study 2003: 54.

Far-reaching consequences

In the age of the Internet, the *Guardian* story, with all its imperialistic, techno-determinist biases, lives on. 'Television killed Shangri-La' has become one of the overarching narratives of international reporting of Bhutan. William Langley, reporting for the UK's *Telegraph*, covered the coronation of King Khesar in 2008 through the prism of Bhutan as a kingdom in decline since television was introduced. It is subtitled 'The prince who brought satellite TV to Shangri-La'.

> He dreamed of hauling his remote realm into the 21st century, so now it has crime and corruption and 46 channels, and a steeply declining Gross National Happiness.
>
> He [the Fifth King] was in a hurry to get back and begin bouncing Bhutan into the 21st century. So, upon his return from Oxford, he quickly convinced his father to embark on a fast and furious programme of modernisation. And this is where the current problems began. The first event to shake the Kingdom out of its millennial slumber was the arrival of television... Crime, vandalism and anti-social behaviour – the blight of many advanced societies, but barely known in Bhutan – started to become commonplace.
>
> (Langley 2008)

Langley's story, like the *Guardian* story, is demonstrably wrong.[6] The fourth king introduced television as part of a long and considered programme of modernization that began with his father, the third king. And, as discussed earlier, Bhutan has always had crime.

The *Guardian* story is quoted in Wikipedia, under its 'Crime in Bhutan' section. The story is also referenced in blogs,[7] news sites,[8] mass market books,[9] and education syllabuses.[10] It is referenced in academic books[11] and journals[12] as a case study 'proving' media effects. UK film theorist Sue Clayton is one of the few media scholars to be critical of the *Guardian* story:

> This coverage overlooked two important points. Firstly, that Bhutan is not a passive victim of new media as they suggest: The introduction of these media and their likely effects has been, and continues to be, the subject of much academic and popular debate within Bhutanese society
>
> (Clayton 2007)

The *Guardian* story has become part of a pernicious cycle. Scott-Clark and Levy visited Bhutan believing television is addictive, encourages violence and obliterates cultures. Through that simplistic (and imperialistic) prism they wrote their story. A decade later, their version of Bhutan continues to be presented as a case study 'proving' that television is addictive, encourages violence and obliterates cultures.

In February 2013 a Russian man provided a link to the story via Twitter, ready for a new generation to be misinformed:

Not all of Bhutan's early experiences with television were good. But nor has it caused the neutron bomb effect experienced by the Inuits or the crime wave of Scott-Clark and Levy's imaginings. It is a resilient culture, able to adopt and adapt new technologies to serve its own cultural purposes.

In April 2012 a lightning strike on the transmission tower in remote Pemagatshel took BBS TV off air for two weeks. *Bhutan Observer* reported that the villagers and farmers were most disappointed to miss the popular *Druk Superstar* programme. They explained why.

> 'We really miss Superstar show,' Sonam, an ardent follower said. She makes telephone calls to her friends living in other dzongkhags to keep herself updated on the show. Dema, a farmer in her late twenties, said she was frustrated by BBS going off air. 'After a week of hard work, we look forward to the show to be among friends and watch the show together, passing comments and giving the performers our own marks,' she said.
>
> (Namgyal 2012)

 **Bas Grasmayer**
@Spartz

In 1999, Bhutan introduced television. The effects have not been that great....
gu.com/p/x2c3k/tw via @guardian

8:06pm - 24 Feb 13

Fast forward into trouble

Four years ago, Bhutan, the fabled Himalayan Shangri-la, became the last nation on earth to introduce television. Suddenly a culture, barely changed in centuries, was bombarded by 46 cable channels....

Figure 4.4 A Twitter link sent on 24 February 2013 directed followers to the 2003 *Guardian* story

Bhutan is not merely following the media experiences of other countries. Less than 15 years after its arrival, the Bhutanese are utilizing television in ways that suit their own cultural purposes. The public space that is opening up is a manifestation of Bhutanese citizens' collective experiences and aspirations. It is acting as a counterpoint to outside cultural forces, showing the nation to itself and offering a significant contribution to the construction of its cultural nationhood.

Notes

1 The Census of Bhutan in 2005 listed the population as 634,982 in 2005, with a population projection of 733,004 for 2013 (Royal Government of Bhutan 2005).
2 Some residents already had televisions, which they used to watch video-cassette tapes, mostly in Hindi. By 1980 there where an estimated 1,000 video-cassette recorders and video-cassette players in Bhutan, owned by senior civil servants and business people (Media Impact Study 2003: 24). A 'select few' smuggled illegal satellite dishes over the border from India (Dendup 2002). In the 1970s a handful of cinemas were built in the biggest cities, which showed Hindi films, and in the 1980s the Royal Government of Bhutan experimented with making documentaries (Media Impact Study 2003: 24).

3 The number of languages varies according to the source. According to *Ethnologue* there are 23 languages (SIL 2015); George van Driem numbers them at 19 (van Driem 1994, p.1); Tshering Tashi puts the figure at 18 (Tashi 2013).
4 Readership is much lower than literacy. Reading and writing are largely associated with office and school 'work' (Media Impact Study 2003: 15). There is a joke in Bhutan that if you want to keep a secret, put it in a book. No one will read it (Ongmo 2009a: 5).
5 Religious festival with lama dancing.
6 William Langley also claimed, somewhat bizarrely, that high heels and foreign languages were banned. Neither is true.
7 Rethink the World (2010); Future Salon (2003).
8 Western Voices, World News (2013); Infoshop News (2013).
9 For example, Rubens (2008).
10 For example, Science Net Links (2013).
11 For example, De Vogli (2013).
12 David Adams quotes at length from the article, see Adams (2006); also, Penjore (2004); Norris and Inglehart (2009).

References

Adams, D. (2006) 'Media and development in the Middle East', *Transformation: An International Journal of Holistic Mission Studies*, 23(3): 170–86.

Anderson, B. (2006) *Imagined Communities: Reflections on the Origin and Spread of Nationalism*, revised edn, London: Verso.

BIMIS (2013) *Ministry of Information and Communications*, Thimphu: Royal Government of Bhutan.

Bly, R. (1996) *The Sibling Society*, Reading, MA: Addison-Wesley Publishing Company.

Clayton, S. (2007) 'Film-making in Bhutan: the view from Shangri-La', *New Cinemas: Journal of Contemporary Film*, 5(1): 75–89.

Croteau, D. and Hoynes, W. (2000) *Media Society: Industries, Images, and Audiences*, 2nd edn, Thousand Oaks, CA: Pine Forge Press.

Dendup, T. (2002) 'Bhutan's busiest cable guy', www.pbs.org/frontlineworld/stories/bhutan/interview.html.

De Vogli, R. (2013) *Progress or Collapse: The Crises of Market Greed*, New York: Routledge.

Elliot, J. (1987) 'The modern path to enlightenment', *Financial Times*.

Fischer, T. and Tashi, T. (2009) *Bold Bhutan Beckons: Inhaling Gross National Happiness*, Brisbane: CopyRight Publishing.

Future Salon (2003) www.futuresalon.org/2003/06/guardian_unlimi.html.

Gauntlett, D. (2008) *Media, Gender and Identity: An Introduction*, London: Routledge.

Hershock, P. (2004) 'Trade, development, and the broken promise of interdependence: a Buddhist reflection on the possibility of post-market economics' in K. Ura and K. Galay (eds.) *Gross National Happiness and Development*, Thimphu: Centre for Bhutan Studies.

Infoshop News (2013) http://news.infoshop.org/article.php?story=03/06/14/4899032.

Kaul, N. (2009) 'Bhutan's democracy and the international media', *Kuensel*, 10 January.

Langley, W. (2008) 'The king of Bhutan: the prince who brought satellite TV to Shangri-La', *Telegraph*, 8 November, www.telegraph.co.uk/news/worldnews/asia/bhutan/3408177/Profile-The-King-of-Bhutan-The-prince-who-brought-satellite-TV-to-Shangri-La.html.

72 Bunty Avieson

Lessing, D. (1997) 'The roads of London', *Granta*, 58.

Levo-Henriksson, R. (2007) *Media and Ethnic Identity. Hopi Views on Media, Identity, and Communication*, New York: Routledge.

Lumby, C. and Fine, D. (2006) *Why TV is Good for Kids: Raising 21st Century Children*, Sydney: Macmillan.

Mackay, H. (2002) *Media Mania*, Sydney: UNSW Press.

McDonald, R. (2004) 'Television, materialism and culture: an exploration of imported media and its implications for GNH', *Journal of Bhutan Studies*, 11: 68–9.

McQuail, D. (2005) 'Communication theory and the Western bias' in X. Shi, M. Kienpointner and J. Servaes (eds.) *Read the Cultural Other: Forms of Otherness in the Discourses of Hong Kong's Decolonization*, Berlin: Walter de Gruyter & Co, pp. 21–32.

Media Impact Study (2003) Ministry of Information and Communication, Royal Government of Bhutan, www.unapcict.org/ecohub/resources/bhutan.

Media Impact Study (2008) Ministry of Information and Communication, Royal Government of Bhutan, www.doim.gov.bt/wp-content/uploads/2012/09/mediaimpact_2008.pdf.

Ministry of Information and Communications (2013) *Bhutan Information and Impact Study*, Thimphu: Royal Government of Bhutan, www.bhutanfound.org/wp-content/uploads/2013/06/BIMIS-2013-REPORT_REVISED-DRAFT_21-05-2013Submitted-copy.pdf.

Namgyal, G. (2012) 'Entertainment hungry people frustrated over BBS going off air', *Bhutan Observer*, 27 April, http://bhutanobserver.bt/5629-bo-news-about-entertainment_hungry_people_frustrated_over_bbs_going_off_air.aspx.

Norris, P. and Inglehart, R. (2009) *Cosmopolitan Communications: Cultural Diversity in a Globalized World*, New York: Cambridge University Press.

Ongmo, S. (2009a) 'We want more Bhutanese writers', *Kuensel*, 2 May.

Ongmo, S. (2009b) 'Whose social responsibility?', *Dragon Tales*, www.sonamongmo7.com/2009/10/whose-social-responsibility.html#more.

Penjore, D. (2004) 'Security of Bhutan: walking between the giants', *Journal of Bhutan Studies*, 10.

Powdyel, T. (2006) 'Media and the maverick mind: need for media literacy: a lay view' in *Seminar of Media and Public Culture*, Thimphu: Centre for Bhutan Studies.

Putnam, R.D. (2000) *Bowling Alone: The Collapse and Revival of American Community*, New York: Simon and Schuster.

Rethink the World (2010) http://rethinktheworld.blogspot.com.au/2010/02/tv-incited-violence-vs-gross-national.html.

Roth, L. (2005) *Something New in the Air: The Story of First People's Television Broadcasting in Canada*, Montreal: McGill-Queen's University Press.

Royal Government of Bhutan (2005) *Population and Housing Census of Bhutan*, Thimphu: Royal Government of Bhutan.

Rubens, J. (2008) *Over Success: Healing the American Obsession with Wealth, Fames, Power and Perfection*, Texas: Greenleaf Book Group.

Science Net Links (2013) http://sciencenetlinks.com/lessons/influencing-cultures.

Scott-Clark, C. and Levy, A. (2003) 'Fast forward into trouble', *The Guardian*, 14 June, www.guardian.co.uk/theguardian/2003/jun/14/weekend7.weekend2.

SIL (2015), www.ethnologue.com/country/BT.

Tashi, T. (2013) 'Voice of the fort: how Dzongkha became the national language', *Kuensel*, 11 April, www.kuenselonline.com/voice-of-the-fort/#.UdM9Rus3iAo.

Turner, G. (2010) *Ordinary People and the Media*, London: Sage Publications.

van Driem, G. (1994) 'Language policy in Bhutan' in M. Aris and M. Hutt (eds.) *Bhutan: Aspects of Culture and Development*, Gartmore: Kiscadale Publications, pp. 87–105.

Wangdi, T. (2008) 'TV fever grips Kangpar', *Bhutan Observer*, 15 October, www.bhutanobserver.bt/tv-fever-grips-kangpar.

Washburn, K. and Thornton, J. (eds.) (1996) *Dumbing Down: Essays on the Strip Mining of American Culture*, New York: Norton.

Western Voices, World News (2013) www.wvwnews.net/story.php?id=9763.

Winn, M. (1987) *Unplugging the Plug-in Drug*, New York: Penguin.

Yeshi, S. (2012) 'A wealth of tongues', *Kuensel*, 28 May, www.kuenselonline.com/2011/?p=31686.

Zellen, B. (1988) 'Surf's up! NWT's indigenous communities await a tidal wave of electronic information', *Cultural Survival Quarterly*, 22(1).

5 Battling angels and golden orange blossoms

Thai television and/as the popular public sphere

Brett Farmer

On 19 September 2006, the first indication many people in Thailand received that the country was undergoing another military coup d'état, the eighteenth such putsch since 1932, was when the nation's six free-to-air television networks suddenly suspended regular programming and, channel by channel, started to broadcast a generic mix of royal news and light entertainment (Connors and Hewison 2008). Final confirmation came again via television later that evening in the form of an official announcement, broadcast at regular intervals across all stations from a central feed, in which the armed commanders in chief behind the coup – the awkwardly titled 'Administrative Reform Group under the Democratic System with the King as the Head of State' – explained apologetically that they had temporarily taken control of the nation's airwaves, as indeed of the nation, exhorting viewers to remain calm and reassuring them that normalcy would soon be restored, at which point broadcasting reverted to the same steady flow of innocuous entertainment programming. For all its exceptional gravity, the 2006 coup's strategic blend of direct state interventionist control of broadcasting combined with a more indirect use of escapist entertainment as populist pacifier is arguably a structural characteristic of Thai television history writ large.

From its advent in 1955, when the first Thai TV network was established under the authoritarian prime ministership of Field Marshal Phibun Songkhram, Thai television has been subject to close, even rigorous, state governance. Despite recent moves toward liberalization, all free-to-air TV networks in Thailand remain under the ownership, whether majority or in full, of the Royal Thai Government. Even networks licensed to private commercial operators are subject to close government supervision and have been prone to allegations of politico-corporate collusion (Ubonrat 2000, 2006). Furthermore, the Thai state has long used television as a principal means for the propagation of government policies and nationalist ideologies and maintains strict censorial control over broadcast material deemed to be contrary to hegemonic interests, whether political, economic, cultural or moral (McCargo 2000; Lewis 2006). Television professionals routinely practise additional self-censorship under a strong unwritten code in the industry of what is and is not permissible (Chavarong and Leveau 2007).

Battling angels and golden orange blossoms 75

The restrictive political economy of Thai television has engendered widespread critiques, with many media advocates and scholars arguing it not only hampers the development of a mature civil society but also compromises citizens' communication rights (Servaes et al. 2008; Ubonrat 2007; Brooten and Klangnarong 2009). Indeed, the scholarly literature on Thai television tends to paint an unremittingly bleak picture. Jonathan Woodier (2008: 190) contends that Thai television remains rooted in a repressive ethos of state monopoly and that, despite gestural moves toward increased openness, it remains part of the 'state ideological apparatuses that provide dis-information'. Ubonrat Siriyuvasak (2007: 9) similarly argues that 'seven decades [of] monopoly over the broadcast media by the Thai state' and the corresponding regime of censorship means that 'free expressions find little spaces [sic] in the mainstream media' and 'the struggle for a democratic society continues to be an uphill task'. While Boonrak Boonyaketmala (2008a) concludes bluntly that, 'television in Thailand has acted largely as a tool to produce a culture that will sustain a reigning political order' and that its 'role... as an engine of democracy is therefore curtailed'.[1]

As evidence of the insufficiency of Thai TV's civic cast, these critiques routinely point to the dearth on the nation's airwaves of 'serious' news and current affairs programming and the contrastive surfeit of populist fare or what Glen Lewis (2003: 71) describes as 'the rampant consumerism in entertainment programming' in the form of soap operas, musical varieties, sports and game shows that form the overwhelming majority of TV broadcast content in Thailand (Ubonrat 2000; Somkiat 2008). Duncan McCargo (2000: 23) lambasts what he describes as Thai TV's 'well-established tradition of bland news reporting' where there is 'exhaustive coverage of the activities of the revered royal family' and other such anodyne material 'but little attention paid to controversial issues'. Boonrak Boonyaketmala (2008a) remonstrates that 'the level of professionalism in television has never been high in the area of news' and that 'much of what is on TV in Thailand is designed to please the masses [with] locally-made melodramas about women fighting for rich and handsome men [and] game shows focusing on financial rewards'. While a recent report on Thai media commissioned by the German liberal think tank Konrad Adenauer Stiftung (Vogel et al. 2008: 91) states baldly that 'since the military and the state own virtually all radio and television stations, hard news is neutralised through a diet of "light" information and entertainment rather than serious political discourse'.[2]

As important as these political economy critiques undoubtedly are, they tend to construct a rather limited, monolithic apprehension of Thai TV programming and its social operations. In particular, these readings turn on a somewhat simple, value-laden opposition between serious news and light entertainment in which the former is assumed as the ideal, if not exclusive, province of political discourse, and the latter gets written off as mere apolitical distraction or, worse, depoliticizing 'false consciousness'. It is a widespread, even common-sensical opposition that is a feature of academic

76 *Brett Farmer*

theory and everyday talk alike, but it's not one that is particularly conducive to nuanced critical analysis, nor for that matter at all responsive to the wealth of revisionist work in cultural and media studies essayed over several decades now that has challenged this kind of simplistic oppositional thinking and worked toward a more complicated assessment of media discourses and their multiple valences.

In an attempt to move beyond the constraints of this widespread dualist mapping in critical accounts of Thai broadcast media, this chapter seeks to mount an argument for the polyvocality of Thai television and its provision of competing forms of political publicness. In particular, it explores how popular entertainment genres, far from effecting a defence against or simple escape from political realities as the standard reading of Thai TV suggests, might actually be seen to articulate and process a host of issues, big and small, local, national and global that impact the life circumstances of Thai TV's diverse audiences and that thus obtain an irreducible potential for profound political significance.

In making these claims, the chapter draws from two intersecting traditions of contemporary cultural and critical theory: revisionist accounts of popular culture and cultural politics, and expanded theories of the popular or cultural public sphere. In terms of the former, one of the guiding precepts of the so-called 'cultural turn' in the academy and arguably one of its most distinctive contributions has been the need for a serious, sustained engagement with what, in a foundational text, Raymond Williams (1989) famously terms 'ordinary culture' that is at once unencumbered by the sort of unreconstituted aesthetic or social prejudices that traditionally plagued scholarly responses to the popular, and that is sufficiently cognizant of the inherent complexity of mass culture and its manifold constituencies. A particularly influential variant of this tradition has been post-Gramscian retheorizations of popular culture as less a unified structure or even set of localizable cultural products with knowable forms and effects than a processual field of competing discourses, practices and identities, a site of struggle in which, as Tony Bennett (1986: xii) writes in a now-classic formulation, 'dominant, subordinate and oppositional cultural and ideological values and elements are "mixed" in different permutations'. It is a theoretical model that has enabled, among other things, renewed recognition of the complex socio-political valences of popular culture, the fact that it operates as a vital, if fraught, arena for engaging and negotiating the organization of power and social relations under capitalism and a site of sense-making and self-formation in the everyday lives of ordinary people. If at times this recuperative remapping of mass culture has given rise to a naive celebratory populism – what Meaghan Morris (1990: 24–5) memorably lampoons with the tautological syllogism: 'people in modern mediatized societies are complex and contradictory, mass cultural texts are complex and contradictory, therefore people using them produce complex and contradictory culture' – it has nevertheless been crucial to the critical validation of ordinary culture, its texts, practices and audiences, and

Battling angels and golden orange blossoms   77

a renewed attention to their socio-political operations, demonstrating that as Henry Giroux (2000: 2) asserts, 'struggles over culture are not a weak substitute for "real" politics, but are central to any struggle willing to forge relations of power, theory, and practice, as well as pedagogy and social change'.

An influential variant of this argument, and one that is central to the thinking of this chapter, can be found in recent scholarship on popular culture, especially popular media, as an adjunct or competing public sphere. Inspired by but equally revisionary of traditional Habermasian theories of the liberal public sphere as a vital organ of deliberative democratic governance, a communicative space of public discussion and opinion formation among citizens in a democratic polity, these theories claim a correlative capacity for communicative publicness on the part of popular cultures (Gripsrud et al. 2010). Variously dubbed the 'popular public sphere', 'postmodern public sphere' or simply 'cultural public sphere', the field of popular media is reimagined in this scholarship as a dynamic space of public meaning-making in which various issues of common concern among citizens of a given polity are engaged and political knowledges articulated (Hartley 1996; Couldry 2000; Moores 2005; McGuigan 2010). Unlike the traditional liberal public sphere, however, the popular cultural public sphere is distinguished on two important counts. First, it canvasses a much broader range of socio-political issues than the orthodox public sphere: not just civic and institutional but also private, domestic and subjective; the realm of what, after feminism, has commonly come to be known as 'the politics of the personal': sexuality, bodies, families, ethnicity, age and the myriad coordinates that govern social relations of identity and intersubjectivity and their constitutive networks of power. Second, it engages and processes this material less via rationalist modes of communication, the prescribed ideal of the liberal public sphere, than affective and aesthetic ones: fictional rather than factual, dramatic and personalized rather than cognitive. 'The cultural public sphere,' writes Jim McGuigan (2010: 16) 'trades in pleasures and pains that are experienced vicariously... through entertainment and popular media discourses. Affective communications help people to think reflexively about their own lifeworld situations... provid[ing] vehicles for thought and feeling, for imagination and disputatious argument.'

Where, from a strictly orthodox liberal stance, this expansion of civic discourse in popular media to encompass topics, values and communicative styles formerly deemed private and subjective is typically held to be a *devaluation* of the public sphere, an erosion of its rationalist values and authority, advocates counter that such developments are actually serving to open up civic cultures and make them more accessible to a much broader range of social constituencies. As these critics commonly point out, for all the lofty rhetoric of democratic inclusiveness and open exchange, traditional conceptualizations of the liberal public sphere have more often than not been framed and experienced in ways that are decidedly *non-inclusive*, patterned as they are on white bourgeois male subjectivities and knowledges as normalizing ideals and thus excluding or at least marginalizing large sections of the population

78　*Brett Farmer*

outside this narrow purview: (some) women, working classes, people of colour, immigrants, children and youths, sexual minorities and so forth. That these socially subordinate constituencies are often among the most significant and enthusiastic audiences of popular media is taken by some commentators as proof positive of popular culture's capacity to engage and service new and expanded forms of publicness, allowing a greater range of people access to the realms of civic representation and a space, however limited and compromised, for the articulation of competing political discourses, public and personal. As Peter Dahlgren writes:

> [P]opular culture offers us resources for exploring the political links between public and private spheres, and thus extending and multiplying our civic identities… it provides a continuous flood of topics that touch people in various ways. Some of these topics can, especially if processed through discussion, resonate with core values, suggest practices, mobilize identities, and generate engagement in the public sphere. They can evoke contestation, and further develop the terrain of the political, thereby pumping blood into the body of democracy.
>
> (Dahlgren 2009: 16)

This combined scholarship offers a suggestive framework within which to rethink the political dynamics of Thai TV and move beyond the dead-end constraints of the dualist models of serious political programming versus apolitical popular entertainment that continue to dominate critical commentary in Thai media studies. In particular, it encourages renewed attention to the socio-political communicative capacities of popular Thai TV genres and how they might be seen to operate as a competing or adjunct public sphere for Thai audiences: a space of common cultural exchange that is distinct from more traditional forms of political publicness but that performs not entirely indissociable operations of civic discourse, providing a set of shared discursive resources through which to think and process various issues central to contemporary Thai polities and the heterogeneous lifeworlds of their multiple subjects.

An argument could even be made that, because Thai TV is so straight-jacketed in its ability to provide the sort of overt political discursive material requisite for the provision of a functional liberal public sphere, popular programming has in many ways come to assume an even more significant role in practices of TV-mediated public meaning-making and civic exchange.[3] In her fascinating anthropological research on mass media and Thai national identity, Annette Hamilton contends that popular Thai audiences frequently use fictional media as a central source of coded political critique and counter-discourse. Given the highly controlled information environment of Thai broadcasting and its often paternalistic elitism where the 'views of important and educated people are the only ones that count' (Hamilton 2002a: 298), Hamilton suggests 'ordinary' Thai audiences engage in a form of dual cultural interpretation, outwardly receiving the 'official' discourse of Thai media but then reprocessing a counter-discourse of their own. 'Precisely because everyone knows the news is not what is really happening,' she writes, watching TV 'becomes a major act of cultural interpretation' whereby audiences 're-interpret or deconstruct' official discourse using 'hidden narratives... as explanatory frameworks' (Hamilton 2002a: 292).[4] These hidden narratives stem from a range of sources and assume multiple forms, from gossip and folklore to popular mysticism, but Hamilton singles out fictional narrative media as a particularly fertile site for this practice of popular reinterpretation. Television and film texts enable 'the creation of a para-discourse' where narratives are 'interpreted as being "about" something else – for example, a wealthy eldest son in a current Chinese drama who is having marital problems could be coded for a subject of conversation about the Crown Prince'. In this way, she writes, 'television and film narratives... take their place within a vast signifying chain' of Thai public discursivity, 'meaning much more than they would seem to do at a literal level' and constituting a common cultural repertoire and 'a shared consciousness' among popular Thai audiences (Hamilton 2002b: 165).

Hamilton's work dates from field research conducted in the 1980s and early 1990s but the para-discursive practice of duplicitous media consumption she describes arguably continues apace. Indeed, to the extent that social and legal injunctions against overt political commentary have, if anything, intensified in the Thai public sphere in recent years – as evidenced in, among other things, the exponential escalation in lèse-majesté and defamation cases and the radical increase of state censorship via new laws and agencies such as the Computer Crimes Act of 2007 (Streckfuss 2011) – socio-political discourse, at least of any nominally critical kind, has arguably had to resort even more to indirect communication and the suggestive ambiguities of subtext, metaphor and allegory. A recent crystalline example is offered by the controversial case of the so-called *Hi-S Tales*, an anonymously authored serialized narrative published on a series of Thai websites and social media platforms from 2009 to 2012. Taking the form of an irreverent domestic soap opera, the serial humorously plots the melodramatic machinations of a canned fish factory and the dynastic family that runs it in a way that is quite obviously patterned on, and designed to be interpreted as, the Thai royal family and associated current events in Thai politics but that, because of its allegorical fictional form, still allows all-important scope for plausible deniability. The *Hi-S Tales* operate as what Andrew Walker (2011) terms 'narrative sedition', a practice that draws from 'the vast subaltern world of popular story-telling about Thailand's royals' in order to construct a counter-discourse to official narratives of the Thai public sphere.

That *Hi-S Tales* draws much of its aesthetic inspiration from the popular generic repertoire of soap opera provides a convenient segue into a consideration of TV soaps as a further manifestation of these traditions of para-discursive articulation whereby Thai audiences use popular narrative media as displaced or symbolic reflections on socio-political issues and knowledges. The importance of soap operas to the industrial and aesthetic economies of TV, as well as to broader social contexts, is well-recognized. With their enormous popularity and widespread transnational appeal, Jim McGuigan (2010: 11) suggests that '[p]erhaps television soaps are the most reliable documents of our era'. Certainly, in terms of Thai TV, soaps, or *lakhon* as they are known in Thai, are undoubtedly the local industry's most vital form (Kanokporn 2009; Sirinya 2009). Each year, more than 100 *lakhon* are produced and broadcast on Thai TV and they routinely attract among the nation's biggest viewing audiences. In 2011, for example, six of the year's ten highest rated programmes were soap operas, with average audiences in excess of ten million viewers (Banterng TV 2011). Not surprisingly, *lakhon* are lucrative business and there is intense competition among producers to attract as big a share as possible of the genre's loyal fan base and, by extension, the advertising revenue that follows.

The all-important prime-time market is effectively dominated by the two leading commercial networks, Channel 7 and Channel 3, with a third network, Channel 5, obtaining some minimal market share as a producer of middle-brow quality soaps, generally of an historical and/or literary kind. Traditionally, Channel 7 – the bigger of the competitors, if only because its more advanced satellite broadcasting infrastructure gives it greater national coverage – has tended to pitch its *lakhon* to the working class and provincial sectors with content and styles seen to be *talad*, or luridly populist, with sensationalist and often implausible storylines focused on the plutocratic lives of fabulously wealthy families, melodramatic performance styles and excessively lavish *mise-en-scène*. Channel 3, by contrast, has traditionally courted the urban petit bourgeois and youth audiences via a slightly more realist, if still broadly melodramatic, aesthetic. Recently, however, these industrial distinctions have started to blur as Channel 3 and even Channel 5 adopt a more sensationalist style, a trend noted with some alarm by middle-brow commentators and moral gatekeepers (Amporn 2008).

Thai *lakhon* bear both similarities to and distinctions from Euro-American TV soaps. Like their Western counterparts, *lakhon* focus largely on thematic material drawn from the personal and domestic spheres of everyday life (kinship, sexuality, generational conflict, marriage, birth, illness, death, etc.) all represented via the multi-levelled textual structures of serial narrative and the stylized aesthetic palette of popular melodrama. However, where a Western soap typically runs over a long period of time, screening as short daily episodes for years and in some cases even decades, a Thai *lakhon* runs for a finite period of generally no more than a couple of months with one- to two-hour episodes aired in batched instalments over several nights each week, not unlike the telenovelas of Latin American TV. Additionally, *lakhon* are characterized by a very high degree of formulaicism with stock plots, character types, scenarios, settings and even actors recurring from series to series in an overtly repetitive, conventional manner. In many cases the same story,

Battling angels and golden orange blossoms 81

frequently adapted from a literary source, will be remade as a *lakhon* every few years, updated with a new cast and sensibility, but remaining strikingly similar to preceding versions (Sirinya 2009).

To say that this distinctive combination of domestic melodrama, formulaic textuality and lower-class audience demographics has earned *lakhon* a less than fulsome cultural reception would be putting it mildly. The common Thai epithet applied almost reflexively to *lakhon* is *nam nao* or 'putrid water': a term that Van Fleet (1998) argues originates out of the 1970s student movement where it was used to describe the corruption of the political establishment and that she says 'evokes the look and smell of stagnant water and rotting garbage, conjuring up images of modern Thailand's polluted canals and waterways' (Van Fleet 1998: 298).[5] It's a rhetoric of decay and refuse that neatly highlights the paradoxical dynamics of hegemonic cultural responses to *lakhon* in Thai society where, on the one hand, *lakhon* are routinely disregarded as worthless trash, something of insignificance with no intrinsic value or merit, yet, on the other, are ascribed a quite intense potency as objects of social pollution that need to be expelled or quarantined.[6]

Certainly, for something typically dismissed as little more than dirty dishwater, *lakhon* have attracted a good deal of reproachful attention on the part of some pretty powerful agencies. Several state bureaucracies, such as the Ministry of Culture, for example, the regulatory government body charged with overseeing state cultural policy and planning, have waged high-profile campaigns against TV *lakhon* in recent years (Kultida 2011). Much of the criticism has focused on the perceived social transgressiveness of *lakhon*, their breaking of various moral taboos and/or breaching of social boundaries. Of particular concern is what might be described as 'the spectacle of unruly subalterns' in *lakhon* wherein members of traditionally subordinate social factions – women, most notably, but also lower classes and, increasingly in recent times, non-normative sexual minorities – are seen to exceed culturally prescribed modes of comportment and/or to contravene their appointed position in orthodox social hierarchies.

In 1999, for example, the Public Relations Department under then prime minister Chuan Leekpai issued – and, facing vocal media backlash, subsequently rescinded – a directive to all TV stations asking them to refrain from the increasingly common practice of featuring outrageous transgendered or *kathoei* characters in *lakhon* because they were deemed to be setting 'unfavourable examples' and promoting 'sexual abnormalities' (Jackson 2002: 221). More recently, in 2008, the Ministry of Culture intervened in a public controversy that had embroiled the wildly popular *lakhon Songkhram Nang Fa* ('Battle of Angels'), a sensationalist serial focused on amorous intrigues among a group of Thai flight attendants and pilots. Petitioned by the national carrier, Thai Airways, and the flight attendants union, the Culture Ministry expressed strongly voiced concern over the lewd tenor of the show and, particularly, its 'vulgar display' of uninhibited, even aggressive female sexuality, which was deemed 'insulting

82 *Brett Farmer*

and damaging' to 'the professional image and dignity' of Thai flight crews (*The Nation* 2008). In 2011, the Ministry of Culture once more came out, critical guns blazing, against a popular *lakhon*. This time its ire was raised by *Dok Som Si Tong* ('Golden Orange Blossom'), another sensationalist *lakhon* about familial intrigues and adulterous affairs. The serial possibly pushed some boundaries by featuring slightly more explicit love scenes than usual but the Ministry's chief complaint was not so much the steamy raunch as the central character of Reya, a scheming bad girl played by popular soap star, Araya 'Chompoo' Hargate. Accused of a laundry list of moral offences including sexual aggressiveness, violent language and behaviour and, horror of horrors, showing ingratitude to her mother, Reya was branded 'a threat to public decency' and, in a series of increasingly hysterical press releases, the Ministry called for the show to be censored, then to be banned and even for the broadcasting network to have its licence revoked (Atiya 2011). The following year, 2012, another sensationalist *lakhon*, *Raeng Ngao* ('Strong Shadow'), caused an even wider political storm with not only the Ministry of Culture but also affiliate state agencies, the Senate Committee and the National Broadcasting and Telecommunications Commission (NBTC), waging an escalating war of words over the show's audience-pleasing spectacles of sexual promiscuity and melodramatic violence (Kong 2012). As with *Dok Som*, much of the official disapprobation was levelled at the series' central female protagonist, Munin, a conniving bad girl out to avenge the death of her twin sister, Mutta (both parts played by Janie Tienphosuwan), by wreaking emotional and physical havoc on the wealthy family that had indirectly caused her sister's demise. Munin was roundly castigated by the show's formidable line-up of institutional critics for, among other things, setting a bad example for the nation's youth and tarnishing the national image of Thai femininity (Nattapong 2012).[7]

It is no small irony of course that these controversies merely served to make the offending programmes even more popular. Both *Dok Som* and *Raeng Ngao* were the single biggest hits on Thai TV in their respective seasons with ratings spiking substantially in the wake of government disapproval and ensuing media debates. In the case of *Dok Som*, the Ministry's remonstrations became part of the generalized media ballyhoo surrounding the programme, fuelling a frenzy of public fascination that was quickly dubbed 'Reya fever' after the central *femme fatale* character demonized by state officials but loved by audiences (Maya 2011). *Raeng Ngao* similarly struck a nerve with large segments of the Thai viewing public, scoring a record-breaking 21.9 point audience share in Bangkok, leading some pundits to dub its weekly broadcasts a de facto national holiday due to the fact that much of the country stayed in to watch the latest instalments (Kanokporn 2012).

Even more ironic is that, in the broader scheme, none of the examples singled out for vociferous castigation by state agencies in recent years are particularly distinctive or remarkable. Adultery, seduction, revenge, corruption and other tropes of sexual and social transgression have long been a thematic

Battling angels and golden orange blossoms   83

stock in trade of Thai *lakhon*. Indeed, following aforementioned industrial practice, these recent *lakhon* are remakes of stories that have been told in various forms many times before. The 2012 version of *Raeng Ngao* was the fourth remake of this particular *lakhon* to be broadcast on Thai TV since 1986, while *Dok Som* was based on the second volume of a sprawling family saga penned by popular novelist Taitao Sucharitkul, which had inspired two previous *lakhon, Mongkut Dok Som*, in 1996 and 2009 respectively. Moreover, the scheming *femme fatales* of these two series, Reya and Munin, are fairly stock *lakhon* characters, patterned on the conventional *mia noi* or 'minor wife/mistress' figure that has been a typical feature of *lakhon* for decades 'with the classic low-birth status, towering ambition and super-crass personality' (Atiya 2011). All of which suggests that much of the indignant outrage on the part of bureaucratic agencies like the Culture Ministry and other institutional gatekeepers is ultimately something of a smokescreen hiding, even as it symptomatically indexes, an ulterior set of cultural anxieties beyond mere concern with breaches of sexual decorum and gendered etiquette in TV soaps.

Pavin Chachavalpongpun (2008) argues that behind many, if not most, of these censorial attacks on *lakhon* lies a deeper question, 'the question of Thai identity and its discursive exploitation', of who gets to define and enforce 'the moral identity of being Thai'. Here it is worth recalling that the Ministry of Culture's principal political rationale, its raison d'être, is fundamentally ideological and avowedly conservative. Established in 2002, the Ministry is the latest in a long line of state agencies charged with what Michael Connors (2005: 524) calls 'the minister-ing of Thai-ness', the strategic use of state-sanctioned culture to define and police Thai national identity and, by so doing, to 'create a nationally identifying citizenry that can be mobilized for productive purposes'. Indeed, Ladda Tangsuphachai, the director of the Ministry's Cultural Watch Centre and the public figure most closely associated with the government's crusade against *lakhon* and other deleterious cultural forms, at least till her 'transfer' in late 2012, is disarmingly candid about the ideological agenda of the Ministry's work, describing her agency as the 'culture police' whose role is to 'keep a close eye on Thai culture', 'monitoring the media for anything that might be inappropriate' or 'that affects our cultural identity' (Apichart 2009).

This nakedly ideological programming helps explain some of the incommensurate vehemence of the current Thai state-generated censures of TV *lakhon* and also perhaps why they seem to be intensifying in both frequency and tenor. Gripped by one of the most violent and sustained periods of social and political instability in its history, Thailand today is a nation of deep and seemingly intractable divisions. In the face of what Michael Montesano et al. (2012) term 'a slow-burn civil war', the Thai state or at least hegemonic factions therein have gone into regressive disavowal, redoubling efforts to maintain their grip on power and restore the *status quo ante* generally via recourse to the same obsolescent mechanisms of political control that had served them well in the past: military coups, statist propaganda, censorship, paternalistic

84   Brett Farmer

hierarchism and authoritarian loyalty to narrowly prescribed ideals of Thai-ness (Askew 2010; Ferrara 2011; Montesano et al. 2012). It's an arsenal of blunt political tools that may have worked in previous historical contexts but is proving desperately inadequate to the radically changed conditions of modern Thailand and its increasingly heterogeneous and enfranchised citizenry. 'The cleavages in Thai society,' writes David Streckfuss (2011: 313), 'class, race, ethnic, religious, regional, and political – so long papered over and held together by incessant calls for unity and a century-old construction of an ossified national identity, are no longer deniable or manageable.' Reactionary agencies within the Thai state may continue to try and disavow this truth, burying their head ostrich-like in the nostalgic sands of paternalistic authoritarianism and obsessively seeking to excise any trace of dissent from the realms of official public culture, but the cleavages of which Streckfuss speaks inevitably and inexorably assert themselves in all sorts of disruptive ways... including through the popular discourses of entertainment TV.

While it may be drawing a long bow to claim Reya, Munin and the other misbehaving gadflies of Thai *lakhon* as direct articulations of these massive socio-political upheavals, there can be no doubt that these characters and the TV shows of which they are part have, even if only through the high-profile controversies surrounding them, been explicitly drawn into the discursive orbit of Thai politics. They have in effect become overtly politicized, touching deep social nerves and resonating with a host of issues at play on the national political stage. It is, for example, telling that so much of the recent furore surrounding *lakhon* in the Thai public sphere has focused on what was described earlier as 'the spectacle of unruly subalterns' and the statist desire to have these disruptive figures chastised and recontained. The scheming *mia noi* or 'minor wife/mistress' character may have been a longstanding convention of classic *lakhon* but this character's typical combination of lower class, usually rural, origins, aspirational ambitiousness, and transgressive disruption of traditional social hierarchies (marriage, family, business) has suddenly come to assume radically intensified socio-political resonances in the context of Thailand's present political struggles. Those struggles are exceedingly complex and opaque but one of the dominant ways in which they have been represented, both within Thailand and without, is via a melodramatic narrative of subaltern disruption: redshirts against yellowshirts, *phrai* (commoners) against *amart* (aristocrats), poor against rich, rural against urban, periphery against centre (Askew 2010; Montesano et al. 2012). As David Streckfuss (2010) writes in a representative account, current political unrest

> tap[s] into a long-simmering brew of ethnic and economic tensions bubbling below the surface of Thai society. It is often said there are two Thailands: Bangkok and the rest. After a century of the capital's political and military incursions into the hinterland, the red-shirt demonstration represented the most serious and sustained foray of the hinterland into Bangkok.

Battling angels and golden orange blossoms 85

Against this backdrop, the fictional travails of *lakhon* characters like Reya and Munin, upcountry girls of humble origin who come to the city and challenge the smooth functioning of hegemonic elites, becomes suddenly and deeply suggestive, even provocative.

This type of allegorical interpretation has in fact been a feature of at least some of the media commentary on these *lakhon* and their political controversies. In an influential article that first ran in the liberal *Prachatai* newspaper but that was subsequently reprinted in many online forums, Nattapong Sakulliao (2012) argues for *Raeng Ngao* as a loose parable about Thai social structures and their current political transformations. In this reading, each of the *lakhon*'s characters is apprehended as an archetypal embodiment of variable factions or segments of Thai society, with the active, vengeful Munin seen as a symbolic representation of the 'new insubordinate rural classes' (*chonabot mai phu mai sirorap*) seeking to avenge a history of abuse suffered by her twin sister, Mutta, representative of 'the old-style persecuted rural underclass' (*chonabot baeb gao thuk yiab yam rang gae*), by overthrowing, or at least unsettling, the hegemonic alliance of old aristocracy and new moneyed mercantilists (symbolized in *Raeng Ngao* by the philandering wealthy patriarch, Janepop, and his vindictive high-society wife, Noppa). It is a broad reading that arguably oversimplifies the complex dynamics of contemporary Thai class factionalism and *lakhon* characterization alike. Munin, for example, may embody certain aspects of the rural underclass but, by the same token, she is also encoded with many markers of upper-class privilege: a well-educated, cosmopolitan beauty who, like most major characters in contemporary *lakhon*, is played by a fair-skinned *luk khrueng* or Eurasian actor with a central Thai/Bangkok accent. Nevertheless, Nattapong's reading highlights the extent to which popular *lakhon* like *Raeng Ngao* have been charged with deeply political significances and mobilized as occasions for varying forms of political discursivity in and for the public spheres of contemporary Thai TV.

It also helps underscore, and partially explain, the popular appeal of these TV shows. The Ministry of Culture and other elitist gatekeepers may not much care for the scandalous upstarts of Thai *lakhon* who refuse to know their place and kowtow to orthodox cultural prescriptions, but for their millions of fans – many of whom come from the very subordinate constituencies that are currently challenging and destabilizing the old social order and who, precisely because of this, are also routinely accused of transgressing the dictates of appropriate Thainess (Poowin 2010) – they very well may be topoi of pleasurable identification and even possibly catalysing figures by which to imagine and legitimate possibilities for social and political change. Several commentators in fact claim that the increasing penetration of TV, and more recently other forms of communicative media, into the provincial hinterlands has been crucial to the transformation and growing politicization of the Thai rural classes (Walker 2012; Chairat 2013). Much of this commentary focuses on more traditionally informational forms of TV but research equally

86 *Brett Farmer*

underscores the potential role played by entertainment genres such as *lakhon* in this process of increasing political and social empowerment. In her ethnography of working-class and lower-middle-class TV audiences in the northern city of Chiang Mai, Sarah Van Fleet (1998) links the popularity of *lakhon* among these social groups to their experiences of social fragmentation under capitalist modernity. More recently, Catherine Hesse-Swain (2006, 2011) has researched the ways in which north-east Thai or Isan youths similarly mobilize popular TV genres in the construction and negotiation of enfranchised cultural identities. '*Lakhon* is a potential harbinger of positive social change,' she asserts, 'with the capacity to play an important role in focusing the attention of elites on the raw and challenging social issues of the poor, as well as empowering poor communities to both dream of and fight for change' (Hesse-Swain 2011: 169).

This exploration of the socio-political valences of Thai *lakhon* has of necessity been brief. However, it hopefully gives some sense of the dynamic vitality of this hugely popular form of Thai TV and, more to the point, its potential for productive, if coded, political signification. In the face of an official public sphere that actively, even aggressively, represses dissent and excises most anything that falls beyond the state-sanctioned scripts of hegemonic 'Thainess', entertainment genres such as *lakhon* signal an important alternative forum, however imperfect and attenuated, for the exploration of competing ideas and issues central to the lifeworlds of Thailand's heterogeneous polities. This is not to suggest of course that *lakhon* or any other of the fictional forms of popular Thai TV operate as unbridled points of anti-hegemonic resistance or ideal vehicles of popular oppositionality. They are products, first and foremost, of a state-controlled, market-driven industry and, as such, remain firmly in the service of social and ideological orthodoxy. Nevertheless, they can and do serve to raise a host of competing issues of pressing socio-political concern, often in ways that are more accessible and possibly more meaningful to their diverse audience constituencies than the traditional rational communicative modes of mainstream political discourse. Rather than dismissing these popular genres as apolitical escapism and/or positioning them as a structural other to political communication proper, critical studies of Thai media would do well to recognize and more fully theorize the potential role assumed by fictional entertainment TV as a competing or adjunct popular public sphere for varying forms of socio-political expression and exchange. The political communicative capacities of Thai TV are seriously inhibited by an overdetermined agglomeration of governmental, industrial and ideological constraints but, against these massive odds, varied voices and even whispers of dissent can still be discerned.

Notes

1 Some critics go so far as to suggest that the repressive culture of authoritarian statist control of Thai broadcast media extends equally to academic research in the

Battling angels and golden orange blossoms 87

field. Youngsamart and Fisher (2006: 37) claim that: 'It is not in the interests of the Thai elite groups that benefit from media control to encourage academic research that may be critical of their role' and that this has resulted in the largely apolitical traditions of descriptive historicism, uncritical sociology and vocational training that dominate media studies in the Thai academy.

2 Some commentators claim the prioritization of light entertainment over more serious fare is not unique to Thai TV and may form part of a broader pattern of Thai cultural organization whereby a premium is placed in traditional Thai social value systems on, among other things, ego-oriented social harmony (*kwam-sa-ngop-riab-roi*) and fun-pleasure orientation (*sanuk*), which results in a structural penchant for pleasurable entertainment and a corresponding avoidance of potentially conflictual material (Servaes et al. 2008).

3 In his important historical work on Thai cultural modernity in the early twentieth century, Scot Barmé (2002) details how the emergent Siamese middle classes seized upon the new commercial mass media of the time – popular newspapers, magazines, comics, short stories, films and advertising – to construct novel popular forms of cultural expression and political awareness that contested the social and ideological hegemonies of the royal-noble elite, while serving to articulate and legitimate their own evolving social and moral worldviews. While some of this material was openly political in its critical form – indeed, often surprisingly so – much of it assumed a covert, emblematic status where issues were dealt with symptomatically through the metaphoric vernacular of popular narrativity.

4 Further emphasis to this practice of subtextual encoding is possibly lent by the oft-noted Thai cultural penchant for indirect communication and discursive circumspection keyed to the surface maintenance of smooth social relations – as the title of one recent book on Thai cultural communication put it, 'Thais say it best when they say nothing at all!' (Leo 2007).

5 Van Fleet (1998) also suggests that the widely used term *lakhon nam nao* is only superficially derogatory and that, among fans of the genre at least, it is used with ironic affection.

6 This kind of paradoxical ambivalence, which is another point of commonality between *lakhon* and soap operas elsewhere in the world (Allen 1995), arguably stems from the genre's constitutive association with devalued social constituencies – women, lower classes, young people, etc. – as well as its investment in a thematics of what David Buckingham (1987) terms 'public secrets', the disclosure and exposition of aspects of private life ordinarily concealed from public culture.

7 A slightly different and, at the time of writing, the most recent *lakhon*-fueled controversy came courtesy of *Nuea Mek 2* ('Above the Clouds 2'), a sudsy drama about a 'fictional' prime minister and his corrupt deputy who is involved in shady business dealings. With a supernatural theme, common in many Thai *lakhon*, the hook of the series was that the prime minister was actually a reanimated corpse that was being controlled from afar by a nefarious sorcerer. Sporting some pretty overt potential parallels to real-life political scenarios in Thailand – notably, the incumbent government of Yingluck Shinawatra, widely regarded, at least by political opponents, as a 'puppet' regime controlled by former PM Thaksin Shinawatra from his position in exile abroad; although there has also been contrasting speculation that the narrative was interpretable as a coded critique of royalist interventionism and thus potentially courted *lèse-majesté* – the series proved potentially explosive and it was abruptly pulled from the air by broadcaster Channel 3 amid cries of political interference. Unlike the other examples profiled above, however, *Nuea Mek 2* largely drew diplomatic denials and stony silence from the Ministry of Culture (Atiya 2013, Bangkok Pundit 2013, Hookway 2013).

References

Allen, Robert C. (ed.) (1995) *To Be Continued...: Soap Operas Around the World*, London and New York: Routledge.

Amporn Jirattikorn (2008) ' "Pirated" transnational broadcasting: the consumption of Thai soap operas among Shan communities in Burma', *Sojourn: Journal of Social Issues in Southeast Asia*, 23(1): 30–62.

Apichart Jinakul (2009) 'Volunteers keep a close guard on Thai culture', *The Bangkok Post*, 9 January, p. 11.

Askew, Marc (2010) *Legitimacy Crisis in Thailand*, Chiang Mai: Silkworm.

Atiya Achakulwisut (2011) 'Ministry of over-reacting', *The Bangkok Post*, 3 May, www.bangkokpost.com/opinion/opinion/235049/ministry-of-over-reacting.

Atiya Achakulwisut (2013) 'Soap opera saga will only end in tears', *The Bangkok Post*, 8 January, www.bangkokpost.com/news/local/329697.

Bangkok Pundit (2013) 'Why was the Thai soap opera *Nua Mek 2* pulled from the air?', *Asian Correspondent.com*, 7 January, http://asiancorrespondent.com/94876.

Banterng TV (2011) 'Lakhon Haeng Pi' ('Soap operas of the year'), *Thai Rath Online*, 31 December, www.thairath.co.th/content/ent/227093.

Barmé, Scot (2002) *Woman, Man, Bangkok: Love, Sex, and Popular Culture in Thailand*, Lanham, MD: Rowman and Littlefield.

Bennett, Tony (1986) 'Popular culture and the "turn to Gramsci"' in *Popular Culture and Social Relations*, Milton Keynes: Open University Press, pp. xi–xix.

Boonrak Boonyaketmala (2008a) 'Broadcasting and democracy: whose television and for what?', *The Bangkok Post*, 18 January, p. 6.

Boonrak Boonyaketmala (2008b) 'TV soap operas and national culture: TV angels on verge of causing nervous breakdown', *The Bangkok Post*, 30 January, p. 11.

Brooten, Lisa and Klangnarong, Supinya (2009) 'People's media and reform efforts in Thailand', *International Journal of Media and Cultural Politics*, 5(1/2): 103–17.

Buckingham, David (1987) *Public Secrets: EastEnders and its Audience*, London: British Film Institute.

Chachavalpongpun, Pavin (2008) 'Only one winner in soap-opera clash', *The Nation*, January 25, www.nationmultimedia.com/2008/01/25/opinion/opinion_30063458.php.

Chairat Charoensin-o-larn (2013) 'Redrawing Thai political space: the Red Shirt Movement', in Tim Bunnell, D. Parthasarathy and Eric C. Thompson (eds.) *Cleavage, Connection and Conflict in Rural, Urban and Contemporary Asia*, Dordrecht: Springer.

Chavarong, Limpattamapanee and Leveau, Arnaud (eds.) (2007) *State and Media in Thailand During Political Transition*, Bangkok: IRASEC.

Connors, Michael (2005) 'Ministering culture: hegemony and the politics of culture and identity in Thailand', *Critical Asian Studies*, 37(4): 523–51.

Connors, Michael K. and Hewison, Kevin (eds.) (2008) 'Special issue: Thailand's "good coup": the fall of Thaksin, the military and democracy', *Journal of Contemporary Asia*, 38(1).

Couldry, Nick (2000) *The Place of Media Power: Pilgrims and Witnesses of the Media Age*. London and New York: Routledge.

Dahlgren, Peter (2009) *Media and Political Engagement: Citizens, Democracy and Communication*, Cambridge: Cambridge University Press.

Ferrara, Federico (2011) *Thailand Unhinged: The Death of Thai-Style Democracy*, 2nd edn, Singapore: Equinox Publishing.

Battling angels and golden orange blossoms 89

Giroux, Henry (2000) *Impure Acts: The Practical Politics of Cultural Studies*, London and New York: Routledge.

Gripsrud, Jostein, Hallvard, Moe, Molander, Anders and Eide, Martin (eds.) (2010) *The Idea of the Public Sphere: A Reader*, Plymouth: Lexington Books.

Hamilton, Annette (2002a) 'Rumours, foul calumnies and the safety of the state: mass media and national identity in Thailand' in Craig J. Reynolds (ed.) *National Identity and Its Defenders: Thailand Today*, Chiang Mai: Silkworm Books.

Hamilton, Annette (2002b) 'The national picture: Thai media and cultural identity' in Faye D. Ginsburg, Lila Abu-Lughod and Brian Larkin (eds.) *Media Worlds: Anthropology on New Terrain*, Berkeley: University of California Press, pp. 152–70.

Hartley, John (1996) *Popular Reality*, London: Edward Arnold.

Hesse-Swain, Catherine (2006) 'Programming beauty and the absence of Na Lao: popular Thai TV and identity formation among youth in Northeast Thailand', *GeoJournal*, 66: 257–72.

Hesse-Swain, Catherine (2011) *Speaking in Thai, Dreaming in Isan: Popular Thai Television and Emerging Identities of Lao Isan Youth Living in Northeast Thailand*, doctoral dissertation, Edith Cowan University.

Hookway, James (2013) 'Soap opera stirs the political plot in Thailand', *The Wall Street Journal*, 7 January, http://blogs.wsj.com/searealtime/2013/01/07/soap-opera-stirs-the-political-plot-in-thailand.

Jackson, Peter A. (2002) 'Offending images: gender and sexual minorities, and state control of the media in Thailand' in Russell H.K. Heng (ed.) *Media Fortunes, Changing Times: ASEAN States in Transition*, Singapore: Institute of Southeast Asian Studies, pp. 201–30.

Kanokporn Chanasongkram (2009) 'Our love affair with soaps', *The Bangkok Post*, 22 May, p. R1.

Kanokporn Chanasongkram (2012) 'Wading through putrid water to get to the truth', *The Bangkok Post*, 22 November, www.bangkokpost.com/opinion/opinion/322484.

Kong Rithdee (2008) 'Thai soap makes flight attendants foam', *Variety*, 23 January, www.variety.com/article/VR1117979544?refCatId=14.

Kong Rithdee (2012) 'Bitchfest ends, but morality saga goes on', *The Bangkok Post*, 1 December, www.bangkokpost.com/opinion/opinion/324002.

Kultida Samabuddhi (2011) 'Young culture minister has far to go', *The Bangkok Post*, 19 August, p. 8.

Leo, Annie (2007) *Thais Say It Best When They Say Nothing at All! A Guide to Nonverbal Communication in Thailand*, Bangkok: Bangkok Books.

Lewis, Glen (2003) 'Television, media reform and civil society in "amazing Thailand"' in Philip Kitley (ed.) *Television, Regulation and Civil Society in Asia*, London: Routledge, pp. 61–79.

Lewis, Glen (2006) *Virtual Thailand: The Media and Cultural Politics in Thailand, Malaysia and Singapore*, London and New York: Routledge.

Maya Yunaidted (2011) 'Reya fever', *Siam Dara*, 29 April, www.siamdara.com/ColumnDetail.asp?cid=10720.

McCargo, Duncan (2000) *Politics and the Press in Thailand*, London and New York: Routledge.

McCargo, Duncan (2003) *Media and Politics in Pacific Asia*, London and New York: Routledge.

McGuigan, Jim (2010) 'The cultural public sphere' in *Cultural Analysis*, London: Sage, pp. 8–21.

90 Brett Farmer

Montesano, Michael J., Chachavalpongpun, Pavin and Chongvilaivan, Aekapol (eds.) (2012) *Bangkok May 2010: Perspectives on a Divided Thailand*, Singapore: Institute of Southeast Asian Studies.

Moores, Shaun (2005) *Media/Theory: Thinking About Media and Communications*, London and New York: Routledge.

Morris, Meaghan (1990) 'Banality in cultural studies' in Patricia Mellencamp (ed.) *Logics of Television*, Bloomington: Indiana University Press, pp. 14–43.

The Nation (2008) 'Air hostesses urge "Battle of Angels" to be reasonable', *The Nation*, 22 January, http://nationmultimedia.com/2008/01/22/headlines/headlines_30063001.php.

Nattapong Sakulliao (2012) 'Khrongsang Kwamsamphan Kong Sangkhom Thai Nai "Raeng Ngao"', *Prachatai*, 31 October, http://prachatai.com/journal/2012/10/43405.

Palatino, Mong (2010) 'Thailand: "We're Sick of the Ministry of Culture"', *Global Voices*, 11 January, http://globalvoicesonline.org/2010/01/11/thailand-'were-sick-of-ministry-of-culture'.

Pasuk Pongpaichit and Baker, Chris (2008) 'Thailand: fighting over democracy', *Economic and Political Weekly*, 13 December, pp. 18–21.

Phot Jaicharnsukkit (2011) 'Meua "Dok Som See Thong" Ban Nai Social Media', *DrPhot.com*, 22 May, http://drphot.com/thinkabout/archives/398.

Poowin Bunyavejchewin (2010) 'Constructing the "red" otherness: the role and implications of Thainess on polarised politics', *ASEAS: Austrian Journal of South-East Asian Studies*, 3(2): 241–8.

Sehmer, Alex (2008) 'Bangkok's battle of ethics', *Al-Jazeera News*, 10 July, www.aljazeera.com/news/asia-pacific/2008/03/200852517372773913.html.

Servaes, Jan, Malikhao, Patchanee and Pinprayong, Thaniya (2008) 'Communication rights as human rights for instance in Thailand', *Global Media Journal*, 7(13).

Sirinya Wattanasukchai (2009) 'Thai soaps: tweaking time-tested TV tales', *The Bangkok Post*, 14 October, p. O3.

Somkiat Tangkitvanich (2008) 'The creation of Thai Public Broadcasting Service: Thailand's first public television station', *Thai Development Research Institute Quarterly Review*, 23(2): 3–8.

Streckfuss, David (2010) 'The spring of Thailand's ethnic discontent', *The Wall Street Journal*, 24 May, http://online.wsj.com/article/SB10001424052748704546304575261331886900358.html.

Streckfuss, David (2011) *Truth on Trial in Thailand: Defamation, Treason, and Lèse-Majesté*, London and New York: Routledge.

Sutraphorn Tantiniranat (2005) *Images of Thai Women Presented through Female Antagonists in Thai TV Drama Series*, MA thesis, Chiang Mai University.

Thak Chaloemtiarana (2007) *Thailand: The Politics of Despotic Paternalism*, revised edn, Ithaca: Cornell Southeast Asia Program Publications.

Ubonrat Siriyuvasak (2000) 'The ambiguity of the "emerging" public sphere and the Thai media industry' in Georgette Wang, Jan Servaes and Anura Goonasekera (eds.) *The New Communications Landscape: Demystifying Media Globalization*, London and New York: Routledge.

Ubonrat Siriyuvasak (2006) 'Who owns the Asian media: Thailand media report', *Campaign for Popular Media Reform*, www.media4democracy.com/eng/PDF_file/UBONRAT%20Thailand%20media%20report.pdf.

Ubonrat Siriyuvasak (2007) 'New media for civil society and political censorship in Thailand', *Asia Rights Journal*, 8, http://rspas.anu.edu.au/asiarightsjournal/Issue%20Eight_Siriyuvasak.htm.

Van Fleet, Sarah (1998) *Everyday Dramas: Television and Modern Thai Women*, doctoral dissertation, University of Washington.

Vogel, Bernard, Grabow, Karsten, Korte, Karl-Rudolf and Weissenbach, Kristina (2008) *KAS Democracy Report 2008: Media and Democracy, Volume II*, Berlin: Konrad Adenauer Stiftung.

Walker, Andrew (2011) 'Narrative sedition and democratic consolidation', *New Mandala: New Perspectives on Mainland Southeast Asia*, August 24, http://asiapacific.anu.edu.au/newmandala/2011/08/24/narrative-sedition-and-democratic-consolidation.

Walker, Andrew (2012) *Thailand's Political Peasants: Power in the Modern Rural Economy*, Madison: University of Wisconsin Press.

Williams, Raymond (1989) *Resources of Hope*, ed. Robin Gale, London: Verso, pp. 3–18.

Woodier, Jonathan (2008) *The Media and Political Change in Southeast Asia: Karaoke Culture and the Evolution of Personality Politics*, Cheltenham: Edgar Elgar.

Xavier, Ismail (2004) 'Historical allegory' in Toby Miller and Robert Stam (eds.) *A Companion to Film Theory*, London: Blackwell.

Youngsamart, Daungdau and Fisher, Gregory (2006) 'Governance and administration in a "new" democracy: the case of formal control of the free-to-air television in Thailand (1997–2006)', *JOAAG*, 1(1): 36–46.

6 Dramatizing the nation
Television, history and the construction of Singaporean identity

Jinna Tay

Television dramas, both serials and series, have been a long-term recruiter of large-scale national audiences for television broadcasters as they are potentially able to speak to their audience in affective and imaginative ways (Chan 2011; Sun and Gorfinkel 2014). Usually it is the locally produced drama that resonates most with a national audience, the familiarity of the setting and context often carrying significant implications for social and sometimes political life (Blandford et al. 2011, Chan 2011). These television texts can pick up on popular strands of discourses in the public sphere and succeed in establishing a form of dialogue with audiences; in the instances examined in this chapter, this dialogue is about the formation of national identities or citizenships. There is good reason, then, for broadcasters and governments to attempt to use television drama to educate and persuade, although Sugg and Power (2011: 26–7), long-term drama producers at the BBC World Service Trust, warn that for dramas to succeed in this manner, they first have to be entertaining, otherwise they are unlikely to generate an audience in the first place. Audiences are not easily fooled and can sniff out the difference between being entertained and being preached at in a didactic way. This chapter deals with a period in the history of Singapore where television historical drama played a significant role in creating a national past upon which the promotion of a distinctive national identity might be based. In addition to a consideration of a selection of drama series themselves, the chapter draws upon interviews where viewers are encouraged to share their memories of these dramas, and the part they played in the construction of a Singaporean identity.

Television arrived in Singapore in 1963, a good two years before national independence in 1965; it was in place, then, to capture the tearful announcement by Prime Minister Lee Kuan Yew that Singapore had separated from the Malayan Federation. However, it wasn't until 1977 that colour television arrived and local-flavoured television and content began to be produced specifically for its local audience. It is apt that television began around the time of the nation, since television in particular has played an important, if not *the* main role in the mediascape of Singapore (Tan 2008;

Chan 2011). Chan notes that while the television history of larger nations such as China and Japan has received its fair share of academic analysis, in contrast, smaller ones like Singapore have received little attention (Chan 2011: 115). In fact, we may argue that the history of television in smaller nations is even more critical to the national story due to the impact over its smaller demographic, and sometimes smaller nations offer up alternative models to that of the received wisdom of the bigger hegemonic nations (Blandford et al. 2011; Chua 2011). It may also seem natural to assume that smaller nations, due to their size, are homogenous and therefore offer relatively uncomplicated instances of nation formation; the population of Singapore, however, is made up of a composite of local Malays, Indians, Chinese and a small number of Europeans. This was especially so up until the early 2000s, when more new migrants and guest workers were allowed in on work visas. As a result, television has had to learn to attract such a disparate group of viewers with four official languages and more than eight dialects between them.

In particular, this chapter recognizes the significance of the Mandarin drama serials in contributing to the success of the newly established Singapore Broadcasting Corporation in 1980. These serials captured the imagination of the nation and the interviews for this chapter demonstrate that they left an indelible impression on, and historical legacy for, the memories of its audience. The depth and longevity of the public engagement with these dramas was most apparent at the death of Huang Wen Yong in 2013, one of the lead actors in Mediacorp's first successful big-budget drama serial, *The Awakening*, which screened in 1984. Huang went on to subsequently star in many of the local drama serials, but he was always remembered for his portrayal of the upright, heart-warming and hardworking Ah Shui (Lim 2013). Representing not only the endearing characters, *The Awakening*, which was produced in conjunction with Singapore's 25th anniversary, triggered a sentimental and nostalgic memorializing of the deeds of 'our forefathers' in the building of modern Singapore. The producers explicitly and successfully used the drama to commemorate the national day and it clearly struck a chord with Singaporean audiences then (Leong 1984b), as demonstrated in the interviews I conducted.

The history of television dramas such as *The Awakening* over the 1980s reveals that television was proselytizing a national agenda while successfully educating and entertaining its public. Chan (2011: 115) agrees that, from the beginning of domestic television drama production in 1982, 'television dramas produced by the state-owned television station have served the ideological function of cultivating national identity for this relatively young nation'. Both contemporary and historical dramas evoked localized incidents of everyday life that Singaporeans could identify with; consequently, television spoke to the currency of the social life in the state in meaningful ways that encouraged the audience to also realize their role as citizens in a nation-state.

Television and social life: urbanization, nationalization of land, civic campaigns

During the 1980s, Singapore embarked on a major programme of urbanization that included the residential adjustment that moved citizens from kampongs (traditional villages) and urban squats to government-built high-rise flats or apartments managed by the Housing Development Board (HDB). Beginning in the 1960s and over the course of the 1970s and well into the 1980s, this domestic migration impacted the lives of many villagers. In fact, by 1975, the HDB had built enough flats to rehouse almost half the population of Singapore (NAS 2009: Section 6) and by the 1980s almost 90 per cent of Singaporeans and permanent residents were living in these flats (Chua 2011: 44). By the late 1990s there were no functioning kampongs left. The rapidity of this shift brought with it change and disruption to the social life of the residents. Many of the systems and patterns of social relations, cultural routines, customs, communities and connections in kampongs were ephemeral but structured into the practices of everyday life. As these practices changed in order to make way for progress and modernity in the urban environment, these traditional ways of life were demolished along with their kampongs.

From the 1960s, this relocation began with the compulsory nationalization of vast tracts of land in kampongs and urban squats, often with minimal compensation to the landowners of the kampongs (Chua 2011: 44). The government had counselled the landowners to accept this as a form of land reform and redistribution. Yet, this resettlement involved not just inadequate compensation but the destruction of old communities and the displacement of neighbourhoods build around kinship. The government took care to rehouse all the disrupted communities into new housing estates in areas such as Jurong, Ang Mo Kio, Tampines, Bedok and so on, allocating the relocated residents as many flats as they required to accommodate their families. The government also instituted incentives to own these flats through low mortgage repayments via their CPF accounts (Central Provident Fund), a form of social security fund. Loh Kah Seng, a Singaporean historian, has argued that the 'social history of housing unveils the political motivation behind the development of public housing in Singapore – to transform the semi-autonomous urban kampong population into a model and integrated citizenry' (Loh 2009: 619). Sociologist Chua Beng Huat also argues that the reduced mortgage payment for public housing actually enabled a form of 'transformation and disciplining of the population into an industrial labor force' as the CPF required that mortgage payments should be made through regular employment (Chua 2011). The transformation and disciplining of this citizenry into a model of a modern industrial workforce did not stop at the domestication and urbanization of landscapes, but it was further enabled through the wider apparatuses of media consumption, public civics campaigns and education institutions.

Over the period 1975–85 this residential transformation also resulted in the widespread relocation of itinerant street hawkers and peddlers to fixed coffee shops and hawker centres, with centralized licencing of food sales and higher sanitation practices. While many of these changes were in line with the objectives of modernization and often resulted in improvements, they also alienated many through the forced adaptation to high-rise living away from the shared communal open doorways of kampong life and the corridors of urban squatters. Drama serials such as *Son of Pulau Tekong*, *Five Foot Way*, *Neighbours*, *Kopi-O* and *Good Morning Teacher* depict the emotional and social impact of modernization. Not only did these serials recreate the emotional texture of this journey, they also demonstrated how to adapt to these changes through participating in HDB Community grassroots events and promoted policemen on bicycles as 'our friendly neighbourhood policemen' (NAS 2009: Section 6). Looking back at those television serials now, they might seem like a crude form of popular education, but for an audience that was experiencing both significant social change and mass media for the first time, these television serials examined real issues that the audience/citizens faced.

The establishment of new town centres and community centres functioned to provide governmental grass roots services to encourage an urbanized, centralized and even homogenous form of living practice – for example, providing the modern and material comforts of a nearby wet market, supermarket, food centres, playgrounds, library and kindergartens allowed the suburban-centralization of the population, but also allowed the congregation of an identifiable community, e.g., Bedok residents. However, it underestimated the frictions and difficulties of in adjusting to living in HDBs. Problems included unsecured potted plants falling over the railings and 'killer litter' falling on pedestrians from great height, burglary and the defrauding of elderly folks by people pretending to be postal workers or workmen, people urinating and littering in lifts and snatch thieves along corridors were all widely reported in the local newspapers. In addition to these criminal activities, many other activities were deemed uncivilized and undesirable for the modernizing nation-state: these included spitting in public and vandalizing public property with chewing gum. These undesirable behaviours were punished by the imposition of fines: $200 for littering, $500 for spitting and so on. Heavy public media campaigns aimed at educating the populace to be aware of these sanctions against such behaviours, and the fines connected to them, were conducted through posters, television advertisements and education initiatives in schools. Children who were of school age in the 1980s will remember seeing many of these posters and campaigns at school, as many of these campaigns were not just aimed at deterring particular forms of misbehaviour but were also aimed at inculcating virtues and positive values through projects such as the Courtesy Campaign, the Keep Singapore Clean campaign, the Let's Save Precious Water campaign, and the Speak Mandarin campaign (Teo 2004a, 2004b; Newman 1988; RemSg 2013). Some of these issues were incorporated into the storylines of drama serials, extending the educative reach of the drama and at times opening up a public space for audience dialogue about

96 *Jinna Tay*

these issues. Some of the respondents I spoke to could still sing the Courtesy jingle we were all made to learn in school.

Over this decade, from its beginnings with the nationalization of land, the geographical transformation of the landscape of Singapore was coming to be epitomized by the new modernity of skyscrapers in the business district and the equally tall and widespread public housing estates with the distinctive Mass Rapid Transport (MRT) in 1987 snaking its way through the heart of major city routes. These government-led transformations of the physical landscape, in concert with the public campaigns over cultural and political issues via television advertisements, television dramas, school videos, public posters and news and media reports, had the enclosure effect of a disciplining of the public consciousness, a nationalization of the citizenry. By 'nationalization of the citizenry', I'm referring to a sensitization of the citizenry towards an internalized consciousness of the progress of nation: so that 'what is good for the nation, is good for us'. By putting the good of the nation first, (even if it meant making sacrifices now), the citizens could accept that they would be investing in the future of Singapore. The strategy of nationalizing the citizen through the creation of a national consciousness was particularly focused and comprehensive, and its influence is easily visible in the history of the Mandarin television dramas of the time. Table 6.1 demonstrates how topics addressed within this programme of nationalization were embedded into the storylines of the drama serials in the 1980s. It is not an exhaustive list; rather it illustrates the close relations between social history, the various foci of the nationalization campaigns and the Mandarin-language TV dramas.

The 1980s was also a milestone decade for a series of other modernization achievements; these included international success with the completion of Changi International Airport in 1981, and the subsequent 1988 award for 'Best Airport in the World' from *Business Traveller Magazine*. This reinforced the sense that this little island state was making a name for itself globally. This was further marked by Singapore's Silver Jubilee National Day celebration in 1984, with a number of firsts such as the first 'hit' national theme song for the parade, 'Stand Up for Singapore', and the first evening fireworks. The arrival of the MRT in 1987 was seen as the completion of another public development project that changed the condition and familiarity of everyday life in Singapore for the better. This was especially remarkable when compared to the development of Singapore's neighbours at the time.

Across the mediascape, the developments were equally fast and furious. Television had emerged as the kingpin of all the media industries. After its arrival in 1963, it had a slow uptake but as the population grew more affluent by the mid-1980s most families had a television set in their homes. In my interviews for this chapter, several respondents spoke about owning television sets in the 1980s. PL's earliest memory was going to his neighbour's house to watch television as they had the only set in the street. As many of the respondents had television sets in their own homes by the 1980s, many stated that television was the main form of entertainment in those days as it was a cheap

Dramatizing the nation 97

Table 6.1 Nationalization and Singapore drama

Media/social history background	*Nationalizations 1980s*	*Mandarin-language TV dramas*
Television arrives 1963 Independence of nation 1965 (State broadcaster: media plays a guiding role for nation)	Civic campaigns: across schools, community centres, public spaces: • 'Courtesy our way of life' • POSB Savings Bank • Speak Mandarin campaign • Productivity campaign • Let's not waste water • Stop at 2 (birth control) • No Spitting (fine)	1st SBC TV production: *Seletar Robbery* (1982) *Good Morning Teacher* (*LaoShi ZaoAn*) (1989) *Coffee Shop* (*Kopi O*) (1986) *Army Series* (*XinBingXiao Zhuan*) (1983) *Neighbours* (*ZiMaLuDou*) (1988)
1970s, TV not widely available – shared experiences, consolidation of domestic politics. Programmes bought from Hong Kong, Macau, Taiwan – in dialects.	Urbanization, nationalization of land: eviction of kampongs (villages and urban villages). System of fines, e.g., $300 for litter, $2,000 for 'killer litter', $500 and community work for spitting, $50 for jaywalking.	*Son of Pulau Tekong* (*Yadazi*) (1985) *Five Foot Way* (*WuJiaoJi*) (1987)
1980s, nationalizations across multiple platforms. Partial privatization in 1980 to SBC. 1994 fully privatized as Television Corporation Singapore and Radio Corporation Singapore. 2001 incorporated as Mediacorp Singapore.	Nationalization, celebration of 25 years of nation-building (1984). National Day parade song: 'We are Singapore' (1987) 'Stand Up for Singapore' (1984) 'Five stars arise' (1989).*	*The Awakening* (*WuSuoNanyang*) (1984) *Samsui Women* (*HongTouJing*) (1986) *Flying Fish* (*Xiao Feiyu*) (1983)

*http://en.wikipedia.org/wiki/List_of_Singaporean_patriotic_songs

and simple form of family entertaining, and most were able to still cite their favourite programmes of those days. Yet, behind the programmes, television had undergone tremendous industrial and structural change.

Life of a public broadcaster

Since its black and white one-hour pilot test on 15 February 1963, television has never looked back in Singapore. It was then operated by Radio Television Singapore (RTS), the public service broadcaster and a state monopoly and this was to be the first of its many incarnations before becoming SBC, then

98 *Jinna Tay*

TCS and its eventual form as Mediacorp Singapore. Today it is still the only free-to-air broadcaster in Singapore, offering up to seven channels on terrestrial TV in English (Channel 5), Mandarin (Channel 8), Malay (Suria) and with Vasantham being a channel dedicated to the Indian communities in Tamil, Hindi and other languages. The pride of Mediacorp is Channel News Asia (CNA), its 24-hour English-language news channel launched in 1999, boasting an Asian perspective in news and coverage of regional news and current affairs that is different from Western perspectives. Channel U (Mandarin) was absorbed into Mediacorp as a competitor station that failed and Okto is the latest children's channel. The programmes range from locally produced news segments, features and documentaries for CNA and dramas, variety shows, edutainment, lifestyle and so on for Channel 5, 8, Suria and Vasantham to imported drama on Channel U.

In 1963, even though programming only ran for one hour, within two months of the commencement of transmission, 7,000 television sets were sold to community centres, homes and associations (*The Straits Times* 1963). This meant one in 58 people owned a television. From the outset, the official multiracial/multilingual policy (English, Mandarin, Malay and Tamil are all official languages in Singapore) was evident. It was planned that nightly at least three languages would be broadcast, with the aim of creating deeper understanding between the races through cultural and entertainment forms (Lim 1963: 1) with concurrent subtitling as one of the strategies to enable this cultural exchange to take place. Chinese dialects were still used, especially on radio to reach the various communities, but by 1979 the incorporated Chinese Language Policy dictated that all the dialects had to be dubbed into Mandarin. This affected the popular variety shows and drama programmes imported from Taiwan and Hong Kong that were produced in Hokkien and Cantonese, respectively. Dubbing and subtitling were established early on as a strategy to encourage interracial understanding and also due to the compulsory enforcement of Mandarin; however, this became a significant budgetary constraint due to the restricted operation of RTS as a public broadcaster.

One of the solutions came in 1980 when RTS underwent a partial privatization under the Parliamentary Act to become Singapore Broadcasting Corporation (SBC). This partial privatization gave the broadcaster the right to manage its own finance, personnel, language subtitling, production and programming – key to its subsequent developmental success. It enabled SBC to directly manage their funding, take on the hiring of foreign talents to help develop the fledging drama unit, and to increase media development and local content across its two channels: Channel 5 (in English and Malay languages) and Channel 8 (in Mandarin and Tamil languages). This privatization was pivotal to SBC's long-term success as a broadcaster and media content producer as well as to its regional ambitions in exporting content and then talent; and it gave the organization greater autonomy to set up from scratch the Chinese drama unit that produced so many popular drama hits from 1982 to the late 1990s. More importantly, it also offered some freedom by taking television away from the direct control of the Ministry of Culture.

By 1994, in an attempt to wholly privatize SBC, it was incorporated as Television Corporation of Singapore (TCS) and Radio Corporation of Singapore (RCS). In 2001, it was again revamped to the current Mediacorp Singapore as a media conglomeration owned by the Singapore International Media Group and totally owned by Temasek Holdings, the investment arm of the Singapore government. In its current organizational structure, Mediacorp Singapore encompasses several segments: print, television, radio, interactive platform, production houses and studio training units, media research and consultancy and a whole plethora of other media-related businesses such as satellite uplink, events management and even distribution of film and television products (Mediacorp Singapore 2010). Television is, nonetheless, the most prominent face of Mediacorp, with its local celebrities providing resources for its tabloid newspaper, *Today*, and other celebrity magazines, *8 Days*, *Style* and *Singapore FHM*. The studio training units and production houses scout for new talents into their radio and television programmes with successful in-house actor-directors such as Jack Neo branching out into his own films, distributed under RainTree Productions.

The string of Mandarin mainstream successes in the 1980s were by no means the first local programmes produced by SBC. However, their success in producing their own celebrities and telling their own stories generated the semblance of a national culture – something very new for a young nation. These stories were culturally resonant, attracting mainly the Chinese but also the Indian and Malay viewers in the population. (These dramas – see Table 6.1 – were also the ones most cited by audience members interviewed for this chapter.) While Singaporean television of this early period tried to cater to children and adults across news bulletin development, variety programmes, drama serials and educational segments often in multilingual programming, it was the Chinese viewers, being 80 per cent of the population, that enabled the critical success of Channel 8 to translate into a mass audience for SBC. The Singaporean dramas were qualitatively different to the imported ones from Hong Kong, Taiwan and China, in that they reflected local cultural practices, especially in food and living standards, showing Singaporean streets and stories that referenced Singaporeans' common histories and future. While the producers were imported from Hong Kong to teach the local television producers, the outcomes were stories about *our* kampongs, *our* way of life which is South-East Asian, and markedly different from the East Asian environment, politics and climate. As demonstrated by the responses in the interviews, audiences felt that these dramas were especially authentic and captured the unique multiracial identities and culture that made them Singaporean. The experiential effect of such collectivity has to have wider impact on the national sentiments and psyche of the people.

Local television dramas: a national awakening

From 1982 to 1990, SBC produced close to 90 drama serials for Channel 8. They ranged from historical to romance, horror, mystery, crime, comedy and martial arts (RemSg 2014). The first Mandarin drama ever made was a single episode, *Seletar Robbery* (1982), that lasted 90 minutes. Subsequent to that were two serials, *Army Series* and *Flying Fish* in 1983 comprised of six and eight episodes respectively. These serials were relatively successful, especially for the young actor Wang Yuqing who catapulted to fame in both these serials. *Army Series* dealt with the compulsory National Service that young men in Singapore had to undergo as citizens, especially the emotional and mental struggles many faced in transitioning into a military life of combat and training, with an underlying message of 'doing it for the country'. A few of the male respondents in the interviews cited it fondly as one of the serials that they felt related to them.

Then, in February 1984, SBC made a huge leap into a double series: costing an unprecedented S$1 million to produce (Chan 2011), the 27-episode (first series) and 26-episode (second series) serial *The Awakening* part I and II, (雾锁南洋, *wùsuǒ nányáng*) debuted to more than 800,000 audience on its first night, thus reaching roughly 30 per cent of the population (Leong 1984b), and continued to rate extremely well over subsequent weeks. Screened twice a week, on Mondays and Fridays in the prime-time slot of 7pm, the series was so popular with Mandarin and non-Mandarin speakers in Singapore that it topped the ratings over the staples of imported as well as local variety programmes. Classified as a historical fiction, it is the coming-of-age story of Singapore as seen through the eyes and struggles of its immigrants from the 1920s, arriving as coolies (labourers) from Chinese junks. It deals with Singapore's colonization in World War Two as well as the subsequent rebuilding of modern Singapore. The director, Leung Lap Yan, wanted the story to entertain but also to educate the youth of Singapore so that they would appreciate the work of their forefathers in building the nation and surviving the war (Leong 1984b). The central characters, Ah Shui (Huang YongWen) and Ah Mei (Xiangyun), played by actors who became household names after this serial, were upright, hardworking, poor immigrants who met and got married in Singapore and established a family through honest work. Around them, a cast of other characters showcased local community life.

The serial dramatized the formation and adoption of a distinctive South-East Asian Chinese-Singaporean identity. In the first series, it began with the British colonial government of 1920s and the arrival of the Chinese immigrants as coolies from China, leading up to the Japanese occupation in World War Two. The second series detailed historical events such as the postwar political chaos in the bid for power by communists, trade unionists, political groups and Chinese associations (*hui guans*) as well as gang protectionism in Chinatown. Forming the historical backdrop to the classically heroic nation-forming narrative was the liberation from Britain and

Dramatizing the nation   101

Malaysia, leading to the journey towards self-determination. The depiction of racial prejudice even between dialect groups (Hokkien, Cantonese, Teochew, Hainanese), served to remind the audience of the social discord and chaos of that period in contrast to the peace and prosperity that Singapore experienced in the 1980s. In dealing with these particular historical milestones, the drama reimagines and reinscribes them with ideological meanings for contemporary society. One of the interview respondents, SC, stated in regard to the series' representation of the suffering caused by the Japanese occupation:

> I mean, I feel very touched and I feel sad for them. I really admire them. It's something that I don't know whether nowadays people can really go through that kind of suffering for the sake of the family.
>
> (SC, personal interview, 2013)

For SC, the portrayals captured an authentic aspect of early Singaporean life and of the hardships Singaporeans had to overcome to build a great nation – this is a repetitive trope many of the other respondents expressed. They listed the set locations, costumes and historical backdrop of the serial as being particularly authentic. The producers have stated that they had enlisted the help of historians to recreate an authentic version of the past (Leong 1984b), including building an old street scene, something that was seen as innovative for the SBC at that time. Historical fictions such as *The Awakening* and *Samsui Women* articulated a different form of dialogue with the audience by igniting a temporal and spatial reimagining of the creation journey that, along the way, normalized ideological and philosophical ethics of how to be a moral as well as a good citizen (*zuorendedaoli*).

The actors who played the characters Ah Shui (Huang WenYong) and Ah Mei (Xiangyun) have gone on to become the most popular actors in Singapore over the past 30 or so years. During the 1980s, with the expansion and semi-privatization of Singapore Broadcasting Corporation, these actors blazed a trail with subsequent Channel 8 dramas such as *YaDaZi* (*Son of Pulau Tekong*), *Samsui Women*, *Kopi-O*, *Xiao Feiyu*, *LaoShi ZhaoAn* (*Good Morning Teacher*), *WuJiaoJi* (*Five Foot Way*). In particular, *Son of Pulau Tekong* narrativized the relocation of the villages from Pulau Tekong, a small island east of the mainland that was being cleared due to nationalization of the land for use by the Singapore Armed Forces as a training ground. The drama itself showed the social and emotional upheavals experienced by the villagers as they made their way to living in high-rise flats and negotiated urban life on the mainland. Similarly, *Five Foot Way* dramatized the transition from the traditional old two-level terrace shop homes to flats, and *Kopi-O* centred on the lives of the workers and the owners of a coffee shop, characters known literally as the 'little people' (*xiaorenwu*) in new public housing estates. These texts readily acknowledge the difficulties involved in the transition to modern life and becoming 'little people' – that is, as they have to become part of a massive urban community, rather than a smaller and more personal community, they become unimportant. On the other hand, such stories also focused on the intrinsic happiness that comes from treating your neighbours, your customers and your family right. In that sense, the didactic nature of the text was obvious and in fact readily admitted; however, the sense of it being a 'good' text by encouraging people to do the right thing appealed to audiences, offering them a sense of identification by drawing on these actors as the local heroes of Singapore society.

The success continued by drawing on both historical and contemporary stories as resources to address the rapid changes in society. The justifications for the nationalization of the citizenry are often built into these narratives through didactic scripts reinforcing the interpretive agenda of modernization. Television was the main form of mass entertainment during the 1980s and early 1990s (personal interviews with SC, PL and RT, 2013) and the prime-time slot of 7pm family watching was a large part of local television ritual (much like television rituals globally). In 1984, when the country celebrated its 25th year of independence, these drama serials were charged with the idea of enhancing the celebration by telling the nation's own coming-of-age stories, hence *The Awakening* was an integral part of imagining the nation. Therefore television inserted, consolidated and celebrated the achievements of the everyday citizen and his/her sense of place in modern Singapore through the reimagining of the struggles of their forefathers.

Working in concert with the programme of dramatizing a national history, there was also the range of public civics campaigns mentioned earlier, aimed at modernizing and civilizing the national citizen. Through advertising and jingles, the public campaigns on television validated the achievements of the nation and its progress while continually exhorting improvements through campaigns to encourage courtesy, productivity, saving (thrift), kindness, speaking Mandarin and keeping Singapore clean. These 'virtues' were designed to have civilizing tendencies associated with one's behaviour in public but the underlying factor relates to how one would function and respond to the national body. Traits such as courtesy, kindness and productivity are all virtues one would use in a social environment, especially at work or in public spaces. Courtesy and kindness in particular were framed as ways to greet and interact with international tourists as individual 'representatives' of the nation. To save your money and to speak in Mandarin were tactics for progress, where China was seen as a potential powerhouse and to be educated in simplified Chinese writing as well as speaking Mandarin would allow Singaporeans to operate in Asia and the West. In practice, saving, as opposed to quick and perhaps high-risk investment in bonds or the stock market, was seen as an honest and hardworking means to accumulate wealth. These values were also taught in schools through civic education or moral education classes. While these campaigns promoted values that are seemingly 'rational' and progressive, closer readings by other academics in the field have produced both ideological and political rationales for pursuing them. Television provided the ideal mediated enclosure and a vehicle for bringing these messages into domestic space (Teo 2004a 2004; Newman 1988; RemSg 2013). The performance of citizenship in public and private were conflated with these series of values informing what it means to be a moral, ethical, progressive and modern Singaporean.

Audience memorialization of television texts

In order to substantiate the accounts given in the previous sections with evidence of how the audience of the time experienced these dramas, I conducted ten interviews with members of the television audience in Singapore in 2012. Six of the respondents were self-admitted television addicts, especially to drama programmes. The other four professed to watch television as family time, or sporadically, or only in order to see documentaries and news. All of them, however, remembered and watched some of the popular Mandarin dramas from the 1980s, especially *The Awakening*, *Kopi-O*, *Samsui Women*, *Flying Fish*, *Army Series* and *Good Morning Teacher*. Most said they watched mainly Channel 8 with only a few watching English programmes as well. The other popular programmes tended to be the variety/game/song shows that came after the 7pm drama slots, which many of them also watched. The interview subjects' ages ranged from the youngest of 27 to oldest at 74, with four male and six female. Only one of them was a retiree, whilst the rest were all of working age. In terms of their age breakdown, there was one in their twenties, one in their thirties, three in their forties, three in their fifties, one in their sixties and one in their seventies. Due to the differences in age, it makes sense to explain when they watched these drama serials. Whilst many of those aged 40 and above watched the original screening of these dramas in the 1980s, the two below 40 years of age watched them on reruns on afternoon TV. These serials have been continually rebroadcasted over the years, although I do not have the count for how frequently this has occurred. LY, one of the self-confessed 'TV addicts', said she watched most of these serials in the 3pm afternoon time slot after school.

With the small sample size, the interviews provide qualitative material that adds to our understanding of the television texts from the audience's point of view. The individualized semi-structured interviews all lasted for one to two hours. To begin with, the respondents were asked to name some of the 1980s TV serials they watched or remembered. I also brought stills from the dramas to prompt them to remember the characters or plots when necessary. I also offered them video clips of the theme songs to jog their memory. In most cases, they rejected the video clips but flipped through the stills, which sometimes prompted giggles. With the exception of the two respondents aged under 40, the rest of the respondents remembered the time when TV was in black and white. All could cite in great detail where they first encountered TV and how they usually watched it. In one account, SC, who lived within an extended family then, stated:

104   *Jinna Tay*

> It was like [an] after-dinner kind of thing, that we all watched. I remember the positions, we [the extended family] would all get ourselves into positions of relaxation. Some in front of the TV, some lie on the couch… it was like TV was the centre of the attraction, everybody would just be glued on it and waiting for it to come, there's a serial on, we are watching it all.
>
> (SC, 2013 interview)

It was not only the drama serials that these respondents remembered, however. Most respondents remembered the national civic education campaign jingles without prompting, while some could name almost all the campaigns slogans listed above and could even explain in great detail the content and approach of some of the advertising campaigns. Many could still sing the Courtesy jingle from TV, 'Courtesy is for free, Courtesy is for you and me'. The connection between these programmes of civic transformation and the historical drama series is temporal as well as ideological. The campaigns played throughout the day but were often targeted during prime-time to accompany the screening of the drama serials.

By the 1980s, these respondents tended to be in their own nuclear families as parents, newlyweds or young adults. Rather than watching at community centres, at a neighbour's home or with the extended family, they could afford to own a TV set. Television's material presence in the home was something that most of them commented on, especially how it was acquired in the 1970s or early 1980s, when the TV was still a symbol of aspirational middle-class status. In AT's account, it was an object to be cherished and protected when the instalment collector came, as the father didn't have enough money to pay for the TV repayments. Concurrently, what is interesting is that respondents are not able to recall their relationship with TV in the 1980s without recounting what occurred in the domestic space within familial structures (what they were doing at that point in life, domestic rituals). Second, discussions of TV inevitably brought up questions about the way in which it participated in the process of nation-building (the focus of the campaigns and what the serials meant to say to us). Third, there was clearly a strong affective dimension to the memories drawn on to construct these accounts: their feelings about the authenticity of texts, their empathy with the characters and their identifications with the nation.

From these interviews, there are three main strands that substantiate the arguments made in the discussions of the television texts and their relation to the construction of a national history. In choosing to highlight these strands, I have deliberately left out discussions that are more affective and domestic in nature.

The role of television in creating a national imaginary and shared sense of national belonging

In considering these historical fiction series and their memorializing of the past, one of the respondents, HF, who is in her 50s, comments: 'I think TV is really very powerful. It's one of the most powerful media and all these drama series, I think really very powerful to get people remember their own past.' Beyond memorializing, it is also recognized as an imagining of the past, as stated by LY, who is in her twenties: 'it's nice because that [*The Awakening*] served as my image of what Singapore is. And that became like my benchmark so when my grandparents told me their story I was benchmarking their story against what I watched on TV.' Validated by relatives who had lived through World War Two and who saw the television representations as genuine and authentic, these stories placed the younger audience member at the scene (so to speak), establishing what is *real* and *ours* as common shared televisual memories. This is demonstrated in the comment from another respondent, PL:

> My favourite was *XinBinXiao* (*Army Series*), *WuSuoNanYang* (*The Awakening*) and *Xiao Feiyu* (*Flying Fish*), partly because it was our history in condensation... Partly my grandfather said to me this is how it was, so realistic. Certain portions were so realistic and certain portions is sort of like relive the memories even though I was so young. My grandfather would say, this or that is a historical fact, this scene and that I could identify with story.
>
> (PL, 2013 interview)

Through such corroboration, the impact of the dramas were extended so that there was a sense that television provided these audience members with access to their past:

> At least I got to know what is my past, otherwise you wouldn't know that at all. So I see this is how our forefathers have actually gone through, you know, we hear, but hearing is different. The impact is not there. The visual impact is there, for example, you know, my father-in-law said that he was actually captured by the Japanese, how he was actually helped by one of the soldiers to escape, you know, the route to being slaughtered and that one you can hear it, but you don't really feel what it is, what it was at that time when he went through the current situation. So watching the series then you can see, oh that's actually quite a traumatic experience in having to be caught by the Japanese and then sent to – and then saved in the nick of time by someone who took pity on him.
>
> (RT, 2013 interview)

Among the consequences of the perceived authenticity of the dramas is the successful establishment of these stories as 'our' stories. The ideological payoff is that the historical narrative is aimed at demonstrating not just how far Singapore has progressed as a nation but also as a means of demonstrating the quality and legitimacy of the nation's leadership and their policies:

106   *Jinna Tay*

> So just to let them [children] have an understanding of how life has changed over the years. And Singapore has changed a lot over these 20 or 30 years. From nothing to everything, now we are among the best in the world, with all the… transport system, in terms of housing, all is so different and we are very much better off than a lot of neighbouring countries.
>
> (SC, 2013 interview)

> Most of us agree that our government has done a lot, … for the people to make the country prosper, they've upgraded everything and that life is so much better than those days. Of course, things are getting expensive. […] Actually they are good and bad.
>
> (HF, 2013 interview)

There is an acknowledgement that there are 'bad' outcomes of government policy such as the cost of living being too high (SC) and the loss of our traditional historical environment to make way for modernized flats (HF), however, these are seen as necessary sacrifices for the national progress. This is demonstrated by the success of Singapore in comparison to the histories of other nation-states within the surrounding region (SC). In one breath while mourning the loss of some aspects of community life, SC also acknowledged that 'I feel proud in the sense that I'm proud of Singapore. And I believe when we watch these shows, they tell us that we are very lucky.' In this way, loss and memory become reconciled through the identification with the nation, and placated by pride in what Singapore's people have achieved.

The role of TV and media in the nationalization of citizenry

In our earlier discussion, the externalized elements of nationalization were a force that saw citizens physically relocated across the island, with reconfigured spaces, the development of an urban environment and the rise of sprawling malls across Singapore. The internalization of nationalization is a different matter. The acceptance of nationalization as a logic permeated the rationale for everyday life, as demonstrated by HF's self-reflexive statement about the littering campaigns:

> So many campaigns and so many fines… because we are so small, the campaigns are quite effective. There's jingle everywhere, the TV and the radio and you see all these posters and all that around, and you see all these fines… they slap on you. So these things are quite effective, but not so much now [due to new immigrants] this well-dressed lady… just threw a tissue on the ground. Suddenly you say hey? It's not like she's not educated. It has that kind of effect on us because we… can't bear to see a piece of tissue drop on the floor… but you see how effective

these campaigns are? That we can't even stand to see. I realized that it happened to me.

(HF, 2013 interview)

Indeed, she is surprised by her own response to the situation but could reflexively trace the roots of the influence. However, she is possibly the norm rather than the exception among civic-minded Singaporeans. Whilst it is a benign, even 'good', environmental value to maintain today, this example of an internalization of a nationalized value system is still beleaguered by the fact that it is a civic value that has been directly inculcated by the state. As we have seen, this direct shaping of internal value systems was at its height in the 1980s; the respondents indicate a level of acceptance of this and the following exchange suggests that even if it is propaganda, it is 'good' propaganda so we shouldn't have a problem with it:

My education is through TV watching, especially *BaoQinTian* (*Justice Bao*), I thought he was really upright. The values of then were different because we were building the country, a lot of diversity of values, TV make us focus as one – even propaganda [laughs]. Even productivity was very new, we got to know about productivity.

(PL, 2013 interview)

People like rallying together as a country as one. So I kind of like the idea of propaganda actually [laughs]. Because I think there's no point in swinging in different directions, just to swing in different directions... as a country, you can achieve a lot more things if you rally the resources together. If people swing together ... it doesn't really matter who's leading right?

(LY, 2013 interview)

The value of progress is paramount in the opinions being expressed here; political leaderships are all the same if the country can move as one and in the direction of economic affluence and social stability. Social diversity and the diversity of values all come below the priority of economic progress. This hierarchy of values can be heard commonly expressed across the island because these citizens have seen the rewards of affluence in recent years while, in contrast, history has taught them the cost of social instability and political waywardness. And within this logic, nationalization can be interpreted as the practice of the state logic and its powers to intervene hold sway over everyday life and customary practices. This form of nationalization aims to bring the survival, the success, the production of the nation to the coalface and attention of its public in an attempt to recreate a form of malleable citizenry that the state could work with.

108 *Jinna Tay*

The importance of TV in representing everyday life and banal nationalizations

Michael Billig's (2009) idea of banal nationalism has been used to explain the operation of nationalism in everyday life, with its insistence on the obvious, un-interrogated and unconscious practices and symbols that may be bypassed for analysis because of their everydayness, their banality. In his explanation, the national works through discourses that become so familiar and habitual they pass unnoticed. And yet, Billig acknowledges that the subject does not merely passively receive and incorporate the ideological messages carried by these banal practices. Indeed, it is important to recognize that the media does not offer up a single coherent message about the nation but rather a litany of controversies, debates and dilemmas that pockmark the mediascape, resulting in a need to negotiate the meaning of the nation in different contexts, issues and possibilities.

This could explain the possible meaning-making by audiences, especially when pressed to reconcile the difference between personal sacrifices versus following stringent civic codes. The logic of what is good and better for the nation, *for the community of us*, is always held as a higher virtue. Thus, it is possibly why media cynics attest to the power of television, believing that people will do whatever TV tells us to:

> because being a multiracial cultural society they have to be very careful. Showing the wrong script, it may harm ... another group of people, ... bring in disastrous result. So that part, you know, maybe because if we are not ready yet, unless we are able to discern, ... kind of like weigh the pros and con before we make any decision. But I think we still have a long way to go. People is swayed by TV. If TV tell you this is black, they're able to make almost quite a big number of people to accept that it is black.
>
> (RT, 2013 interview)

Is it possible that people will just believe whatever the television says? Otherwise, why would they obey certain rules and social targets? The internalized logic evident here privileges the national good and that of the wider social community over what might be considered important individual freedoms elsewhere. RT raises what has become an old media adage in Singapore, and in a number of other countries where histories of instability still haunt the polity. This is the proposition that Singapore's multiracial harmony needs to be protected from free speech because social dissent through racial disharmony can easily tear the social fabric. Therefore it is necessary not to allow too much freedom of speech in Singapore because people are not ready to handle it. RT goes on to explain that, due to the heavy price our forefathers had to pay to unite the country, there's a fragility about the nation that needs protection everyday:

> Oh yes. [Drama] is important, because it is through this story that people come to realize that, you know, that actually where we are now, the

people, you know, our forefathers that actually paid a very heavy price and, you know, they come a long way to bring the country, to unite the country as it is today and, you know, it's very fragile.

(RT, 2013 interview)

If the underlying root of this everyday banality incorporates media control, censorship or propaganda, the recognition of national social harmony and the smooth economic progress of the nation is reward enough to pay the price.

Conclusion

In exploring the Singaporean dramas of the 1980s, this chapter is concerned with locating the role occupied by television variously as a social-political object and interlocutor that is intimately tied to the creation and shaping of the national fabric. Dramatic narratives are shown to dovetail with larger governmental goals through public campaigns and education to civilize, educate and build a consensus with the population that had been taught to accede to the political will of the government. But television texts also work to interlocute by reflecting the social pressures, economic struggles and disenfranchisement resulting from urbanization and public policy upheavals in land nationalization. Rather than prompting dissent, the television history of Mandarin drama serials demonstrates how reflecting and capturing the banal details of everyday life and the historical struggles of the people generates a form of identification with and recognition of the nation. This shared form of mediated dialogue relieves rather than exacerbates issues as it enables audiences to internalize the logic of nationalization.

By drawing on the context of the 1980s, it is possible to understand how the serials might interact with the wider social issues of the period and the developmental initiatives of public campaigns in schools, media and public spaces to produce a media enclosure that conditions the citizenry towards the national good and national goals. This slow but progressive disciplining of the national body is enabled through the narrative logic in serials that can appeal to the common shared history and a sense of national belonging. And, lastly, by corroborating these conclusions with the audience interviews, we are able to derive a sense of the value judgements in operation; rather than 'telling us' how to think, as many suppose television does, the audience explanations demonstrate how they negotiate the dilemmas and contestations of texts so that the nation and the common good take priority over individual needs. That such negotiation occurs indicates that there is a choice to be made, while the enclosure boundaries to guide you towards the correct judgement. This study of Singapore's television serials of the 1980s and its context demonstrates the significance of television history as one means of opening the process of nationalization to scrutiny; and rather than a direct indoctrination of its audience it offers up a sophisticated model that demonstrates how deep such banal nationalizations can be.

110 *Jinna Tay*

References

Billig, M. (1995) *Banal Nationalism*, London and Thousand Oaks, CA: Sage.

Blandford, S., Lacey, S., McElroy, R. and Williams R. (2011) 'Editorial on television drama and national identity: the case of "small nations"', *Critical Studies in Television: The International Journal of Television Studies*, 6(2): xiv–xvii.

Chan, B. (2011) 'Home, identities and transnational appeal: the case of Singaporean television dramas', *Critical Studies in Television: The International Journal of Television Studies*, 62(2): 114–26.

Chua, B.H. (1991) 'Not depoliticized but ideologically successful: the public housing programme in Singapore', *International Journal of Urban and Regional Research*, 15(1): 24–41.

Chua, B.H. (1997) *Political Legitimacy and Housing Stakeholding in Singapore*, London: Routledge.

Chua, B.H. (2011) 'Singapore as model: planning innovations, knowledge experts' in A. Roy and A. Ong (eds.) *Worlding Cities: Asian Experiments and the Art of Being Global*, Oxford: Wiley-Blackwell, pp. 29–53.

Chua, B.H. (2012) 'Aesthetics of the pathetic: the portrayal of the abject in Singaporean cinema', *ACCESS: Critical Perspectives on Communication, Cultural & Policy Studies*, 31(2): 67–78.

Leong, W.K. (1984a) 'Fiction set in the past: accurate events, fictitious characters', *The Straits Times*, 20 January, p. 30.

Leong, W.K. (1984b) '*The Awakening* is top: local shows head the charts', *The Straits Times*, 26 April, p. 1.

Lim, K. (2013) 'Farewell Ah Shui: Huang Wen Yong's breakout role in *The Awakening*', *My Paper*, 22 April, http://news.asiaone.com/News/Latest+News/Showbiz/Story/A1Story20130422-417495.html.

Lim, K.S. (1963) 'Pilot service exceeded expectations', *The Straits Times*, 2 April, p. 1, http://eresources.nlb.gov.sg/newspapers/Digitised/Article.aspx?articleid=straitstimes19630402-1.2.138.

Loh, K.S. (2009) 'Kampong, fire, nation: towards a social history of postwar Singapore', *Journal of Southeast Asian Studies*, 40(3): 613–43.

Mediacorp Singapore (2010) *Our Business: Print, Television, Radio, Interactive Media, Productions, Other Business*, www.mediacorp.sg/en/corporate/television.

National Archives Singapore (NAS) (2009) *The Second Decade: Nation Building in Progress 1975–1985, Section 6, Housing a Nation: Changing Times, Changing Needs*, www.nas.gov.sg/1stcab/7585/travel_exh_Sec6.html.

Newman, J. (1988) 'Singapore's Speak Mandarin campaign', *Journal of Multilingual and Multicultural Development*, 9(5): 437–48.

RemSg (2011) 'From black and white to colour', *Remember Singapore Blog*, 13 August, http://remembersingapore.wordpress.com/2011/08/13/from-black-white-to-colour.

RemSg (2013) 'Singapore campaigns of the 70s/80s', *Remember Singapore Blog*, 18 January, http://remembersingapore.wordpress.com/2013/01/18/singapore-campaigns-of-the-past.

RemSg (2014) '20 most memorable SBC Channel 8 dramas of the 1980s', *Remember Singapore Blog*, 10 March, http://remembersingapore.wordpress.com/2014/03/10/sbc-dramas-of-1980s.

Skuse, A. (2011) 'Re-framing drama for development' in A. Skuse, M. Gillespie and G. Power (eds.) *Drama for Development: Cultural Translation and Social Change*, London: Sage, pp.1–22.

SOFT (2009) *Forum on Son of Pulau Tekong*, www.soft.com.sg/forum/showthread.php?t=159644&page=2&s=9524b18abacbd2e4198fc375dd9b4e6e.

The Straits Times (1963) '7000 Singapore homes now have TV sets', *The Straits Times*, 1 April, p. 1, http://eresources.nlb.gov.sg/newspapers/Digitised/Article.aspx?articleid=straitstimes19630402-1.2.140.

Sugg, C. and Power. G. (2011) 'Great expectations and creative evolution' in A. Skuse, M. Gillespie and G. Power (eds.) *Drama for Development: Cultural Translation and Social Change*, London: Sage, pp. 23–46.

Sun, W. and Gorfinkel, L. (2015) 'Television, scale and place-identity in the PRC: provincial, national and global influences from 1958–2013' in J. Tay and G. Turner (eds.) *Television Studies in Asia: Contexts and Issues*, London: Routledge.

Tan, K.P. (2008) *Cinema and Television in Singapore: Resistance in One Dimension*, Boston: Brill Academic Publishers.

Teo, P. (2004a) 'Clean and green – that's the way we like it: greening a country, building a nation', *Journal of Language and Politics*, 3(3): 485–505.

Teo, P. (2004b) 'Ideological dissonances in Singapore's national campaign posters: a semiotic deconstruction', *Visual Communication*, 3(2): 189–212.

Watson, J.K. (2011) 'Seoul and Singapore as "new Asian cities": literature, urban transformation, and the concentricity of power', *Positions: East Asia Cultures Critique*, 19(1): 193.

7 Working women and romance on Japanese television dramas

Changes since *Tokyo Love Story*

Alisa Freedman

Since their development in their current format in the early 1990s as a means to attract female viewers in their twenties, Japanese prime-time television dramas—known commonly as '*dorama*'[1]—have featured working women. Even police procedurals, medical dramas, and serials based on '*shōjo manga*' (graphic novels for girls) depict women working outside the home. The *dorama* most watched by Japanese audiences older than age 25, and those that continue to attract global fans, present the daily lives of independent women working in Tokyo. The protagonists enact fantasies about female professionals while depicting real issues facing the larger generations they represent. Viewers may not want to be these characters, but they can see aspects of themselves in them.

While various categories of working women have emerged, the narratives through which they have been portrayed all support the family as the nation's backbone, and work as a rewarding and necessary part of life. These stories show employment to be integral to women's self-cultivation, a notion perhaps rooted in discussions about working women in interwar Tokyo (see, for example, Tipton 2013). I argue that *dorama* have played an important role in nation-building processes and the construction of gender norms, tending to support dominant discourses. *Dorama* cannot take controversial stances as easily as novels and other media, due to the need for mass audiences, advertisers, and state support of commercial networks. Yet *dorama* express women's choices empathetically and thereby are a barometer of the emotional impact of historical change.

I will present an overview of working women on Japanese dramas and survey commonalities in their portrayals, especially from 1990 to the present. What has not changed is as illuminating as what has: both show how *dorama* negotiate social norms for women. Then I will analyze *Tokyo Love Story* (*Tokyo rabu sutorī*, 1991), which marked a turning point in the history of *dorama* and was popular because of its exuberant protagonist Akana Rika (played by Suzuki Honami). *Tokyo Love Story* had many television firsts: it was one of the first *dorama* to be based on manga, to attract global fans, and to have an unhappy ending in terms of love. Most notably, for the first time, the heroine aggressively pursued romance and took the initiative at work, a character type scorned in earlier series. Yet Rika's inability to have all she desired was what captivated audiences. By watching this series with more than 20 years of hindsight, we can see the genesis of career women characters and television's unwavering promotion of the family.

Working women characters in the early years of Japanese television

Since the beginning of television broadcasting, Japanese dramas have idealized the stability of the home and have presented in a good light those characters who maintain the family. Japan's first television drama *Before Dinner* (*Yūgemae*, NHK) aired on April 13, 1940, 13 years before NHK public television started regular programming on February 1, 1953 (a limited schedule from around 2pm to 8:45pm) and 15 years before the five commercial networks—NTV, Fuji TV, TBS, Asahi TV, and TV Tokyo—began in 1955. This 12-minute family drama about a mother, son, and daughter was shown on a television set in an electronics exhibit at Tokyo's Mitsukoshi department store. Although seen by few people, *Before Dinner* established two tropes of later drama series: the dominant mother figure and the depiction of meals to show a family's social status and emotional health. In part because they demanded audience attention in ways different from the earliest programming of sports, concerts, puppet shows, and stage plays aired on the radio, all events where cameras could easily be present, serialized dramas did not develop until television became an attraction possible for families. A 14-inch television set cost upwards of the astronomical figure of 140,000 yen in 1955, at a time a small house with a plot of land in cities sold for 200,000 yen and a male factory worker earned around 7,000 yen a month (Itō 1988: 16–17; Partner 1999: 71–2, 165). Most people watched television as a public or a neighborhood, as crowds, sometimes numbering in the hundreds, even thousands, gathered around appliance shop windows or television sets placed on pedestals in outdoor spaces. The popularity of television was fueled by live NHK broadcasts of national events, especially the royal wedding of future Heisei Emperor Akihito and Michiko Shōda on April 10, 1959, which was watched by 540,000 viewers at a time when only 24 percent of the population owned televisions (Partner 1999: 174–5), and the 1964 Tokyo Olympics, shown in color, as well as by technological advances, decreasing costs of television sets, advertising, and the extension and diversification of programming. In the 1950s and 1960s, the Japanese public came to see owning electronic household appliances as a means toward a comfortable middle-class life and thus, by 1965, 90 percent of Japanese households had purchased televisions, and programs had become a primary form of entertainment (Schilling 1997: 35).

Three kinds of serials—'home dramas' (*hōmu dorama*), 'morning television novels' (*renzoku terebi shōsetsu*), and '*taiga dorama*', historical dramas that developed in the late 1950s and early 1960s—presented the notion that women, even as they work, should prioritize the roles of wife and mother. Home dramas, with a name derived from English, were inspired by American television series (such as *I Love Lucy*, aired on NHK, 1957, and *The Donna Reed Show*, TBS, 1959) and Japanese theater-release films about lower and middle-class families (such as movies by directors Ozu Yasujirō and Naruse Mikio). They depicted the daily lives of seemingly ordinary middle- or lower-middle-class multigenerational families. Home dramas did not mirror reality as lived; for example, several dramas portrayed large families centered around a patriarch—e.g., *Seven Grandchildren* (*Shichi-nin no mago*, TBS, 1964) and *There are Eleven of Us Now* (*Tadaima jyūichi-nin*, 1964)— during the construction boom leading up to the 1964 Tokyo Olympics, a time when many youth were moving alone to cities to find work and the number of nuclear families living in apartments was increasing ((See, for example, Clements, J. and Tamamuro). The broadcasting period was lengthened from 30 minutes to an hour, and extended families provided more plotlines (Sata and Hirahara 1991: 113). Female characters, especially mothers, ran small family businesses. Examples include the beauty shop owner in *Off the Bus Route* (*Basu dōri ura*, 1958–63), NHK's first prime-time serialized drama; the proprietress of a soba shop in *Courageous Mother* (*Kimottama kaasan*, 1968–72); and the bathhouse manager in *It's Time, Everybody!* (*Jikan desu yo*, 1970).

Since they first began in March 1961 with *Daughter and Me* (*Musume to watashi*), NHK morning dramas, nicknamed '*asadora*' ('morning' (*asa*) plus '*dora*' from '*dorama*'), have focused on young women from undistinguished backgrounds who come of age by overcoming hardships, including those caused by poverty, war, and urbanization. (In 1966, NHK made it a policy to always center around a female protagonist; TBS's 'Pola Television Novels' (*Pola terebi shōsetsu*) airing from 1968 to 1986 followed suit.) Set in either the historical past or the present moment, the struggles of the heroine often parallel those of the nation. These dramas also exemplify the ethic (that hard work and perseverance will always be rewarded) that propels Japanese society. The most famous morning drama was *Oshin* (1983, viewer rating of 62.9 percent), which followed the life of a poor woman who moves to the city (NHK 2003: 54–55), and was set before and immediately after World War II. Airing during a time of economic prosperity, *Oshin* showed the hardships of the older generation. Several *asadora* heroines train for traditional service professions (for example, *ryokan okami* (inn manager) in *Perfect Blue Sky* (*Dondo hare*, 2007)) or to master classical Japanese male-dominated arts (e.g. *rakugo* (comedic storytelling) in *Chiritotechin*, 2007–8). Others have been based on historical women who set modern trends and raised children alone after their husbands died: for example, *Aguri* (1997) about Yoshiyuki Aguri, owner of one of Japan's first Western-style beauty salons in the 1920s and mother of novelist Yoshiyuki Junnosuke and actress and essayist Yoshiyuki Kazuko, and *Carnation* (*Kānēshon*, 2011–12) about Koshino Ayako and her three daughters, Koshino Hiroko, Koshino Junko, and Koshino Michiko, all of whom were fashion designers. No recent *asadora* has depicted a university-educated career woman in contemporary Japan. Two of the most popular *asadora* have featured female doctors, but both were set in the past: *Ohanahan* (1966, average rating of 45.8 percent) in the early twentieth century and *Dr. Ume-chan* (*Umechan sensei*, 2012) about a woman balancing career, marriage, and motherhood in the 1940s through 1960s (Harada 1983: 140–1). *Umechan sensei* was the first *asadora* to top average ratings over 20 percent since *Kokoro* in 2003 (Yomiuri shimbunsha 2012).

Yearlong *taiga* historical dramas, airing since 1964, are fictionalized biographies of men who helped Japanese growth before the twentieth century; even when the main characters are female, their role is to support men in political power. This is evident in *Princess Atsu (Atsuhime)*, one of the most popular television series of 2008, about women of the Tokugawa Shogunate and 'worked' through their involvement in politics. Gou, the title character of *Gou: Princesses' Warring States Period (Gou: Himetachi no Sengoku*, 2011), was the third daughter of the sister to Oda Nobunaga (the first of three warriors who helped unify Japan in the sixteenth century) and *daimyō* Azai Nagamasa, and the wife of the second Tokugawa Shogun, Hidetaka; her older sisters married Toyotomi Hideyoshi (the second of the three unifiers) and *daimyō* Kyogoku Takutsugu. *Gou* marked Suzuki Honami's return to television after spending 11 years as a full-time mother (Poole and Takaya 2011).

Working women of the *dorama* generation

Prime-time commercial dramas dropped in popularity in the mid-1970s; ratings fell to an all-time low of 2.7 percent in 1982 (Sata and Hirahara 1991: 168).[2] Based on successful earlier dramas about youth in the city, commercial networks developed so-called 'trendy dramas' (*torendi dorama*) in the late 1980s, one of the first being *Seven People of Summer (Danjo nana-nin natsu monogatari*, 1986–7). Trendy dramas depicted intertwining lateral relationships of love and friendship rather than hierarchical family relationships. The emphasis was on the fashionable lifestyles believed possible in Tokyo, and on romance, as reflected in such titles as *I Want to Hold You!* (*Dakashimetai!*, 1988, and *Aishiatteru kai!*, 1989). After a few flops, producers, including Fuji network's Ōta Tōru, who created *Tokyo Love Story*, further revised the genre in the early 1990s, and the resulting formula has remained largely unchanged.

Dorama, which are divided into four seasons, air weekly for around 11 episodes (shorter than the older 13-week season) in night-time slots that carry certain connotations. *Tokyo Love Story* helped associate Monday 9pm on Fuji (or '*gekku*') with love stories (see Matsumoto et al. 1999: 30–3). In recent years, *dorama* that depict women's problems at work air on NTV on Thursday at 10pm. *Dorama* have theme songs that climb the pop charts. Their ties to tourism, book publishing, and film exemplify the dominant marketing strategy of cross-media promotion. Most are set in Tokyo; characters have a favorite restaurant where they have heart-to-heart talks with friends.[3] Tokyo's impact upon the characters' mindsets is evident in the titles and the

116   *Alisa Freedman*

establishing shots, which often feature urban panoramas. *Dorama* are successful because of the star power of their casts, who are usually hired before scripts are written. This is a reason why actresses tend to be typecast in similar roles. For example, Suzuki Honami, Amami Yuki, Shinohara Ryoko, Kanno Miho, and Mizuki Arisa have played strong working women. Unless specifically featuring themes of immigration, almost all female protagonists on serials to date have been heterosexual Japanese nationals, thus revealing how mainstream television producers have chosen to depict the composition of the country's population. Originally made solely for domestic audiences, they have attracted fandoms worldwide and have shaped global images of Japanese women (see, for example, Iwabuchi 2004). They have inspired and have been influenced by similar programs in Taiwan and Korea, a topic that lies outside the focus of this chapter.

The development of *dorama* has paralleled the coming of age of a generation born in the 1960s. These viewers, who were in their twenties at the time of *Tokyo Love Story,* consumed televised images of affluence during high economic growth in 1970s, came of age during the Bubble Economy Era (around 1986–91), and entered the workforce shortly after the 1985 Equal Opportunity Law and supporting legislation were being implemented to reduce the protective legislation that had restricted women's working hours and thus prevented them from attaining high-level positions that have traditionally required compulsory overtime. Because of legal, educational, and economic developments, and thanks to activist movements, women of this generation, in theory, have had more choices in employment, marriage, and childbearing than earlier generations. In general, legislation that allows women to have careers and to be mothers has not been promulgated for the main goal of promoting a gender-equal society. Instead, it has been instituted to augment the labor force and increase the number of children as Japanese society ages (see, for example, Itō 2008). For most of their lives, women of this generation have been in the media spotlight and targeted as a prime consumer market, and television producers and advertising sponsors have continued to create characters with whom they can empathize. Having grown up before the Internet, women older than 40 presumably have been accustomed to viewing television differently from younger generations who have come of age while television programs have been more readily available online. For example, in the 1990s and early 2000s, Japanese female viewers, along with their counterparts in Taiwan and Korea, bonded in conversations about *dorama,* just as women worldwide did over *Sex and the City,* a series, as especially evident in the last season, that depicts marriage as one of women's main life goals, with the role of female friends being to support it.

As is generally acknowledged, most Japanese middle-class women of this generation are married with children and work at least part-time outside the home. Yet the single, highly educated members who work full-time have been perceived as marking the greatest break with women of the past. As extra-marital births are the exception in Japan, trends toward less and later marriage that have occurred over the past three decades (NIPSSR 2010) have been directly linked to the declining fertility rate, making socio-cultural transformation a source of government concern. These marital patterns became more a topic of political interest around 2005. Then, for the first time in Japanese history, population decline was not due to war or famine but rather to falling below replacement-level fertility. That year, birthrates reached an all-time low of 1.26, prompting then prime minister Koizumi to declare the fertility crisis a national problem (Kitazumi 2006). In 1990, the average marriage age for women was 25.9, rising to 27.8 in 2004 (NIPSSR 2008). On one hand, the emergence of single career women shows the advancement of gender equality from the 1980s through to the present; their work is being taken seriously in a country that still has fewer female corporate managers and politicians than other developed nations. On the other hand, the focus of single women on professional careers instead of homemaking has been interpreted by the media as prioritizing personal happiness over that of the family or the nation. These women, in general, have been painted in media discourses as representing the difficulties of individual freedom and have been described as hard to satisfy and selfish in the spate of television programs, books, and magazines for and about them (see Freedman and Iwata-Weickgenannt 2011). Another reason for the abundance of media for career-oriented, single women is that they are often perceived as having more money to spend on themselves than other social groups do.

The evolution of *dorama* since the early 1990s has reflected media discourses on working women of this generation in particular. Characters working in businesses comment on women's adverse treatment and reveal unexpected positive ways women have supported corporate structures underpinning the Japanese economy. To give a few example categories – 'OL' or 'office lady secretaries' characters of such series as *Shomuni* (1988, 2000, 2002 and 2013, based on a manga by Yasuda Gumi) enacted plots of revenge to satirize workplace hierarchies and to light-heartedly expose darker sides of companies during economic recession. The spate of *dorama* that pit established anchorwomen against younger rivals portray regrets of prioritizing careers over family and friendship. This is evident in *Tabloid* (1998), *Newscaster Kasumi Ryoko* (*Nuusu kyasutā Kasumi Ryoko*, 1999) *Newswoman* (*Nuusu no onna*, 1998—one of a few 1998 *dorama* about working single mothers), *Top Anchor* (*Toppo kyasutā*, 2006), and *Fake Bride* (*Hanayome wa yakudoshi*, 2006). Especially since the 1950s, flight attendants have been promoted as model workers and ideal marriage partners. In *dorama*, they are shown to gain self-worth through helping others and by maintaining attractive appearances. This notion is romanticized in *Stewardess Story* (*Shichuwadesu monogatari*, 1983) and parodied in *Perfect Woman* (*Yamato nadeshiko*, 2000) and *Attention Please* (*Atenshun puriizu*, 2006). In *Perfect Woman* the heroine uses her career as a way to meet wealthy men, motivated in part by the hardships she suffered as a child, but in the end she marries for love instead of money and moves with a poor academic to the United States. Renegade female detectives working on their own or leading a force of women or male misfits, as exemplified in *Unfair* (*Anfea*, 2006, followed by a 2006 special, and feature films in 2007 and 2011) and *BOSS 1* and *2* (2009, 2011), have a powerful role outside the company but are less respected and more poorly compensated than their male colleagues. In many cases, these women do not fit into usual corporate models and chose their jobs because of failures in love.

Especially after 2005, there has been a proliferation of romantic leads who pursue success in both their high-level careers and personal lives. Before, most female professionals were cast in supporting roles or as main characters forced to choose between career and romance. Although these recent heroines embody progressive transformations in corporate structures, educational institutions, and attitudes toward working women, their appearance during national concern over low fertility rates does not subvert the belief that women should prioritize becoming wives and mothers. In 1990s dramas, the question seemed to be if the main character would marry or not. Now that the characters are older, the more pressing question is if they will have children. Although fertility rose slightly in 2006, the Ministry of Health, Labor and Welfare predicts that the Japanese population will drop by 30 percent over the next 50 years, and 40.5 percent of the nation will be over the age of 65 in 2055 (BBC News 2007). Characters, particularly those in *The Man Who Cannot Marry* (*Kekkon dekinai otoko*, 2007) and *Around 40: Demanding Women* (*Araundo 40 ~ chūmon no ooi onnatachi*, 2008), react to media discourses that make single women turning 40, an age seen as the social, if not medical, cut-off for giving birth, seem a social problem (Freedman and Iwata-Weickgenannt 2011). *Being Born* (*Umareru*), airing from April to July 2011 on TBS Friday nights at 10pm, the time slot for *dorama* about social problems, depicts a woman who gives birth at age 51. During economic restructuring, these *dorama* encourage women to love their careers and to feel comfortable with the life courses they have chosen. Unlike earlier characters, these professionals are integral parts of their companies. Still, they are not corporate leaders and instead hold jobs with elements of freelance or that are associated with creativity. If team leaders, they work as teachers or medical professionals, fields long available to women.

Dorama have reacted to changes in Japan's employment system by showing new kinds of workers, such as *haken* (dispatch staff). More women have been able to enter corporations as *haken*, while men have been forced into the part-time tracks once reserved for women. An example is *Dignity of the Temp* (*Haken no hinkaku*, 2007) about a *haken* with superpowers, created in response to a 2006 government report that Japan's proportion of temporary to permanent employees had doubled in eight years. While the fictional series presents real problems, it does not offer solutions but advocates coping with the status quo. It teaches that work gives women's lives meaning and that they must unite with their coworkers to ensure corporate Japan's survival. Female temps gain acceptance, but they are still seen as fungible.

Female characters who prioritize careers share other similarities. For example, they are paired with younger female characters who are less devoted to work and seek their advice. Their love interests are younger men, whose careers they foster. These men, in turn, teach them that there is more to life than work. Marriage is always these women's end goal, or at least weighs heavily in their thoughts, but it is not often reached. These are all true in *Tokyo Love Story*.

Akana Rika as a new kind of working woman

Tokyo Love Story aired from January to March 1991 and was watched by a respectable average of 23 percent of the national audience.[4] Arguably, the fame of *Tokyo Love Story* increased in Japan after it spread to other parts of Asia.[5] Around Valentine's Day 1993, a special—a *dorama* convention that reviews the plot through flashbacks and shows what has happened to the characters—was watched by 30 percent of Japan's viewers, showing how influential *Tokyo Love Story* had become.

Tokyo Love Story set television trends. It was one of the first adult programs adopted from manga, at a time when the global fad for Japanese manga was beginning. Created by Saimon Fumi, the manga was serialized from 1988 in *Big Comic Spirits* (*Biggu komikku supirittsu*), a weekly magazine targeting men in their twenties, and published as a bestselling four-volume book in 1990. *Dorama* based on Saimon Fumi's manga became a staple of Fuji television. Her first was *Classmates* (*Dōkyūsei*, 1989). Later series include *Women's Company* (*Oshigoto desu*, 1998) about female friends who open a store. *Tokyo Love Story* was one of the first dramas to portray characters who came to Tokyo and were not raised there. In a way, the series put a new spin on the literary narrative, dating back to the Meiji period (1868–1912), of youth moving to the capital for their emotional coming-of-age and financial futures, as evident in Natsume Sōseki's 1908 novel *Sanshirō*. In *dorama* that followed, women moved to Tokyo seeking love and work, the latter a means to the former, as evident in *Tokyo Elevator Girl* (*Tokyo erebātā gāru*, 1992). *Tokyo Love Story*'s tagline was 'In Tokyo, everyone becomes the star of a love story' (*Tokyo de wa dare mo rabu sutōrī no shujinko ni naru*). This notion was reinforced by Oda Kazumasa's theme song 'A love story comes suddenly' (*Rabu sutōrī no totsuzen ni*), which sold more than 2.58 million copies and still ranks as the eighth-bestselling single in Japanese music history (*Oricon Style* 2004). The theme song sequence, a convention of *dorama* and a means to convey the characters' thoughts, presents Tokyo at work and play and then fashionable technology, including Toyota sports cars, a major sponsor. Several scenes display Tokyo under construction at a time when the real estate bubble was bursting. Rika gazes at the city when she needs to think. Her important conversations with Kanji occur on the roofs of buildings or in parks.

The plot follows one year in the romantic relationships of three women and two men, a formula adopted in later series, including *Long Vacation* (*Rongu bakēshun*, 1996) and *Love Generation* (*Rabu jenerēshun*, 1997) (Itō 2004: 29). *Tokyo Love Story* grabbed media and viewer attention because of the main character Rika. Through camerawork, especially close-ups of her face, Rika is made the focus of viewers' empathy. Rika, who grew up in Los Angeles, is an important employee of the First Sales Division of Heart Sports. The story begins as she greets her new junior colleague, Nagao Kanji (played by Oda Yuji, who had starred in dramas since the 1970s), at Haneda Airport. 'Kanchi,' as Rika nicknames him, has moved from Ehime and feels unsure of his Tokyo future. From the start, Rika advises him in matters of love and work. Although she is having an affair with her married section head, Waga, Rika soon falls for Kanji, who still has feelings for his former classmate Sekiguchi Satomi (played by Arimori Narimi), now a nursery school teacher. Satomi first chooses Kanji's classmate and rival Mikami Ken'ichi (played by Eguchi Yosuke), a medical student who is more concerned with seducing women than going to class. Ken'ichi soon becomes enamored with his classmate Nagasaki Naoko (played by Sendo Akiho), who is engaged to a man chosen by her parents. Through coincidences possible only on *dorama*, the characters become friends and seek each other's love advice in their apartments, a shot bar, and a favorite restaurant. Kanji and his classmates turn from 23 to 24; Rika's age is undisclosed, but it is implied that she is older. Career women in later series were also older than their love interests, as seen in *Around 40* and *Ohitorisama* (2009). Much of the story revolves around Kanji's decision of whom to love and marry—Rika or Satomi. There are many differences from the manga, which is told from Kanji's perspective. Rika, mostly drawn angry at or trying to seduce Kanji, is a less sympathetic character. Having grown up in the 'African wilds,' she cannot adjust to Tokyo manners (for example, Saimon 1990: Vol 1, 223). She and Kanji work at an eight-person advertising firm, owned by Waga. Kanji and Satomi become a couple while Rika is studying in the United States.

Previous romantic leads were like Satomi. Their rivals were like Rika. Producer Ōta decided to do the reverse in *Tokyo Love Story*. He instead made the two women a pair of opposites (as is true of Kanji and Ken'ichi), a notion reinforced through parallel scenes. Rika becomes more independent, as Satomi hesitates to make her own decisions and asks Rika and Kanji for advice. Both women initiate relationships with Kanji, who is cast in the role, usually given to female characters, of having to choose between suitors. Rika seduces Kanji after he sees Satomi kissing Ken'ichi. Her scandalous proposition—'Let's have sex' (*Ne, Kanchi, SEX shiyo*)—made media headlines (Tokyo News Mook 1994: 580).

Tokyo Love Story launched a fad for '*junai*' or 'pure love' stories in which all characters try to find true love, a goal that proves unobtainable to at least one of them. Ōta's aim was to entice viewers by making them cry for Rika. Aomori Narimi, who played Satomi, received threatening letters from viewers. Ōta remarked that many dramas between 1991 and 1996, such as *Long Vacation*, included characters like 'Kanji the indecisive guy, Satomi, the hateful woman, and Rika, the poor adorable woman' (Ōta 2004: 74 and Itō 2004: 29–30). The concept also appeared in such bestselling novels as Murakami Haruki's 1987 *Norwegian Wood* (*Noruwei no mori*).

Like other female leads, Rika meets her love interest through work, and much of the *dorama* is shot at Heart Sports. The series promotes sports, especially skiing and golf, as choice leisure activities for fashionable urban youth of the Bubble Era. Heart Sports appears in later *dorama* starring Oda Yuji, including *Last Christmas* (*Rasto Kurisumasu*, 2004) and *Loss Time Life* (*Rosu: taimu: raifu*, 2008). Rika balanced viewer expectations for female characters consumed with love but depicted them in a new light—as more competent at work than men. Rika is the one everyone at Heart Sports turns to in times of crisis. She works overtime alone and fixes Kanji's mistakes. She goes on business trips, while Kanji remains in the Tokyo office. No men challenge her authority. Customers request her. Kanji, however, suspects that she was able to secure a sales contract for him because she slept with the business owner. Yet the story focuses more on how a man becomes a high-level salaryman in a prospering company. As I will explain, Rika quits the company, but Kanji becomes an integral member.

The key to understanding working women is in the ending (watched by 32.3 percent of the national audience), which went against precedent and was not happy for the female lead in terms of love (Ishida 1999: 42). In the manga, Rika becomes pregnant with Waga's baby. Kanji urges her to marry Waga, who might leave his family for her. Kanji celebrates by lighting fireworks with Satomi. Four of the main characters of the story marry, which tames Ken'ichi. Rika is the only one who does not marry the person she loves. Years later, Kanji mistakes a woman for Rika walking in front of the hospital where Satomi has just given birth to Kanji's son. He speaks directly to readers asking, if Rika is in Tokyo and they see her, please give his regards to her, for she is the woman he loves. He thereby leaving the impression he will not be happy without her (Saimon 1990: Vol. 4, 226).

In the drama, Rika, sensing Kanji has chosen Satomi, accepts a transfer to the Los Angeles branch, making it easier for him to marry a woman who, it is implied, will be a full-time wife and mother. Rika feels she belongs more in the United States, where she believes people are as cheerful and frank as she is. Women who chose work over love in 1990s *dorama* were often transferred to the United States. The ability to speak English has been a shorthand way to indicate sophistication on Japanese television since around the 1980s, but this plot device also shows that the kind of women they represent was not an accepted norm or would face difficulties in Japan. Rika, however, wavers in her decision, not wanting to leave Kanji. She asks him to convince her not to go. Kanji refuses, telling her that he does not want to impede her career. Satomi deters Kanji from meeting Rika to discuss his future with her.

Living in Tokyo provides opportunities for freedom in love and marriage on most *dorama*, but the romantic couples usually leave the city during the key turning point that determines the fate of their relationship. Rika takes an emergency vacation from work and goes to Ehime to carve her name next to Kanji's on the storehouse at his elementary school. Kanji joins her, and the two enjoy a nostalgic tour of important places from his youth. Rika intentionally returns to Tokyo on a train earlier than the one she told Kanji she would take with him. She writes 'goodbye' on a handkerchief and ties it to the Baishinji Station fence, a gesture later mimicked by fans. Rika cries (for the first time in the series) on the train, the sunset over the Inland Sea framed by the window behind her.

In a coda to the last episode, a common *dorama* convention, three years have passed. Kanji is confident at work. Waga compliments him, saying he is finally ready to bear the weight of Rika's love. Through their conversation, viewers learn that Rika quit the Los Angeles office after only six months for an undisclosed reason and has not been in touch with the company since. Later that evening, Kanji and Satomi meet Rika after Ken'ichi and Naoko's wedding ceremony. As Satomi squats down on the sidewalk to tie Kanji's shoelaces for him, he spots Rika walking toward him in the urban crowd. Rika calls him 'Nagao-kun,' showing their relationship has grown distant. She is not surprised that he and Satomi have married. Satomi allows Kanji and Rika a private reunion. Kanji and Rika enact their common routines, but this time, Rika seems more self-assured. As they talk on a rooftop, Rika states, with a reassuring smile, that she has gotten used to being on her own and will treasure the memories of their time together. She refuses to give Kanji her contact information. She merely suggests that someday they will meet again by chance, for Tokyo brings everyone together. Kanji is more reluctant than Rika to part. Rika affectionately calls him 'Kanchi' one last time and then confidently strides through Tokyo, swinging her briefcase, as the theme song plays. In the end, she gazes down at the city from the roof of Shinjuku's Nihon Seinenkan hotel. After an extreme close-up of her content face, the camera cuts to a panorama of West Shinjuku under construction. This shows that Rika realizes the possibilities for her in the city. In the special, Rika, still single, takes a business trip to Ehime with a junior male colleague (played by Tsutsui Michitaka) and revisits Kanji's elementary school. Memories of her relationship with Kanji flood back to her, but she voices no regrets. The drama, popular for bringing viewers to tears, ended on a hopeful note.

What has changed for working women on television

Woman Workaholic (*Hatarakiman*, 2007), which, in many ways, seems an updated version *Tokyo Love Story*, provides a means to see what has changed and what has not in *dorama*, and how women have been accepted into corporations. *Woman Workaholic* was based on a 2004 manga by Anno Moyoco and was adapted into an anime series in 2006. The story depicts the busy life of the 28-year-old journalist and editor Matsukata Hiroko at the Gotansha company (a play on Kondansha, publisher of the manga) who is trying to balance her career and her five-year relationship with her boyfriend

Women and romance on Japanese television 123

Shinji. She always chooses the former over the later. Shinji, an engineer at a construction firm, becomes disillusioned with his job during the course of the *dorama*. When she becomes most busy, Hiroko is able focus single-mindedly on work, even going for days without bathing. Her colleagues call these moments her switch into 'male mode' (*otoko suicchi irimasu*). Hiroko eats *nato*, fermented beans supposedly rich in female hormones, to balance these so-called masculine work habits. Most of the action takes place in the office, and the viewer is invited to have an intimate look at a family of coworkers. On one hand, the female lead is depicted as a positive role model, promoting a progressive lifestyle to viewers through the use of voiceovers. On the other hand, she is portrayed as needing male colleagues to help her through emotional crises. It is implied that she cannot marry or have children if she continues to pursue a high-powered career.

These notions are reinforced in the last episode, which takes place on Hiroko's 29th birthday. Hiroko has a few choices. She is being recruited to be chief editor of a new magazine for working women. She could follow Shinji, who finally begins to enjoy his job when he is transferred to Kyushu. (Men rarely get transferred abroad on Japanese dramas.) Hiroko instead decides to remain at the tabloid magazine, working as she has been since her early twenties. Hiroko dashes to Haneda Airport to say goodbye to Shinji, who has broken up with her. When Hiroko receives a text message, cutting short their meeting, Shinji gives her an encouraging push and laughs as she runs, as usual, back to work. In a final voiceover, Hiroko tells the viewer that being a workaholic is sometimes lonely and may damage her and Japan's future, but she is not ready to give up the life she has at the company and with her colleagues. The scene ends with Hiroko and her coworkers happily strolling through Tokyo at night on their way to sing karaoke, for business socializing is a common part of Japanese work life. The series encourages women to love their careers and be satisfied with their lives. They can find meaning in work; their coworkers can become a replacement family. Both characters acknowledge—Rika to Kanji and Hiroko to the audience—that they will remain single as long as they keep their current priorities. Both are shown content with not having it all, a feeling expressed in both cases while the viewer is shown the expanse of Tokyo.

Dorama, from the earliest to now, have taught that, because women can never achieve all they desire, they should be content with the lives that they have. Viewers more poignantly reacted to Rika's unrequited love, rather than her job troubles, but, significantly, the hopeful message of *Tokyo Love Story* was about work not in love, marriage, and family. Whether intentionally or not, Rika furthered beliefs that women who prioritize their careers are sexually liberal and cannot be wives and mothers. The ending of the series is telling in this regard and demonstrates that *dorama* are also coming-of-age stories for men, showing how women can help them fit their roles in the family and workplace. Unlike the working mothers on home dramas, young workers on NHK morning dramas, and historical women in

124   *Alisa Freedman*

taiga dramas, women in prime-time *dorama* need to choose between having careers and families of their own. They cannot have both, whether to remain empathetic characters or to comment on women's realities. Although often shown as more skilled than their male colleagues, female employees cannot be seen as more successful.

The most positive change has been the diversification of the kinds of work fictional women can do. Women are currently portrayed as integral to Japanese companies, especially during a time when lifetime employment is breaking down and hiring patterns are becoming more differentiated. *Dorama* convey the message that women, like men, need to work together to ensure the future of corporate Japan. While designed to be entertainment rather than a means of edification, *dorama* exemplify the continued influence of television in classifying gender roles and give an emotional face to discussions about women that are taking place in the mass media.

Notes

1 Other terms include Japanese 'idol dramas' (*aidoru dorama*, coined by Taiwan Star TV), 'pure-love dramas' (*junai dorama*), and 'J-drama.'
2 Although some current *dorama*, such as *Train Man* (*Densha otoko*, 2005), are watched by more than 25 percent of the national audience, ratings for most *dorama* now seem to be between 8 and 20 percent. The actual viewing rates are most likely higher than these percentages, for surveys do not usually take into account people who watch programs online or record them (Freedman 2009).
3 The neighborhood bar, café, or restaurant is also a staple of United States sitcoms, especially those that feature friendships between young, unmarried characters.
4 The most popular program that year was *101st Proposal* with a 36.7 percent viewer average (Matsumoto et al. 1999: 33).
5 The 1992 Korean program *Jealousy* (*Jiltu*) was rumored to have taken its premise from *Tokyo Love Story*, an accusation denied by producer Seung-Ryul Lee (Lee 2004: 267).

References

Anno Moyoco (2004) *Hatarakiman*, Vols 1–4, Tokyo: Kōdansha.
BBC News (2007) 'Japan birth rate shows rare rise,' January 1, http://news.bbc.co.uk/2/hi/asia-pacific/6222257.stm (accessed June 3, 2013).
Clements, J. and Tamamuro, M. (2003) *The Dorama Encyclopedia: A Guide to Japanese TV Drama Since 1953*, Berkeley: Stone Bridge Press.
Freedman, A. (2009) '*Train Man* and the gender politics of Japanese "Otaku" culture: the rise of new media, nerd heroes, and consumer communities,' *Intersections*, 20, http://intersections.anu.edu.au/issue20/freedman.htm (accessed June 3, 2013).
Freedman, A. and Iwata-Weickgenannt, K. (2011) ' "Count what you have now. Don't count what you don't have": the Japanese television drama *Around 40* and the politics of women's happiness,' *Asian Studies Review* 35(3): 295–313.
Harada, N. (1983) *Terebi dorama 30 nen*, Tokyo: Yomiuri shimbunsha.

Ishida, Y. (1999) *TV dorama ōru fairu – 90s minhōhan*, Tokyo: Asupekuto.

Itō, M. (2004) 'The representation of femininity in Japanese television dramas of the 1990s' in K. Iwabuchi (ed.) *Feeling Asian Modernities: Transnational Consumption of Japanese TV Dramas*, Hong Kong: Hong Kong University Press.

Itō, M. (2008) 'Work–life balance starts at home,' *Japan Times*, January 9, http://search.japantimes.co.jp/cgi-bin/nn20080109f2.html (accessed June 3, 2013).

Itō, T. (1988) *Terebi – We are TV's Children*, Tokyo: INAX.

Iwabuchi, K. (ed.) (2004) *Feeling Asian Modernities: Transnational Consumption of Japanese TV Dramas*, Hong Kong: Hong Kong University Press.

Kitazumi, T. (2006) 'Low birthrate threatens Japan's future: support, job flexibility may prompt couples to have more children,' *Japan Times*, November 9, http://search.japantimes.co.jp/cgi-bin/nb20061109d1.html (accessed June 3, 2013).

Lee, D.-H. (2004) 'Cultural contact with Japanese TV dramas: modes of reception and narrative transparency' in K. Iwabuchi (ed.) *Feeling Asian Modernities: Transnational Consumption of Japanese TV Dramas*, Hong Kong: Hong Kong University Press.

Matsumoto, Y. et al. (1999) *That's terebi dorama 90's*, Tokyo: Daiyamondosha.

Nagayama, K. (1991) *Tokyo rabu sutorī*, Fuji Television.

Nagumo, S. and Sakuma, N. (2007) *Hatarakiman*. Nippon Television.

Natsume, S. (1977) *Sanshirō*, trans. Jay Rubin, New York: Perigee Books.

NIPSSR (2008) 'Shōshika no genjō to shōrai no mitōshi – zenkon'in oyobi shokon no heikin kon'in nenrei: 1899–2004,' www.ipss.go.jp/syoushika/tohkei/Relation/1_Future/Fu_Detail.asp?fname.3_marriage/1-1-C09.htm&title1.%82b%81j%8C%8B%8D%A5%82%A8%82%E6%82%D1%94z%8B%F4%8A%D6%8CW%82%C9%8A%D6%82%B7%82%E9%93%9D%8Cv&title2.%91S%8D%A5%88%F7%8By%82%D1%8F%89%8D%A5%82%CC%95%BD%8B%CF%8D%A5%88%F7%94N%97%EE%81F1899%81%602004%94N (accessed June 3, 2013).

NIPSSR (2010) 'Jinkō tōkei shiryō shū 2010 – sei, nenrei (5sai kaikyū), haigū kankei betsu wariai: 1920–2005nen,' www.ipss.go.jp/syoushika/tohkei/Popular/Popular2010.asp?chap.0 (accessed June 3, 2013).

Oricon Style (2004) 'SMAP "Sekai ni hitotsu dake no hana," shinguru uriage rekidai 9-i ni,' *Oricon Style*, August 3, www.oricon.co.jp/news/ranking/5139 (accessed June 3, 2013).

Ōta, T. (2004) 'Producing (post-) trendy Japanese TV dramas,' in K. Iwabuchi (ed.) *Feeling Asian Modernities: Transnational Consumption of Japanese TV Dramas*, Hong Kong: Hong Kong University Press.

Partner, S. (1999) *Assembled in Japan: Electrical Goods and the Making of the Japanese Consumer*, Berkeley: University of California Press.

Poole, R.M. and Takaya, R. (2011) 'Honami Suzuki reflects on stardom, family and a middle-aged comeback,' *CNN Travel*, March 11, http://travel.cnn.com/tokyo/play/actress-honami-suzuki-reflects-stardom-family-and-middle-aged-comeback-450940 (accessed May 28, 2013).

Saimon, F. (1990) *Tokyo rabu sutorī*, Vols 1–4, Tokyo: Shogakukan.

Sata, M. and Hirahara, H. (1991) (eds.) *A History of Japanese Television Drama*, Tokyo: Japan Association of Broadcasting Art.

Schilling, M. (1997) *The Encyclopedia of Japanese Pop Culture*, New York: Weatherhill, Inc.

Tipton, E. (2013) 'Moving up and out: the "shop girl" in interwar Japan' in A. Freedman, L. Miller and C. Yano (eds.) *Modern Girls on the Go: Gender, Mobility, and Labor in Japan*, Palo Alto: Stanford University Press.

126 *Alisa Freedman*

Tokyo News Mook (1994) *Terebi dorama zen shi: 1953 1994 tīvui gaido*, Tokyo: tōkyō nyūsu tsūshinsha.

Yomiuri shimbunsha (2012) 'Harikita "Umechan sensei" kaikyo! Asadora 9 nen buri heikin shichōritsu 20% koe!' *Yomiuri Online*, http://hochi.yomiuri.co.jp/entertainment/news/20121002-OHT1T00009.htm (accessed June 3, 2013).

8 Unpacking multiculturalism and Islam in Malaysia

State–corporate television celebrations of Bangsa Malaysia

Umi Khattab

This chapter presents a critical analysis of media and change in postcolonial Malaysia, a South-East Asian nation of 29 million multicultural people, with a focus on the role of television in the nation's transformation following independence from British rule in 1957. Despite having inherited the basic democratic institutions of the British political tradition, Malaysia continues to debate the transition from soft authoritarianism to democracy (Means 1996: 103). Since 1957, Malaysia has been led by a single political party, the Barisan Nasional (BN). While the BN is a coalition of three major ethnic-based political groups, the United Malays National Organisation (UMNO), Malaysian Chinese Association (MCA) and the Malaysian Indian Congress (MIC), it is, in effect, a symbol of Malay-Muslim supremacy (Ketuanan Melayu). UMNO, the dominant group within the party, has, since its formation, aspired to uphold Malay culture as national culture and Islam as the official religion for the country. From the first general elections in 1959 until the 2008 general elections, the BN held two-thirds of the 222 seats in the Dewan Rakyat (House of Representatives). Malaysian media scholar Karthigesu (1987, 1994) contends this was largely due to the role of public television, which was launched and promoted by government itself, broadcasting in its colonial service model. In fact, the arrival of state television in 1963 coincided with the formation of the Federation of Malaysia (Moten and Mokhtar 2013). In this chapter I argue that television has been pivotal in shaping and transforming the political and cultural landscape of Malaysia as the medium evolved from a strictly national to a loosely global and then fluidly trans-local orientation. While television first enabled the BN to hold its two-thirds majority and build the nation premised on Malay supremacy policies, it subsequently played a part in weakening the BN's grip over the multiethnic electorate as the UMNO Ketuanan Melayu ideology, layered deep beneath the powdered face of television, surfaced in the digital media era.

Any discussion about television and modernization in Malaysia will be futile without reference being made to the man behind the scenes of media power. In examining the role of television in the transformation of Malaysia, this chapter looks closely at the impact of the 22-year regime of Mahathir Mohamad. Mahathir was Malaysia's longest serving prime minister, winning

128   *Umi Khattab*

five general elections between1981 and 2003. Mahathir's influence on the political and socio-cultural scene, including his media tactics and strategies, were apparent prior to his ascendency to the premiership and have continued following his retirement from political office. Mahathir is known to have used the media for a long time to captivate and influence the masses. He used the pseudonym C.H.E. Det for his column in the *Straits Times* during his early years and his books, in particular the *Malay Dilemma*, have had significant influence on the mindset of the Malay-bumiputera (indigenous Malays) who make up 60 per cent of the population. Today, Mahathir, in his role as advisor to the non-government Malay supremacy organization, Perkasa, and via his blog 'Chedet' (http://chedet.cc), continues to shape the political and media trajectory and wield influence and power in the country. His online presence and mischievous comments on Malay rights, Islam, zionism and imperialism, even as he approaches the age of 90, continue to be newsworthy and tend to instigate public controversies that set the news agenda on a regular basis in both the mainstream and alternative contexts. In recent times, his blog postings have regularly lent support to the extremist views of Malay rights leader Ibrahim Ali, fuelling debate in the country.

This chapter firstly maps Malaysia's postcolonial nation-building projects, which were designed and taken on by Mahathir and his hand-picked successors. It engages with the ideas of Anderson, Billig, Hobsbawm, Appadurai, Scannell and Hall, as well as Asian thinkers, to critically assess the mediatized imagining of a new Malaysian nation. Then it examines the history and growth of Malaysian television in the context of national transformation and globalization, and analyses how television has been utilized to 'aid and abet' the implementation of racialized and discriminatory policies and campaigns designed by the Mahathir administration and reinvented by Najib Razak, which are underpinned by Mahathir's medicalization theory of the Malay-bumiputera and his authoritarian media laws.

Nation-building tales

Malaya achieved independence from British rule in 1957, and the formation of Malaysia in 1963 (when Malaya, Sabah, Sarawak and Singapore merged), was followed by the separation of Singapore from Malaysia in 1965. The difficulty of constructing a unified nation from these beginnings was graphically demonstrated by the bloody ethnic riots of 1969. Since that time, almost all nation-building projects (spelt out in the first to the current tenth Malaysia Plan – Rancangan Malaysia 1–10 – and envisioned through a range of development policies, namely, the New Economic Policy, New Development Policy, Look East Policy, Privatisation Policy, New Economic Model, Wawasan 2020 and 1Malaysia) have been implemented through the utilization of the media, primarily television, to construct the identity of postcolonial Malaysia as a sovereign nation-state. In the current decade, the project has been to elevate Malaysia to the status of a developed, high-income, world-class nation.

Introduced in 1991 by Mahathir, Wawasan 2020 remains one of the most significant nation-building projects. The project was initiated with the aim of producing a new and united Malaysian society that was 'ethnically integrated, living in harmony with full and fair partnership, made up of one Bangsa Malaysia (Malaysia "race" or "nationhood"), with political loyalty and dedication to the nation' (Lee 2004: 83–4). Instead of maintaining ethnic identities such as being Malay, Chinese, Indian, Iban, Bajau, Murut or Kadazandusun, or territorialized identities such as Sabahan, Sarawakian, Kelantanese or Kedahan, Wawasan 2020 articulates the aspiration to create a nation whose 'people identify themselves with the country, speak Bahasa Malaysia and accept the Constitution' by the year 2020 (*Asiaweek* 1995). Malaysian social anthropologist Shamsul (2004: 129) contends that non-Malays overwhelmingly embraced the idea of a single Bangsa Malaysia as they believed 'the framework promised, to a certain extent, equal treatment to all ethnic groups in Malaysia through the eventual dismantling of the New Economic Policy', an affirmative policy that had been designed to help uplift the social-economic status of the Malay-bumiputra. Not surprisingly, then, the Malay-bumiputra reacted with less enthusiasm to Mahathir's aspiration. Cheah (2002: 66) argues that few Malays were willing to give up their special status and rights for the sake of sharing equality with the non-Malays.

In order to realize Wawasan 2020, the mass media was tasked with the responsibility of actively promoting the concept of a unified Malaysian national identity, to help raise awareness among the different ethnic groups (*The New Straits Times*, 15 October 1992). Raja Ariffin Raja Sulaiman, the then deputy minister in the Prime Minister's Department, maintained that to attain a cohesive society, 'Malaysians… should identify themselves as a Malaysian and not as a Malay, Chinese or Indian' (*The New Straits Times*, 15 October 1992). Likewise, politicians in Mahathir's cabinet were encouraged to expound the ideals of Bangsa Malaysia to bolster support among the different ethnic communities. Mahathir's Bangsa Malaysia policy has dominated political discourse since the 1990s and was effectively reinvented as the 1Malaysia policy under Najib Razak in 2010, who is noted to have said:

> At the heart of the 1Malaysia concept is a quiet simplicity: a belief in the importance of national unity irrespective of race or religious belief. Malaysia's diversity is what makes us unique, but in order to fully benefit from what is undoubtedly a source of strength we need to come together and build upon our common values. That is the central goal of 1Malaysia, but it is much more than just an abstract ideology, delivering real improvements on the ground.
>
> (www.1Malaysia.com.my)

Hall (1992: 293) argues that a national culture is a discourse, a way of constructing meaning that we can identify, and that these meanings are contained in the stories we are told and the memories which connect the present with the past. What is clear is that the UMNO orthodox discourse is being recycled and repackaged to suit the changing Malaysian population. The ethnic unity and equity tales seem reinvented and narrated via new media tactics. From analogue to digital television times, the core values underscoring these messages have remained constant. Najib Razak continues to build the multiethnic nation based on the values of Malay supremacy and he is doing this through retaining the service of APCO Worldwide.

Despite the continuity between the past and the present apparent in this history and despite decades of policy aimed at such an outcome, the ideology of a united Malaysian nation is far from being achieved. Ethnic divisions, most notably among young Malaysians, seem more prominent and more prevalent than ever before. The rapid development of both legal and illegal diasporas in recent times appears to make the ethnic composition of Malaysia far more diverse and the definition of 'Malaysian' even more complex and challenging. For example, the inflow of Indonesian migrants alone (who are mostly Malay-speaking Muslims) is said to be approximately 2 million (Chin 2002; Kaur 2008) and, as they continue to penetrate Malaysian borders, the question 'who is Malay-bumiputera?' becomes more daunting than the question 'who is Malaysian?'

Schools in Malaysia are no longer a neutral platform for the building of ethnic integration and citizenship as public, private and vernacular schools have become overwhelmingly single-race (Teoh 2007; Khattab 2002). To look into allegations of ethnic segregation, a special committee was set up by the Education Ministry which found only 2.1 per cent of the pupils in national/public primary schools were Chinese, although the Chinese made up 26 per cent of the population, while Indians made up 4.3 per cent of the pupils in these schools despite comprising 7.7 per cent of the national population (Teoh 2007). A state-commissioned study carried out by researchers from the National University of Malaysia found ethnic divisions on the rise in university campuses across the country (Lee 2004: 83). Shamsul (2004: 115) considers these studies to be alarming because he contends that schools are expected to be 'civilizing' institutions, shaping perceptions of what social reality is while simultaneously playing a role in producing moral and productive citizens. Hng (2004) points out that the current education system and state policies are core perpetrators in widening the gap between Malaysia's different ethnic groups. He maintains that Malaysia's education system is both 'victim and perpetrator' for failing unequivocally to fulfil its first and most basic function, that of citizen-building (Hng 2004: x). As a result, he argues, one generation of citizens has grown up painfully aware of the fact that their place in society is largely dependent on whether they are Malay or non-Malay, East or West Malaysian and bumiputera or non-bumiputera (Hng 2004: x).

Emerging television ideas

Continuing with the media infrastructure left behind by the British colonialists, the Information Department was seen to have played a major role in bringing together people of diverse ethnicity to celebrate the birth of a nation. However, media served in essence to construct Malaysia in ethnically polarized terms as a bumiputera (indigenous), non-bumiputra (non-indigenous) or majority–minority nation. National media (in particular television networks), developed along ethnic lines, have been serving Malay, Chinese, Indian and East Malaysian audiences through various vernacular news outlets (Khattab 2006). Television Malaysia was born on 28 December 1963, and, merging with the earlier-established Radio Malaysia, it was named Radio Television Malaysia (RTM), broadcasting centrally from Angkasapuri Complex under the then new Ministry of Information established in 1969. A second television channel was soon developed and named Rangkaian Kedua (2nd channel) and Television Malaysia was renamed Rangkaian Pertama (1st channel). In 1979, the two channels were renamed RTM1 and RTM2 and since 1987 have been conveniently named TV1 and TV2. RTM enjoyed being the sole broadcaster until deregulation policies in the 1980s, under the Mahathir regime, saw the arrival of private terrestrial analogue free-to-air (FTA) channels such as TV3 in 1984. These were followed by cable TV (Mega TV launched in 1994 and closed in 2001) and the direct-broadcast satellite pay TV service ASTRO (All-Asian Satellite Television and Radio Operator) in 1996. Other private FTA networks such as NTV7, 8TV and TV9 emerged subsequently: these included TV Alhijrah in December 2010, a third state network offering Islamic affairs programming in Bahasa Malaysia, and the Worldview Broadcasting Channel, as well as 24/7 ASTRO Malaysian news channels such as, BERNAMA TV (BERTV) and ASTRO AWANI. While privatization and commercialization enabled the mushrooming of diverse television networks and products, it is important to note the political-economy base of these networks. UMNO, through Media Prima, has a significant stake in TV3, 8TV and TV9, including state television – RTM and TV Alhijrah – as well as BERTV and ASTRO AWANI. ASTRO Malaysia Holdings Bhd. is believed to be owned by the family of T. Ananda Krishna, one of the wealthiest men in South-East Asia, who is said to be a good friend of Mahathir Mohamad (Mohd Sani 2004).

It has often been said (for example, by Lee Kuan Yew and Mahathir Mohamad) that ASTRO, BBC World (BBCW) and CNN International (CNNI) present a Western twist to world events. However, in 1998 Malaysia saw the arrival of television news programming from the Arab world delivered in Arabic to a largely Muslim audience. Aljazeera Arabic (AJA) was well-received by Arabic-speaking Muslims in South-East Asia generally because of their cultural proximity. Soon after, in 2006, ASTRO facilitated the transmission of Aljazeera English (AJE) from Kuala Lumpur, which offered a range of programmes as an 'alternative' to the earlier AJA and as an

132   *Umi Khattab*

alternative to the established CNNI and BBCW. AJE, in its official discourse, boasts of offering new nation-states a means to project their voice, their policies and their interpretations of events in the global media (http://english.aljazeera.net). It also claims to balance the information flow from south to north, providing accurate, impartial and objective news for a global audience from a grassroots level, giving voice to different perspectives from underreported regions around the world (http://english.aljazeera.net). While the Malaysian government initially welcomed AJE, over time it came to be seen as offering challenging and contradictory perspectives to what the national media such as RTM, TV3, AWANI ASTRO and BERTV were delivering. This was evident in the way Malaysia's 2008 pre-election issues were covered – such as the Hindu Rights Action Front (HINDRAF) street protests on the marginalization of Indian minorities – and also the 2013 pre-election issues, such as, among others, the Malay-language Bible-burning protests emanating from the use of the word 'Allah' for God (www.themalaysianinsider.com/malaysia).

AJE's perspectives ultimately came to be seen as aligned to those of BBCW and CNNI. AJE's 'alterity' was questioned by UMNO individuals, in particular the then Malaysian minister of information, Zainuddin bin Maidin, who argued that AJE was not keeping its promise of contributing to a balanced flow of information from south to north, nor was it offering an Arabic or national/local perspective to events and issues considered 'sensitive' (see, for example, Lent 1979) in the Malaysian context. Annoyed by AJE's 'Western twist' to the reporting of Malaysian events, UMNO elites recently proposed cooperation between Malaysia and Indonesia in the setting up of the Indonesian TV Nusantara as a global player disseminating local and global news from a local Malay archipelago perspective in the Malay language (https://my.news.yahoo.com/shabery-proses-tv-nusantara-better-ties-between-malaysian-043026448.html).

On the other hand, proponents of media democratization were pleased by AJE's investigative and objective news and applauded AJE for offering an alternative Islamic stance on Middle East affairs and an independent voice to local/national issues, enabling rational debate and transforming politics in Malaysia. Evidence of this transformation included the shocking performance of the incumbent Barisan Nasional (BN) consecutively in the 2008 and 2013 general elections. Adding fuel to fiery politics is the online news portal Malaysiakini (www.malaysiakini.com) and KiniTV (www.youtube.com/user/malaysiakini) that are thriving in the public arena on account of Mahathir's promise not to control the Internet, in accordance with his vision of building a multimedia super corridor in Malaysia. Neither of Mahathir's hand-picked successors, Abdullah Ahmad Badawi (2003–8) and Najib Razak (2009–current), have been able to curtail the Internet in an atmosphere where Mahathir himself has a prominent online presence, stirring controversies and invoking feuds within the Malay-bumiputera community and between the Malay-bumiputera and non-bumiputera communities. Most of these public controversies have centred on Islam, Malay-bumiputera rights and the plight of ethnic minorities in Malaysia.

Redesigning Bangsa Malaysia

Under the current national climate of media convergence, transnational mediatization of local events, rising Islamic fundamentalism, growing ethnic tensions and declining support for the BN as opposition seats in the Dewan Rakyat increase, maintaining commitment to the various themes underlying these long-running nation-building projects (such as patriotism, social inclusiveness and national unity) for the purpose of creating a 'national' consciousness under a single national banner called 'Malaysia', has become difficult, to say the least. How do 29 million multiethnic Malaysians, in an ethnically polarized and media globalized world, identify themselves and imagine their home as Malaysia? Historically, Anderson (1983: 40) contends 'imagining the nation' has been achieved through the advent of print capitalism. He singles out the novel and the newspaper as the technical means for re-presenting the kind of imagined community that is 'the nation', arguing that they lay the basis for national consciousness in a number of ways (Anderson 1983: 47–8). Drawing from Anderson, Appadurai (1996) argues that electronic capitalism can have similar, even more powerful effects, for it does not work only at the level of the nation-state, but instead offers new resources and new disciplines for the construction of imagined selves and imagined worlds (Appadurai 1996: 8). Billig (1995) points out that television news is a particularly rich site to uncover what he has termed instances of 'banal nationalism': that is, the reproduction of the national identity and the habitual assumption of belonging operating through the deixis of the homeland, which makes use of small, prosaic and oftentimes routine words like 'we', 'this', 'here' and 'them'. According to Billig, these words offer constant, but barely conscious, reminders of the homeland, making 'our' national identity unforgettable (Billig 1995: 93). Like Hobsbawm's (1983) invention of tradition, no qualification is needed for the routine interpellation of the national identity; the routine in talking and listening about 'our' nation naturalizes 'our' national identity as a norm, while hegemonic understandings of 'the way the world is' are absorbed as common sense (Billig 1995: 106). Scannell (1989: 138) points out that television is significant in this regard, because it plays a key role in constructing the collective life and culture of whole populations, while Hartley also contends that 'television is one of the prime sites upon which a given nation is constructed for its members' (cited in Morley and Robins 1995: 67)

Television thus is seen as playing a crucial role in facilitating the nation's survival in the eyes of both its people and those outside the community. Clearly the nation is an abstract collectivity, one too big to be directly experienced by the people, but through the existence of mediated rituals and news discourses, the imagined communities are provided a sense of the sacred and, thus, feelings of patriotism that bind the nation together. However, the advent of new global media forms is seen as producing new kinds of attachment and belonging that extends beyond the 'national', the 'regional' or the 'local'. Further, attempts to deploy national television to (re)form and (re)negotiate national identity appear much more complex than Billig might suggest in nations, such as Malaysia, which are divided by ethnic and religious, as well as political, tensions. Television, as the key institution for the transmission of culture (Haynes 2007), epitomizes rather than resolves the evolving ethnic and religious (Islamic) forms and tensions as they dominate political discourses and the everyday lives of postcolonial Malaysians. Despite the Federal Constitution's guarantee of freedom of religious practice, Islam remains the pillar of policy, governance and everyday life in modernizing multiethnic Malaysia. As a result, Islam seems to implicitly underpin these nation-building projects and the lyric of a united Malaysian community, Bangsa Malaysia – sung throughout the 22-year regime of Mahathir Mohamad – continues to trouble the multiethnic and multi-religious people of Malaysia.

Morris (2002) argues that, in the wake of globalization, while identities may be resilient, cultures are ever-changing and this is evident in the hybridity of Malaysia's evolving culture. What seems problematic to elites in the construction and reconstruction of the Malaysian nationhood is determining the right proportion of Islamic values (liberal or fundamental), Malay traditional values, Chinese (foreign) and Indian (foreign) values and inevitably Western secular values for a perfect national blend to be circulated via national television. Billig, Hobsbawm and Scannell theorized the role of television in the imagining of nations and in the construction of collective life clearly in the context of Western established democratic nations.

In the current climate of global flows, multiculturalism, and new nations in the making, collective national identity-building, let alone imagining, appears difficult. Needless to say, the resourceful and the privileged pick and choose cultural ingredients from which to manufacture an identity they perceive as the best for the nation. Generally, the closer the media is to the centre(s) of power, the easier it tends to be for ruling elites to effectively utilize media for change and for this kind of nation-building. Indeed, Malaysian television in the pre-Internet and Internet media eras appears to have served its master through restrictive media laws and cosy state–business liaisons. In fact, the longer the ruling elites remain in power (as in the case of Malaysia and Singapore), the more systematized and naturalized the ideological discourses in play and the quicker the pace for change. In such a context, democracy – ideally seen to provide a favourable climate for a public sphere (Habermas 1989) – constitutes a hindrance to the ruling elites' aspiration for a smooth transition from a colonial to an independent state and to the rapid transformation from an agrarian to an urban state. In Malaysia, the official state view of the role of television remains that it should function as a tool for promoting national development, national harmony and national security (Annuar 2002). Mahathir, for instance, has expressed distaste over the role of activists and lobbyists in democracies, who he claims exert pressure on ruling governments and thus pose obstacles to smooth progress. In response to the political turmoil in the former Soviet Union and Eastern Europe after the collapse of communism, he is noted to have remarked:

> It's not easy to suddenly switch from an autocratic government to a democratic government... Look at what's happened in Albania. That's democracy gone crazy. We tell the people that you can demonstrate in the streets and you can bring down the government. So they demonstrated, brought down the government and now what do they have? Anarchy.
>
> (Khoo 2002: 58)

'Reformasi' is what Malaysia continues to hear chanted on- and offline following the sacking of Anwar Ibrahim in September 1998 from Mahathir's cabinet. Significantly, a month before Anwar was dismissed, editors of the *Utusan Malaysia* and *Berita Harian* resigned, as Mahathir shrewdly clamped down on media closely aligned to Anwar (Wang 1998). However, many websites, such as the Free Anwar Campaign, Laman Reformasi and Justice for Anwar, sprang up on the Internet (Ling 2003). Since the Printing Presses and Publications Act, which grants the home affairs minister power to issue or withdraw printing licences, does not apply to the Internet, the alternative media site, Malaysiakini.com, was able to establish itself and has been running since 1999 without a permit.

Nonetheless, Internet media activity has been tamed primarily through a number of inherited colonial laws: these include the Official Secrets Act of 1972, which prevents journalists from accessing information in any official document labelled secret; the Internal Security Act of 1960 that detains without trial; the Printing Presses and Publications Act of 1984 that requires all publications to apply for an annual license from the Home Affairs Ministry, which can be withdrawn without judicial review; and the Sedition Act 1948 (amended in 1971) that prosecutes anyone who questions Malay special rights, Malay rulers' sovereignty or utters any seditious word. The Broadcasting Act of 1988, which gave the minister of information wide control over what was aired, was repealed with the establishment of the Malaysian Communications and Multimedia Commission (MCMC) under the jurisdiction of the Ministry of Communication and Multimedia (previously Ministry of Information, Communication and Culture). MCMC regulates the converging media and communication industry in Malaysia in accordance with national policy set out in the Communication and Multimedia Act 1998 (www.skmm.gov.my).

Since the ethnic riots of 13 May 1969 culminating in *The Malay Dilemma*, and under the UMNO flagship of the ruling BN, the Malay-bumiputera have been the focus of change and development. In Malaysia's modernization process, the Malay-bumiputera, whom Mahathir contends are deserving of 'constructive protection' (Mahathir 1970), have enjoyed a host of socio-economic benefits that have in a brief generational span shifted the bulk of them from

136 *Umi Khattab*

fishing villages to cyber cities. The slogan 'Malaysia Boleh' (Malaysia Can Do) was coined to inspire the Malay-bumiputera to move to great heights. In this process, native values and supposedly 'sick' hereditary characteristics (Mahathir 1970) appear 'treated' as the doctor-leader diagnosed and healed these as he challenged the Malay to move from an old primitive state to that of urban and global sophistication. Thus values and practices such as fatalism, contentment, laziness and animism were condemned and replaced with capitalism and Islamism. The cliché 'Melayu baru' (new Malay) was promoted loud and clear through televised songs and campaigns, and linked with Western capitalist values such as materialism and individualism.

The influence of imported television programmes over the Malay native was hardly seen as problematic in the early years of the New Economic Policy (1970–90). In this period, Malaysia consumed more television products than it produced. Despite cries to indigenize television products, Malaysia continues to consume and imitate, if not from the USA, then from Japan, India, South Korea, Indonesia and the Middle East. Echoing Schramm, Lerner and Rogers and Shoemaker, Malaysian development communication academics in various ways contended that these imported programmes created 'rising expectations' that were necessary attitudinal forces for modernization, overlooking the obvious problems in processes, structure and policy. Further, the Malay-bumiputera were advised in the 1970s to look to their ethnic Chinese neighbours and learn to become as industrious as they were. In fact, the central goal of Mahathir's *Malay Dilemma* was the changing of Malay values, attitudes and customs that he saw as contributory to their economic backwardness vis-à-vis the Chinese community. In *The Challenge* (1986), Mahathir continued to criticize the Malay for clinging to values influenced by the West and for deviant Islamic groupings.

In engineering change for Malaysia, and in designing a Bangsa Malaysia, Mahathir seemed to have medicalized the Malay-bumiputera (Mahathir 1970), justifying emergency aid and substantial subsidies to them and in the process denying amenities, let alone rights, to those labelled non-bumiputera. As argued by Nain (2000a), the Mahathir administration, using the New Economic Policy as a guideline, introduced a variety of policies and strategies all of which formed part of Vision 2020, which was introduced in 1991 following the expiry of the New Economic Policy. Nain (2000b) contends that these policies focused on attitudinal and behavioural change and psychological liberation for the Malay-bumiputera. In pointing out that the first challenge to Vision 2020 is ethnic integration, Mahathir is noted to have said:

> By the year 2020, Malaysia can be a united nation, with a confident Malaysian society [Bangsa Malaysia] infused by strong moral and ethical values, living in a society that is democratic, liberal and tolerant, caring, economically just and equitable, progressive and prosperous, and in full possession of an economy that is competitive, dynamic, robust and resilient.
>
> (cited in Khattab 2004: 174)

The imagining of a Bangsa Malaysia in some ways helped to legitimize the nation-building agenda but failed to be represented in the desired form, whether through national television and media images or in real-world terms. In other words, Bangsa Malaysia has been reduced to mere rhetoric, which seems to have become a mocked and street-parodied political slogan of the Mahathir administration. As argued by Silk (2002: 791), based on his analysis of the 1998 Kuala Lumpur Commonwealth Games, Bangsa Malaysia was an ideological initiative to erase ethnic tensions: 'the political tensions at the conclusion of the Kuala Lumpur 98 highlighted the ephemeral and mythical nature of such "virtual ethnic cleansing"'.

Under the ambit of the Ministry of Information (revamped as the Ministry of Information, Communication and Culture in 2009 and as the Ministry of Communication and Multimedia in 2013), Radio Television Malaysia (RTM) was mobilized extensively throughout the 1970s and beyond to recreate a new Malay(sia). Subsequently, the wave of privatization spearheaded under CEO Mahathir in the 1980s led to further utilization of diverse media and television channels for the nation-building agenda. While the currents of globalization may have brought new global television and Internet media into Malaysia, upsetting state policies and (direct and indirect) control of mainstream media, the drive to de-indigenize and reconstitute the Malay-bumiputera identity continued. In fact, televised public campaigns and public service announcements in the form of jingles repeatedly introduced information technology (IT) use to the Malay-bumiputera to enable them to become technology savvy and cyber-active.

Since the turn of the twenty-first century, however, the development challenge has been to resist 'Western' cultural products, emulate Japanese work ethics and re-proselytize Islamic Malay(sia) into the old cultural form. When former deputy prime minister Anwar Ibrahim was sacked and sentenced (1998–9), Malay-bumiputera village folks then spoke of 'how he had challenged his father in an un-Malay/un-indigenous manner and therefore tradition justified his punishment'. However, closer to his retirement from office, as his popularity waned and as the political tides changed, and as sympathy and support for Anwar Ibrahim triumphed, Mahathir was noted to have diagnosed a new dilemma in the Malay-bumiputera: that of being crippled and needy of crutches as they continued to be dependent on and cling to state handouts that they had enjoyed since 1970. Mahathir's medicalization of the Malay-bumiputera and mediatized discourse of Malay-bashing, including Anwar-bashing, in many ways contributed to his declining popularity and tearful resignation from office in 2003.

Deconstructing television campaigns

Despite the waning popularity of RTM and TV3 in an Internet media climate, state agencies such as the Ministry of Health, Ministry of Women and Family Affairs continued to depend on terrestrial FTA public and private television stations to reach target audiences in the promotion of national celebrations, festivals and social change. This includes government (UMNO)-linked companies, such as Tenaga Nasional, Telekom, TV3 and Maybank, to name a few, that participate in the state's nation-building agenda particularly during national celebrations such as Independence Day (Merdeka) and ethnic festivities such as Chinese New Year, Diwali, Aidilfitri and Christmas. Since the 1990s, these public and commercial campaigns have struggled to make sense of and represent Malaysian society in a socially cohesive manner (see Hall 1997). Campaign producers appear to have interpreted the notion of 1Malaysia in accordance with their reading of its ideological underpinnings – its investment in Malay supremacy. In the 1990s, for example, public campaigns on healthy lifestyle, road safety, family values and recycling all represented the Malay-bumiputera as the primary actor, as though no other ethnic community existed in Malaysia. If and when an individual from an ethnic minority group was depicted, as in the case of the respect for public property campaign or the diabetic campaign, it was in a bad light. For instance, in some of these campaigns, an Indian-looking male was portrayed as destroying public toilets and an Indian-looking male was portrayed as a diabetic patient being advised by a Malay-looking medical doctor. The healthy lifestyle campaign and the happy family campaign portrayed only urban Malay-Muslim-looking families and imparted values relevant only to Malay-Muslims. Most of these public campaigns were delivered via TV1 and TV2.

In more recent times, under the banner of 1Malaysia, festival television campaigns initiated by linked companies associated with the government (UMNO) have provoked Internet-based protest for their lack of attention to cultural sensitivities. For example, in August 2010, TV3 aired a national Aidilfitri festival campaign (see for example www.youtube.com/watch?v=pMPnplExls8) to continue to position Najib Razak's 1Malaysia brand. This occurred at a time when the issue of ethnic minority rights, religious freedom and human rights had resurfaced via alternative media such as Malaysiakini.com, KiniTV, Malaysian Insider and Malaysia Today as well as social media sites. The campaign commercial depicted symbols that appeared to offend fundamentalist Malay-Muslims. For example, the portrayal of an old Malay man with a white songkok (hat) riding a trishaw-like vehicle flying across the sky was read as reflective of Santa Claus on a sleigh; the symbol of a lotus was read as reflective of Buddhism and the showcasing of lamps was interpreted as reflective of Hinduism. After just a few days the TV3 commercial was removed and the government body Malaysian Communication and Multimedia Commission (MCMC) imposed a RM50,000 fine on TV3 for displaying an Aidifitri festival greeting that was culturally insensitive and disrespectful of Islam. Further, a national apology was issued to all Muslims in Malaysia by TV3 in its 8pm main news bulletin. Primarily, the apologetic message expressed regret for hurting the feelings of Muslims. The Information, Communication and Culture Ministry (now Ministry of Communication and Multimedia) immediately called for a screening of all television commercials by the MCMC.

Soon after, in November of the same year, a Diwali greetings commercial designed by the National Film Development Corporation (FINAS) and aired on RTM including ASTRO (see, for example, www.youtube.com/watch?v=Ybjr3irTsZs) stirred online protest as it depicted a simple Hindu man with a pregnant Malay-Muslim wife visiting the protagonist's parents' home where the issue of the halal-ness of the food served to his Malay-Muslim wife was subtly depicted. The advertisement was read by Malaysian Indians as encouraging Indians to convert to Islam and as reiterating Malaysian Islamic values and imposing Islam on a non-Muslim. It was interpreted as insulting Hindus and continuing to represent Malay-Muslims as being the superior race in Malaysia and attempting to instil the fear of apostasy among Malay-Muslims. Unlike the TV3 Aidilfitri advertisement, however, no apology was issued to Malaysian Hindus by FINAS or RTM and the advertisement was not banned either.

It is instructive to point out that Malaysia has a dual system of law – civil law, which is federal, and sharia law, which is state. While the sharia courts have no jurisdiction over non-Muslims, sharia law in Malaysia requires a non-Muslim to convert to Islam prior to marriage to a Muslim. A Muslim convert is rarely ever able to leave Islam despite the guarantee of religious freedom under the federal constitution. This has been a key obstacle to ethnic integration in Malaysia and a major international human rights violation.

Returning to television celebrations, on a positive note, Petroliem Nasional (Petronas) another UMNO-linked company, was often praised for designing nation-building television festival commercials that were postmodern, reflective of reality and heart-warming and that truly portrayed the spirit of Malaysia (see for example the National Day commercial at www.youtube.com/watch?v=J8cGKY9U46Q and the Diwali festival commercial at www.youtube.com/watch?v=QuHFDck9GbM). These campaigns were designed by the late Yasmin Ahmad, while she was creative director at Leo Burnett Kuala Lumpur, an award-winning filmmaker and artist who was never afraid to challenge social norms (http://e.advertising.com.my/petronas-festival-television-commercials). However, following her death, a 2012 Petronas Diwali television festival commercial caused an outcry. Malaysian Hindus asked why Petronas had selected to portray a South Indian Dappankuthu dance in the commercial for Diwali, as it was a type of dance performed to shed feelings of sadness during moments such as death, and why it had chosen a theme that was culturally more relevant to and appropriate for Hindus in India than Malaysian Hindus. The commercial was eventually pulled with an explanation by Petronas (see 'Do the Dappan', www.youtube.com/watch?v=nPaKW6geBeg).

Conclusion

In the Malaysian television world of nation-building campaigns, there seems to be turmoil in the showcasing of a collective Malaysian nationhood.

140   *Umi Khattab*

There are still questions, such as 'What is Bangsa Malaysia?' and 'What is 1Malaysia?' It is not at all clear how APCO Worldwide has contributed to making the rebranded and reinvented 1Malaysia nation-building campaign reflective of national transformation. Further, Malaysians are entitled to ask what is Najib's real transformation goal in a country where, in the twenty-first century, marriage between Muslims and non-Muslims is apparently restricted and denied by primitive ideological thought frames. More often than not, television carelessly and disrespectfully dismisses the values of ethnic minority groups while Islamic values and Malay supremacy continue to underpin televised campaign discourses and symbols. Even when we compare the Mahathir and post-Mahathir administration national campaigns, we are not able to see how the 1Malaysia rebranding exercise has made any significant positive impact on nation-building. Clearly, the deliberate exclusion and misrepresentation of the 'other' in these campaigns and the intentional focus on some actors, and some issues and some values, are elitist and ethnocentric. Campaigns, whether in the pre-Internet or Internet media times, Mahathir or post-Mahathir regimes, depict an ethnocentric Malaysia, and a skewed national vision that delimits ethnic rights and territories. While Mahathir's Vision 2020 and Najib's 1Malaysia aspire to create an integrated multiracial society called Bangsa Malaysia, this has not been televised and mediatized in a culturally appropriate manner.

It can be argued that national television campaigns have been designed without input from minority ethnic groups and this makes sense when we come to understand that those who design and implement these campaigns are largely Malay-bumiputera themselves, who hold key positions in the broadcast industry and the civil service (itself an outcome of the New Economic Policy). An exception, however, is Yasmin Ahmad's work. There is a yearning for Yasmin's ideas to continue to live and rejuvenate in Malaysia; the 2012 Diwali Petronas commercial speaks of the emptiness of cultural understanding and the deep absence of local, postmodern culture-rich television products that have the potency to generate feelings of nationhood in the hearts of Malaysians and encourage them to engage collectively in redesigning the nation, Malaysia. In a context very different to the one in which the analysis of Billig, Hobsbawm, Scannell and Hartley were generated, Malaysian television does not appear to be the key site for the enabling of collective imagination or collective membership. I say this because the notion of a national collective identity (in the form of Bangsa Malaysia) is being resisted as it is being manufactured and mediatized. As pointed out by Shamsul (1998: 25), Malaysia may in fact be a nationless state or a nation-of-intent. Do 'we' really need a collective identity? If so, why, how and who constructs it for 'us'? Clearly, it is the UMNO elites who are imagining the nation. While the elites do the imagining, the masses are realistically carving out their own individual cultural identities and spaces. As part of the everyday life of its people, television appears to empower Malaysians to rethink their national identity and citizenship and generate oppositional readings for the remaking of a new democratic nation. The Bangsa Malaysia political wish perpetuated through the 1Malaysia brand appears to contradict the communal nature of the ruling BN, the communal nature of its education policy as well as local ethnic-based television programming. Unless the communal nature of the political landscape, the media, the civil service and the education system changes, the achievement of a Bangsa Malaysia through its rebranded 1Malaysia campaign may remain nothing but a national mythology. The social engineering of a modern Malay(sia) seems to have been conceived by the *Malay Dilemma* that, by 2020, may indeed witness a Malaysian dilemma if attempts are not made to correct present injustices. If television mirrors society, then it is clear that the social face of Malaysia needs to be urgently reconstructed, shifting gear away from the orthodox Mahathir mantra of 'Ketuanan Melayu'.

References

Anderson, B. (1983) *Imagined Communities: Reflections on the Origins and Spread of Nationalism*, London: Verso.

Annuar, M.K. (2002) 'Defining democratic discourses: the mainstream press' in K.W.F. Loh and B.K. Khoo (eds.) *Democracy in Malaysia: Discourses and Practices*, Richmond, Surrey: Curzon Press, pp. 138–64.

Annuar, M.K. (2007) 'History of local media', *The Sun*, 24 August.

Appadurai, A. (1996) *Modernity at Large: Cultural Dimension of Globalization*, London: University of Minnesota Press.

Asiaweek (1995) 'One nation, one people', *Asiaweek*, 6 October.

Billig, M. (1995) *Banal Nationalism*, London: Sage Publications.

Cheah, B.K. (2002) *Malaysia: The Making of a Nation*, Singapore: Institute of Southeast Asian Studies.

Chin, C.B.N. (2002) 'The "host" state and the "guest worker" in Malaysia: public management of migrant labour in times of economic prosperity and crisis' in Y.A. Debrah (ed.) *Migrant Workers in Pacific Asia*, London and Portland, OR: Frank Cass, pp. 19–40.

Habermas, J. (1989) *The Structural Transformation of the Public Sphere: An Inquiry into a Category of Bourgeois Society*, Cambridge: Polity Press.

Hall, S. (1992) 'The question of cultural identity' in S. Hall, D. Held and T. McGrew (eds.) *Modernity and its Futures*, Cambridge: Open University, pp. 273–325.

Hall, S. (1997) 'The work of representation' in S. Hall (ed.) *Representation: Cultural Representations and Signifying Practices*, London: Sage, pp. 13–74.

Haynes, A. (2007) 'Mass media re-presentations of the social world: ethnicity and "race"' in E. Devereux (ed.) *Media Studies: Key Issues and Debates*, Los Angeles: Sage Publications, pp. 162–90.

Hng, H.Y. (2004) *Five Men and Five Ideas: Building National Identity*, Malaysia: Pelanduk Publications.

Hobsbawm, E. (1983) 'Introduction: inventing traditions' in E. Hobsbawm and T. Ranger (eds.) *The Invention of Tradition*, Cambridge: Cambridge University Press, pp. 1–14.

Karthigesu, R (1987) 'Commercial competition to government monopoly in television: implications of the Malaysian experience', *Kajian Malaysia*, 5: 76–86.

142   *Umi Khattab*

Karthigesu, R. (1994) 'Television in the Asian cultural map', *Media Information Australia*, 73: 90–6.

Kaur, A. (2008) 'International migration and governance in Malaysia: policy and performance', *UNFAC Asia Papers*, No. 22, pp. 1–18.

Khattab, U. (2002) 'The system needs skilled, wholesale doctoring', *The New Straits Times*, 7 December.

Khattab, U. (2004) 'Wawasan 2020: engineering a modern Malay(sia): state campaigns and minority stakes', *Media Asia* 3(3): 170–7.

Khattab, U. (2006) ' "Non" mediated images: public culture and state television in Malaysia', *The International Communication Gazette*, 68(4): 347–61.

Khoo, B.K. (2002) 'Nationalism, capitalism and "Asian values"' in K.W.F. Loh and B.K. Khoo (eds.) *Democracy in Malaysia: Discourses and Practices*, Richmond, Surrey: Curzon Press, pp. 51–73.

Lee, K.H. (2004) 'Differing perspectives on integration and nation-building in Malaysia' in L. Suryadinata (ed.) *Ethnic Relations and Nation-Building in Southeast Asia: The Case of the Ethnic Chinese*, Singapore: Utopia Press Pte Ltd, pp. 82–108.

Lent, J.A. (1979) 'The mass media in Malaysia' in J.A. Lent (ed.) *Cultural Pluralism in Malaysia: Polity, Military, Mass Media, Education, Religion and Social Class*, Michigan: The Center for Southeast Asian Studies, pp. 32–42.

Lerner, D. (1958) *The Passing of Traditional Society*, New York: Free Press.

Ling, S. (2003) 'The alternative media in Malaysia: their potential and limitations' in N. Couldry and J. Curran (eds.) *Contesting Media Power: Alternative Media in an Networked World*, Ianham: Rowman & Littlefield, pp. 289–302.

Mahathir, M. (1970) *The Malay Dilemma*, Singapore: Times Book International.

Mahathir, M. (1986) *The Challenge*, Kuala Lumpur: Pelanduk.

Means, G.P. (1996) 'Soft authoritarianism in Malaysia and Singapore', *Journal of Democracy*, 7(4): 103–17.

Mohd Sani, M.A. (2004) 'Media freedom in Malaysia', *Journal of Contemporary Asia*, 35(3): 341–67.

Morley, D. and Robins, K. (1995) *Spaces of Identity: Global Media, Electronic Landscapes and Cultural Boundaries*, London: Routledge.

Morris, N. (2002) 'The myth of unadulterated culture meets the threat of imported media', *Media, Culture and Society*, 24: 278–89.

Moten, A.R. and Mokhtar, T.M. (2013) 'The 2004 general elections in Malaysia: a mandate to rule', *Asian Survey*, 46(2): 319–40.

Nain, Z. (2000a) 'Portraying poverty: the media and the poor in Malaysia' in *Media and Human Rights*, Singapore: AMIC, pp. 232–52.

Nain, Z. (2000b) 'Globalised theories and national controls: the state, the market and the Malaysian media' in J. Curran and Myung-Jin Park (eds.) *De-Westernising Media Studies*, London: Routledge, pp. 139–52.

Rogers, E.M. and Shoemaker, F. (1971) *Communication of Innovation*, New York: Free Press.

Scannell, P. (1989) 'Public service broadcasting and modern public life', *Media, Culture & Society*, 11: 135–66.

Schramm, W. (1964) *Mass Media and National Development*, Stanford: UNESCO and Stanford University Press.

Shamsul, A.B. (1998) 'Debating about identity in Malaysia: a discourse analysis' in Z. Ibrahim (ed.) *Cultural Contestations: Mediating Identities in a Changing Malaysian Society*, London: Asean Academic Press, pp. 17–50.

Shamsul, A.B. (2004) 'Text and collective memories: the construction of "Chinese" and "Chineseness" from the perspective of a Malay' in L. Suryadinata (ed.) *Ethnic Relations and Nation-Building in Southeast Asia: The Case of the Ethnic Chinese*, Singapore: Utopia Press Pte Ltd, pp. 109–44.

Silk, M. (2002) 'Bangsa Malaysia: global sport, the city and the mediated refurbishment of local identities', *Media, Culture & Society*, 24: 775–94.

Teoh, A. (2007) 'Education's rocky path to national unity', *The Sun*, August 23.

Wang, L.K. (1998) 'Malaysia: ownership and control', *Development Dialogue, The Journal of the Dag Hammarskjold Foundation* 2: 61–82.

9 The television of intervention

Mediating patron–client ties in the Philippines

Jonathan Corpus Ong

Similar to the other countries discussed in this volume, elite dominance over mass media has been a main characteristic of Filipino history. Foreign-educated Filipino intellectuals from wealthy families founded the early periodicals that demanded reform and/or independence from Spanish colonization in the late nineteenth century (Anderson 1983). Today, 'old rich' landowning families own and operate television networks, radio stations, and newspapers not only as part of prestigious and profitable media conglomerates, but also in connection with their interests in industries as varied as oil and agriculture to insurance, shipping, and mining.

Most of the popular history of Filipino television is written and published by media owners and practitioners themselves, in the form of anthologies that celebrate the anniversaries of the inauguration of television stations, such as GMA Network's *GMA Gold* (2001) and ABS-CBN's *The Story of ABS-CBN—the Medium of Our Lives* (1999), or as biographies of their entrepreneurial and visionary founders, such as ABS-CBN's *Kapitan* (*The Captain*) (Rodrigo 2006). These texts chronicle not only the stories behind the most popular programs and actors of these privately owned companies, but also discuss the ethos of community- and nation-building held by media owners and producers, captured for instance in ABS-CBN's brand tagline 'In the service of the Filipino.' These books also recount the many charitable and interventionist projects that the TV networks themselves (through their corporate personnel, but also journalists, news anchors, and celebrities) have provided to poor or disaster-stricken communities around the country, such as the distribution of food and clothes and the building of shelter and class-rooms (see Figure 9.1).

Alongside this tradition of positive and celebratory historiography of media and the press—seen here as revolutionary, nationalistic, honest, and service-oriented—is a more critical tradition. This approach, taken mostly by independent journalists and academics, highlights the history of televi-sion as an instrument of elite rule in its powers of framing and propaganda (e.g., Abaya 1968; Maglipon 1972; Rimban 1999; Teodoro 1998). They would draw attention to the overlooked origins of Filipino television as originally a 'propaganda machine' for the re-election campaign of the embattled president

Figure 9.1 Fisherfolk on Bantayan Island received livelihood assistance from GMA Network following Typhoon Haiyan
Source: Image from www.gmakapusofoundation.com

Elpidio Quirino in 1953 (del Mundo 1989: 73). They would also highlight the continuing 'semi-feudal' and 'semi-colonial' structure of Filipino media, where media oligarchs observe careful alliances with other elite families and foreign power players (Almario 1972: 19), forming what Alfred McCoy (2009) calls an 'anarchy of families' that possess among them an intense concentration of political, economic, and symbolic power in the context of a weak Philippine state.

While this critical tradition provokes reflection about the negative social consequences of symbolic power being concentrated to a select few families, it is ultimately unable to account for the enduring popularity of television programs, journalists, and celebrities in what is supposedly a grossly unjust society, not to mention the affective relationship that ordinary Filipinos have with particular TV networks. While elite-owned and supposedly serving only elite interests, Filipino television content today curiously 'overrepresents' the

146 *Jonathan Corpus Ong*

poor across genres of news and reality television, soap opera, and documentary. In stark contrast with other Asian television systems criticized as being 'in denial' about poverty, such as India (Sainath 2009) and Korea (Kim 2007), Filipino television content is thematically about the suffering and patient endurance of the Filipino poor and working-class (Flores 2001).

Crucially, the close focus on media ownership of Filipino TV historiography—in both the positive and critical traditions—is unable to explain what I argue is its most defining feature as a social institution: Filipino television today is a television of intervention. Not only does Filipino television mediate in symbolic terms, such as in the circulation of representations of the Filipino poor, it mediates in material terms as well. Operating not only as intermediaries between donors from the private sector and the poor, or between the government and the masses, television networks themselves engage in interventionist projects directed at poor individuals and communities, such as charity and disaster-relief (see Figure 9.1), but also in its 'wealth-sharing' game shows and the operation of the TV station itself as a site of 'media pilgrimage' (Couldry 2003) for social services, such as free medical consultation, free legal advice, and money-lending. This chapter aims to show how the television of intervention works in the context of a weak state unable to serve its citizens, and occasionally during times of crisis, 'acts as the government' (De Quiros 2009).

This chapter retells a history of Filipino television, then, not solely from the perspective of elite ownership, but in the everyday context of ordinary people's diverse and dynamic interactions with both television content (symbolic mediations) and interventionist media practice (material mediations). In media studies, this follows the 'mediational approach' to the study of television as involving a concern of the interrelationships between 'moments' of production, text, and reception (Couldry 2003; Livingstone 2009; Madianou 2005; Ong 2012). This perspective acknowledges that audiences—in this case, low-income audiences assumed by many academics and cultural elites as 'abused' and 'exploited' by elite media producers (Cordova 2011)—are fully capable of creatively interpreting and rejecting hegemonic discourses in media content. As such, I draw from archival research as well as my previous ethnographic work with Filipino television audiences in Manila, who not only engaged in traditional 'fan' practices toward particular TV shows or celebrities but also visited TV studios to avail themselves of promised economic rewards and social services (Ong 2015).

Consistent with mediation theory, this paper further traces the historical development of interventionist Filipino television through the anthropological framework of patron–client ties. This framework, I argue, helps explain how the wide gap between the elite class and the poor is bridged and resolved by the symbolic and material transactions enabled by interventionist television. While this approach has been used extensively in Philippine studies to explain the operation of mutually beneficial transactions in the context of grossly asymmetrical interpersonal relationships—between landowners and

The television of intervention 147

peasants (Kerkvliet 1995), politicians and constituents (Rafael 1990; Sidel 1989; Yean 2008), and those in power and 'those who have nothing' (Cannell 1999)—it has not been used in the study of Filipino media. My argument here for the Philippine studies literature is that the television of intervention draws from historical and cultural normativities of a good patron–client relationship and is used to resolve and justify the contradictory tensions that have faced mass media in the Philippines and elsewhere, such as the tension between profitable programming and quality programming, and the conflict between media freedom and media regulation.

In the next three sections, I discuss key historical eras for the development of television: 1) the early years, marked by a television whose ownership and content were elite-oriented, yet influenced by narrative themes of suffering already present in older media forms; 2) the martial law years, which momentarily suspended the control of television by elite families due to government seizure and control of mass media, although this was challenged by reactionary (and revolutionary) critique in alternative media; and 3) the post-martial law years, defined by a return to oligarchic control of mass media, an amplification of neoliberal values, and the emergence of television as a central social institution in the context of a 'weak state' unable to serve the lower class. In the final section, 'The mediation of patronage', I argue that enduring logics of patron–client ties shape the operations of Filipino television in occasional tension—and frequent conflation—with highly neoliberal values.

The early years of elite television

Contrary to today's television environment of elite ownership with mass-oriented content, the origins of Filipino television reveal a more exclusivist history of the medium. History books assert that the 'father of Philippine television' is an American named James Lindenberg, who imported television from the United States to the Philippines, which was granted independence by the United States in 1946 (Rodrigo 2006: 12). In 1952, Lindenberg's Bolinao Broadcasting Company was bought by Antonio Quirino, brother of then-president Elpidio Quirino. The company was renamed as Alto Broadcasting System (ABS) and was responsible for the first telecast in 1953. The central reason for the buyout was not economic but political: President Quirino was seeking re-election and hoped to harness the gloss and strength of the new medium for his campaign. But because TV catered only to the narrow audience demographic able to afford its high cost, Quirino's strategy failed, especially in contrast with his rival Ramon Magsaysay's populism. Magsaysay's media strategy leveraged the existing popularity of radio, where his memorable jingle 'Magsaysay is my Guy' dominated the airwaves (del Mundo 2003: 6). In 1957, ABS was bought by the Chronicle Broadcasting Network (CBN), owned by the oligarchic Lopez family, who also owned public utilities firms and sugar plantations. This merger paved the way for the launch of ABS-CBN, now the country's largest network (Rodrigo 2006). It was only in the 1960s that four other privately

148   *Jonathan Corpus Ong*

owned TV stations began broadcasting and challenged ABS-CBN's market dominance.

In its early years, Filipino television content consisted of mostly American programming. From several decades of being a US colony (1898–1946), with English instituted during this period as the 'medium of instruction' in basic education over the 70 other languages and dialects in the country (Tovera 1975: 41), the Philippines became an ideal market for American shows and advertising. Drawing evidence from the dominance of US-produced English-language content in the daily TV schedule, nationalist academics criticized America's continued cultural imperialism as well as Filipinos' 'colonial mentality' and 'white love' (Rafael 2000; Tolentino 2011). Nevertheless, early TV culture was restricted to an elite class. Due to the high cost of television, the TV box as well as the receiver antennas perched above houses became status symbols. A 1955 UNESCO survey indicated that among the 12 million population, only one out of 2,000 people owned a TV. The practice of TV viewing is described by historians as largely a community affair, where windows and doors of wealthier TV-owning households were opened so that neighbors could gather and watch (del Mundo 2003).

The most popular media forms of this period continued to be the radio drama, with its melodramatic narratives of suffering and tragedy that derived too from the spoken and sung religious text of the *pasyon* (Christ's passion) (Ileto 1979; Reyes 1986). Cultural elites criticized radio as a medium that perpetuated a 'ghetto' or 'trash' mentality (*bakya*, or *jologs*) by glorifying human suffering in its fictional genres (a critiqued leveled at television today, as I discuss in a later section). However, news and public affairs programs on radio that catered to the basic needs of the poor were more positively received. The early public affairs programs that were precursors to today's interventionist media activities included radio shows that broadcast bulletins of missing children and farm animals and educated listeners about effective farming techniques (Lent 1965).

As a response to radio's popularity, television networks slowly incorporated mass-oriented programming into their schedules. Popular radio programs were adapted to television, such as the long-running radio serial *Gulong ng Palad* (*Wheel of Fortune*), known for its message of hope in the midst of oppression (Gimenez-Maceda 1996: 39), and the talent show *Tawag ng Tanghalan* (*The Callback*), known to launch the singing careers of ordinary people. It is crucial to note that Filipino television evolved and grew as a medium not only by modernizing and innovating, such as by being the second in Asia to broadcast in color (ABS-CBN Broadcasting Corporation 1999), but also by adopting the grammars and narratives of the growing working class and poor populations. As the percentage of people living in poverty increased after the 1960s, with the Philippine peso devalued by around 50 percent, the first crucial move by television to become a central institution in Filipino public life was to follow shifts in market conditions and make available symbolic and material resources that the majority of audiences would need and desire.

The martial law years: repression and revolution

The martial law rule of president Ferdinand Marcos from 1972 to 1986 temporarily interrupted the trajectory of television as an elite-oligarchic medium attempting to reach larger audiences, because the Marcos government wrested privately owned media from their owners. Nevertheless, as this section will show, government-controlled television in this period continued to adopt more and more interventionist practices than in its early years, as it was used for explicit propaganda (that audiences would reject) and for more benign charitable projects that continued to draw inspiration from the successful programming of early community-oriented radio (that has proven popular among audiences to this day).

Marcos' first instruction issued under martial law included the identification of mass media personnel critical of his totalitarian administration as 'enemies of the state' and the turnover of TV companies to a 'new breed of oligarchs' sympathetic to Marcos' vision of 'The New Society' (Maslog 1990: 38). The suppression of freedoms of speech and organization also came in the form of physical abuse, arrest, exile, or killing of journalists, publishers, and even TV owners—such as the exiled Eugenio Lopez III, owner of ABS-CBN (Nieva 1983). During martial law, children's educational programs, variety shows, and game shows became the new popular genres, alongside a steady stream of American-produced content, including the soaps *Dallas* and *Falcon Crest*. News and public affairs programs as well as newspapers followed government propaganda and projected only a positive image of 'The New Society', consistent with urban redevelopment programs that erected artificial walls and decoration to cover up the squalor of shanties and dump sites (Tadiar 2004). As in the previous era, television programs continued to air in English. Even locally produced content, such as news and public affairs shows, aired in English in line with Marcos' use of the medium as a technology for mass pedagogy (Rimban 1999).

In response to intense government censorship and the 'crony journalism' of the Marcos era, low-circulation 'mosquito publications' revived the revolutionary and anti-authoritarian spirit of those earliest Filipino newspapers that were critical of Spanish rule. Anti-Marcos writers informed publics about the government's distortion of information (CMFR 2005; Maslog 1990; Teodoro and Kabatay 1998), while in cinema, filmmakers adopted social realist aesthetics in tackling themes of urban poverty and corruption starkly absent from free-to-air television and radio (Campos 2011). Film actress Nora Aunor became a celebrated icon among audiences for starring in an entire genre of movies that depict what the scholar Patrick Flores (2001) calls 'sufferance'—that is, the patient endurance of suffering among the poor and marginalized.

It was during the 1980s that television slowly became a real 'mass medium', particularly in urban centers such as Metro Manila, where 80 percent of households came to own a television. Nevertheless, provincial areas only reported TV ownership rates of between 14 percent and 50 percent (PIA

150   *Jonathan Corpus Ong*

1987), as English-language and highbrow 'educational' content alienated most of the uneducated and poor population. To address this gap, however, producers introduced more interventionist practices in genres such as the talk show in order to appeal to mass audiences' needs and interests. For instance, the public affairs talk show *Damayan* (*Empathy for Each Other*), hosted by the head of the Philippine Red Cross, Rosa Rosal, would become among the first TV programs with an institutional linkage to a charitable organization. The show not only broadcast expert medical and legal advice to mass audiences, but it also engaged ordinary people in confessional interviews about their life struggles. In its later years, the show began seeking donations from television viewers at home to aid people they identified as in need of medical assistance, and also featured segments aimed at helping people reunite with lost family members, related both to urban resettlements and migrations as well as to extrajudicial killings and exiles during martial law (Lapeña 2010; Donato 2010).

Perhaps the most enduring legacy of martial law to Filipino mass media to this day is the continued skepticism toward any government regulation of media institutions. This extends far beyond traditional journalistic concerns over press freedom, censorship, and libel, but also toward the continued expansion of interventionist practices by elite-oligarchic television.

The mass audience of post-1986

The present day landscape of a highly interventionist television system characterized by 1) strong media/weak state and 2) elite-owned television acting as patrons to low-income audiences (or 'clients') is configured in the immediate aftermath of Marcos' totalitarian regime. In particular, four important moves enabled the establishment and acceptance of interventionism as a defining logic of Filipino television. First, mass media consolidated an heroic image for themselves when they played a crucial role in the overthrow of Marcos' unpopular regime in February 1986. Media institutions became enabling platforms for the success of the 'People Power Revolution' that marked three days of peaceful protest by 500,000 people in the streets of metropolitan Manila, ending in the exile of Marcos to the United States and the appointment of his rival, Corazon Aquino, as president. Such was Aquino's debt to the TV owners, personalities, and journalists that supported People Power and critiqued Marcos throughout the martial law period that among her first orders in office was the return of government-sequestered media companies to their original owners (McCoy 2009). In a speech that also referenced the spread of democracy in Eastern Europe, Aquino said:

> It was in Asia, it was in the Philippines where it all began. It was here that the power of media, exposing the truth about bad government, showed itself able to galvanize a nation for its own liberation. It was in the Philippines that the ability of human flesh, charged with courage and

fortified by faith, to prevail over steel and oppression was first demonstrated by a people and reported by the media.

(Aquino 1982: 155)

Media's heroism, cultivated in their revolutionary practices during martial law and confirmed in their advocacy of People Power, was also rewarded by Aquino in the form of lax government regulation of media and the enshrining of press freedom in the 1987 Constitution, which is still used to this day (CMFR 2007). Privately owned television companies now draw their 'unbridled freedom' and independence from regulatory policies framed in the context of the enduring public association of media control with the dark era of propaganda and totalitarianism under Marcos. And, while self-regulatory bodies were established for mass media institutions, these inter-organizational bodies were of little consequence to operations, as television networks could freely evade sanction simply by withdrawing their membership to these groups (Ong 2010).

The second crucial phase of television's expansion of interventionist practice was the translation of this unregulated heroism into the formats for popular TV shows. For instance, post-martial television became awash with news and public affairs shows since 'the people were hungry for information after 14 years of censorship' (Stuart Santiago 2011). Unlike the Marcos era and the early years of TV, post-1986 news and public affairs programs became more inclusive toward mass audiences by shifting languages from English to Filipino, with the first Filipino-language talk show, *Public Forum*, launched in the late 1980s. Entertainment genres such as the soap opera broke free from directives to represent only positive images of 'The New Society' and revived the themes of suffering and oppression from radio melodrama and older media forms such as the *pasyon*. Television drama enjoyed narrative license to depict 'the same bitter and oppressive conditions of [people's] lives' (Gimenez-Maceda 1996: 39):

> The dramas ... entertained by squeezing one's tear glands dry and making a river of one's nose ... empathizing with facile stories about poor-but-beautiful-[housemaid] drowning in a torrent of abusive words from wicked [rich master], or about maudlin moppets subjected to physical violence by [evil women], or of tubercular husbands coughing their life away in the arms of wives who eke out pitiful life from washing other people's clothes.
>
> (Tiongson, quoted in Gimenez-Maceda 1996: 40)

Other factual entertainment genres such as game shows and talent shows incorporated generic elements of soap opera and talk shows to focus on individual contestants' emotional backstories of separation, poverty, and personal tragedy. Ordinary people now embark on 'media pilgrimages' to television studios not only to partake in the magical aura of the 'media

152 Jonathan Corpus Ong

world' absent from the 'ordinary world' (Couldry 2003), but for the attractive wealth-sharing of cash prizes, groceries, livelihood packages, and houses offered by these mass-oriented game shows. The popularity of the landmark game show *Wowowee*, in fact, caused a stampede that killed 71 people and injured 800 others, as more than 25,000 people gathered outside a stadium that could only hold 10,000 (Coronel 2006). In spite of public criticism for irresponsible event planning, TV station ABS-CBN evaded any criminal, civil, or inter-organizational sanction, in part through their formal establishment of a charitable foundation that promised to care for the families of the 71 victims.

Indeed, the third crucial manifestation of the television of intervention was the establishment of charitable organizations whose operations work in synergy with their television news departments. For instance, ABS-CBN Foundation, operating since 1989, commits to making 'a significant impact in the strategic areas of child care, environment, education, and disaster management' (ABS-CBN Foundation Incorporated 2013). Perhaps its most visible project is *Bantay Bata* (*Child Watch*), which offers a 24-hour hotline for ordinary people in need of 'home visit, rescue, legal assistance, medical assistance, educational assistance, and supplemental feeding to children' (ABS-CBN Foundation Incorporated 2013). ABS-CBN Foundation's activities are regularly featured on the network's prime-time news, as their beneficiaries of economic aid and assistance would become 'packaged' as 'human interest' stories as the bittersweet final act of the evening news (compare with Silverstone 1988: 26).

Similarly, GMA Network has its own Kapuso Foundation, headed by their respected prime-time news anchor Mel Tiangco. Its vision as an organization is 'to uplift the quality of life of marginalized Filipino families... [through] direct provisions of resources and services in the areas of education, health and disaster relief, referrals and other social services' (GMA Kapuso Foundation 2013). Tiangco links the establishment of her media charity to an extension of the responsibility of television journalists as the most efficient 'first responders' during a crisis:

> The reason why Kapuso Foundation is tied to the news is because, from our news desk, we learn days beforehand of the possibility of, say, a typhoon, and therefore we are able to prepare and help the victims. Why, who arrives on the site first anyway? It's always us [the TV networks]. And it's just irresponsible if we arrive and do nothing but just cover, when people are actually dying, or buried in [rubble]... But when Red Cross and the government and the other charities arrive, then we [Kapuso Foundation] would pull out. But Kapuso Foundation is always there as the first to respond.
>
> (Tiangco, quoted in Ong 2015: 63)

Tiangco's statement highlights media companies' corporatized efficiency over that of underresourced and bureaucratic government departments, perceived as inept, particularly when it comes to crisis management. For instance, when a major typhoon hit Metro Manila in September 2009 and submerged 80 percent of the nation's capital, journalists quickly reported on the lack of facilities of the National Disaster Coordinating Council (NDCC), which admittedly was said to only have 13 lifeboats available for rescue operations (Padilla 2009). This led TV journalists and celebrities to use their own helicopters and speedboats to rescue stranded victims, provide them with food, and subsequently broadcast these stories of 'heroic' rescues and benevolent donations by media people on television. In the words of writer Conrado de Quiros:

> In fact the monumental thing that happened was the complete absence of government. The only government there was were the media, notably [privately owned television networks] ABS-CBN and GMA-7. You can forgive both for advertising their wares, or relief efforts, under the extenuating circumstances. They were the government. They were the central authority apprising the public of the situation. They were the central authority coming to the aid of victims. They were running the country.
>
> (De Quiros 2009)

As mass-oriented TV stations,[1] ABS-CBN and rival GMA (and now a recent third player, TV5) would become involved in what commentators describe as a 'ratings war... for the hearts and minds [of ordinary Filipinos]' (Rimban 1999) that would be played out in both head-to-head television programming and the expansion of interventionist projects intended to cultivate loyalty among *masa* viewers. Overtaking radio as the top medium, with a 98 percent ownership rate in the mid-2000s (McCann-Erickson Philippines 2009), television owes its popularity to its strategic 'overrepresentation' of the poor in both fictional and factual television genres, despite upper-/middle-class critique of television being a *jologs* and patronizing medium that 'targets the least common denominator... feeding one kind of food, the easiest to digest, yes, baby food to adults with teeth' (De Jesus 2011). Needless to say, many upper-/middle-class audiences have 'switched off' from Filipino television and spend their leisure time with American entertainment (now available only on cable television) and social media, where class boundaries between elite and *masa* users are strictly maintained (Ong and Cabañes 2011).

In the next section, I discuss the history of interventionist television in the Philippines through the analytical prism of patron–client ties. I argue that the emergence of television as a central institution in Filipino society that empowers it to even 'act as the government' draws from its adoption—and reshaping—of enduring normativities of the patron–client relationship. While primarily a medium for one-to-many communication, television in the Philippines adopts practices of *direct intervention* and *personalization* in order to approximate the dyadic personalism and mutual aid of the patron/client relationship in the television/audience relationship. The consequence of this

154 *Jonathan Corpus Ong*

personal relationship is the ability to command *reciprocal exchange*, and in this context, this is evident in the implicit (and occasionally explicit) obligation to act as a loyal television viewer to the TV station.

The contemporary context in which interventionist television is situated, of course, is that of high neoliberalism in Filipino public life, where private companies fill in the gap left by a weak state unable to serve its citizens (De Quiros 2009; Tolentino 2009). I argue that just as interventionist television is informed by longstanding historical and cultural normativities of patronage, in its most current iteration it is also simultaneously 1) fueled by neoliberal imperatives for profit and 2) justifying the market- and *masa*-orientedness of what is increasingly criticized by cultural elites as 'dumbed down' *jologs* Filipino television. Drawing from my previous ethnographic work with television audiences in Manila, I finally argue that interventionist television should not be regarded through simple binaries of 'authentic assistance' or 'exploitation' but, rather, should be understood in relation to continuing struggles for social recognition and redistribution in a widely unequal society.

The mediation of patronage

The anthropologist Benedict Kerkvliet defines patron–client relationships as:

> built by face-to-face exchanges between two non-relatives, one of whom (the patron) clearly has a superior capacity to grant goods and services to protect and/or benefit the client, often in an immediate, tangible way. The client reciprocates by giving services, assistance, and general support that are frequently less tangible than, and nearly always different from, what he or she receives. This special relationship typically begins as a limited, particular interaction but evolves, through actions of both individuals, into a flexible, multi-stranded association or even friendship that is dependable for each individual.
>
> (Kerkvliet 1995: 412)

While this framework has been also been used in the study of *caciquismo* in Latin America and warlordism in China (Sidel 1989), in the Philippines it is particularly animated with local cultural normativities of *utang na loob* (debt of gratitude or, more literally, debt of the inside) and *hiya* (shame). As scholars in various fields have pointed out, interpersonal relationships are strictly yet informally regulated by norms of reciprocity or debt repayment, such that individuals (especially low-status clients) feel morally obliged to repay favors in order to avoid being stigmatized as *walang utang na loob* (without debt of gratitude) or *walang hiya* (without shame)—'the worst possible thing a Filipino should be seen as exhibiting' (Miller and Madianou 2012: 24). Being extended assistance from a patron incurs a debt that is interiorized in the client (hence: *utang na loob*), as the patron is viewed to have gone beyond the norms of kinship or friendship in extending help (Rafael 1990). Relationships between

The television of intervention   155

landlords and tenants, lenders and borrowers, landholders and agricultural workers, employers and employees, and politicians and constituents have been examined through this prism in historical and contemporary contexts (Hollnsteiner 1973; Sidel 1989; Yean 2008).

The common argument in the literature is that the Philippines' 'underdeveloped' politics is caused by the proliferation of oligarchic elite families with total control over the state and that patron–client relationships have continued to thrive due to inefficient bureaucracy, a weak economy, and the cultural values of *utang na loob* and *hiya* (for a comprehensive review, see Yean 2008: 415). Although the framework has also been criticized for its 'orientalizing of so-called Filipino values as the negative other of Western, or more specifically American, values' (Yean 2008: 416) as well as its longstanding concern with traditional politics rather than an 'everyday politics' of resistance that account for clients' need not only for material goods but also for symbolic recognition (Cannell 1999; Kerkvliet 1995), such is its resonance that its critics demand its contemporary updating rather than complete revision (Yean 2008).

While I do not wish to endorse a wholesale adoption of this framework in this historical analysis of Filipino television operations, I argue that it lays open the 'hidden transcript' of interventionism as the unique and defining logic of Filipino mass media. Although Filipino media scholarship has previously gestured to patron–client ties in more micro-analyses of relationships between fan audiences and charismatic celebrities or game show hosts (Cornelio in Valisno and Marcelo 2011), these analyses fail to link these practices to the organized and vertical infrastructure of interventionism that television networks have historically cultivated and updated.

Indeed, the history of Filipino television points towards a cooptation of popular interventionist practices from both community radio and newspapers into a more organized system of intervention coordinated on a national scale, yet deployed in local contexts. As we saw in the 'Early years' section, Filipino television slowly broadened its reach and popularity by borrowing from mass-oriented radio programming that directly addressed local community needs (such as locating missing farm animals and children, and so on). While early television content was caught in tension between elite-oriented programming imported from the United States and radio-adapted soaps and talent shows that played on cultural and religious tropes of suffering and pity, over time television oligarchs would rely more on mass-oriented programming and the expansion of direct services to broaden their market and cultivate loyalty among their client-audiences. As discussed earlier in both the 'Martial law' and 'Post-1986' sections above, we also saw how media intervention of the most popular and effective kinds were ones that operated outside of government control or regulation, where propagandistic television during martial law was rejected, yet extra-governmental charity and assistance was popularly received.

As an agent outside of formal government yet nevertheless a staunch representative of the nation, Filipino television references and consolidates the

156   *Jonathan Corpus Ong*

historical image of the nationalistic, revolutionary heroes behind the earliest Filipino media critical of Spanish colonization. The revolution against Marcos' martial law in 1986 provides a more contemporary reference for this imaging and is mundanely cultivated through the circulation of nationalistic branding in television networks' taglines, as we discussed in the introduction (e.g., ABS-CBN's 'In the Service of the Filipino'), and today's news and public affairs programs (e.g., ABS-CBN's prime-time newscast *Bandila*, or 'flag', prominently displays in its opening titles the Philippines flag juxtaposed with images of journalists alongside face-painted youth activists that work to reference historical and contemporary nationalist movements).

The systematized intervention of Filipino television in public life now requires deeper analysis of its contemporary operations. As the patron–client framework dictates the requirement of *face-to-face* exchanges, it seems to run contrary to the assumed operations of television as a *one-to-many* communications medium premised on 'dissemination' rather than 'dialogue' as primary mode of address (Peters 1999). In the Filipino context, however, television's embeddedness in public life significantly operates on the level of *face-to-face* exchange and *dialogue* in its diverse practices of intervention. We see this in 'media pilgrimages' (Couldry 2003) where ordinary people come to the television networks for gestural forms of social redistribution practiced across various entertainment genres, news and public affairs shows, and projects of media charities. We also observe this in 'reverse pilgrimages' (Couldry 2003) where media personnel themselves leave the television center to visit disaster zones and administer emergency relief operations, as we saw in earlier sections. These 'media pilgrimages' and 'reverse pilgrimages', although individually operating with differences according to the specific exigencies of media genre and social context, are nevertheless shaped by television's systematized patronage, where obligations of mutual exchange are subtly enforced, and the television *network* is personalized as a benevolent patron in its embodiment as a celebrity or media employee directly interacting with a client-audience/fan, and thereby materializing a kinship network rather than the strictly dyadic relationship of traditional patron–client ties. Occasionally, this interaction is also captured by television cameras and through the process of representation, one can argue that the client-recipient on television becomes a proxy for viewers at home who claim to 'see themselves' in the mediated stories shared by people who belong to the same kin network by virtue of loyal viewership (Ong 2015).

On the first point of obligations of mutual exchange, it is important to emphasize that television's hospitality toward low-income people within the specially demarcated 'media world' is not unconditional. While they extend invitations for people to travel to and visit their offices as actual venues not only for entertainment but also for legal advice or medical assistance, referrals to NGOs and other government offices, and even moneylending, depend on the specific *mediator* of the interventionist practice. Whether it is the particular

The television of intervention   157

genre of the game show, the talk show, or media charity, the recipient is required to observe conditions of exchange. For instance, broadcast-worthy 'entertaining' public testimonies of personal tragedy are required of media pilgrims seeking assistance through game shows or talk shows, just as material and visible evidence of urgent need is required to avail oneself of medical assistance through media charities. It is unsurprising then that a regular sight at television network exteriors are queues of people, often women carrying sick children to display tangible evidence of 'authentic' need, to justify *their particular* deservedness of television's economy of symbolic recognition and economic assistance over the many other poor people seeking similar help.

Related to this first point of debt obligation is the second issue of a *personal* and extended kin relationship that is cultivated in 'media pilgrimages' and 'reverse pilgrimages'. This second issue refers to the concurrent move by media institutions to deploy contemporary practices of branding that reference and reshape the normativities of patron–client relationships. In the branding of the top three privately owned TV networks as ABS-CBN *Kapamilya* (Of One Family), GMA *Kapuso* (Of One Heart), and TV5 *Kapatid* (Sibling), kinship bonds are extended to diverse audiences on a daily basis through the various genres and services that they offer, and become more strongly consolidated into debt obligations in the context of direct intervention. Perhaps the most striking evidence of the successful personalization of interventionist practices through contemporary branding (such as in these branding taglines used in the post-1986 context) are quantitative and qualitative industry surveys that suggest that the majority of television viewers tend to be viewers of *entire channels*, rather than selective viewers of individual programs across multiple channels (GMA Research Department 2004). In my own ethnographic research with television audiences in Metro Manila, I also found that it is common practice for ordinary people to self-identify as *Kapamilya* or *Kapuso*, and that slum neighborhoods *as a community* converge in their attention and loyalty to a particular TV station, such that one neighborhood 'adopts' the moniker of *Kapamilya* or *Kapuso* (Ong 2015).

In the context of intervention, then, the use of pseudo-family idioms can be seen as inordinately extending the conditions of exchange beyond the immediate transaction of personal-story-for-material-assistance toward a more lasting relationship of viewership and fandom, where loyalty to the television network broadens out from a personal affinity towards a specific celebrity, show, service, or genre, onto the wider *network* of other celebrities, shows, services, and genres on offer in the present and still to come in the future. Of course, these pseudo-family idioms work simultaneously as contemporary corporate strategies of branding that leverage on affinity-building that is hoped to translate into high TV ratings, but in a more critical light are ways to 'mystify the inequality [of patronage] to the point that makes it seem not only historically inevitable but also morally desirable' (Rafael 1988: 296).

158 *Jonathan Corpus Ong*

As sources of seemingly inexhaustible patronage across its multiple plat-forms that achieve nationwide reach and trust beyond that of government and individual politicians, television institutions nevertheless contend with contrasting discourses of being, on one hand, one of the most trusted social institutions in the Philippines (Garcia 2013) and, on the other, profit-seeking corporations that glorify and exploit the *masa*'s poverty and further 'condi-tion them to be poor' (Koh 2006). Both optimistic and pessimistic discourses should be seen working not in complete opposition but rather in a relation-ship of reinforcement and justification. My argument here is that, while elite media owners are widely criticized by other cultural elites for eschew-ing quality content for lowest-common-denominator programs that further infantilize *masa* audiences, the justification of this marketing strategy is the visualization and circulation of evidence of symbolic recognition and mater-ial redistribution for 'those who have nothing' (Cannell 1999). By claiming to not only represent the *masa* through the fictional narratives of soap but also to help the *masa* through direct intervention, television networks construct a shibboleth against the critique of exploitation and demands for media regu-lation and control—be it on economic issues of limiting advertising min-utes on television, or security issues of live broadcasting a hostage crisis and negotiating with hostage-takers (Ong 2010). Furthermore, these elite-owned media institutions find potential allies among other (aspiring) political elites who need a communications platform that might endear them to those seen as the constitutive vote during elections, and local and transnational corpo-rations that leverage on the 'sachet economy' business model to reach mass consumers.

In another light, the established cultural normativities of patron–client ties (which include personalization, mutual aid, and reciprocity) soften the edges of what are highly neoliberal and impersonal imperatives that dictate the explicitly profit-oriented direction of Filipino television, as we recall the statement above of ABS-CBN's Lopez to focus on economic concerns over political concerns after martial law. Patron–client ties additionally provide a readily available vocabulary for Filipino audiences to make sense of the often amorphous and ambiguous processes of crossing the bound-ary to the 'media world' as part of the ordinary cosmology of 'testing fate' and 'taking a leap of faith' (*pagbabakasakali*), which are the common idi-oms also used by clients when interacting with patrons in everyday life (Cannell 1999; Ong 2015). The client-audience recuperates agency in what is seen by many academics and cultural critics as purely exploitative or self-exploitative practices by asserting that these experiences of displaying the self and 'performing suffering' in media spaces are dignified forms of physical labor (in contrast with passive activities of staying at home) and creative emotional labor (in the skillful manipulation of generic codes and social expectations in the practice of demanding pity and recognition from people in power).

Conclusion: the neoliberal patronage of Filipino television

As discussed in this chapter, one of the 'hidden transcripts' in Filipino history is the media's story of intervention in public life: revolutions, social movements, political critique, and charitable services have been enabled, if not orchestrated, by media personnel at different periods of the nation's history. Today's television exists in continuity with older media of revolutionary and 'mosquito' newspapers and development-oriented community radio in sustaining a national (even global, if we count Filipino transnational TV) communicative infrastructure that forges patron–client relationships between TV networks and their audiences. Television's unique form of symbolic power in the Filipino setting relies on its traditional capacities for one-to-many broadcasting and the staging of grand media events, but also on the ways in which it has reanimated local Filipino cosmologies centered around gift-giving, mutual aid, and reciprocity through its various TV programs, personas, and projects. Television's centrality in Filipino public life depends much upon its modern expansion of intervention through the mundane *circulation* of images and narratives of benevolent intervention in the context of a weak state, its contemporary use of *personalization* through branding strategies, and its strategic *mediation* of pseudo-family idioms that situate interpersonal exchanges in the 'media world' within an extended family (and TV!) network with obligations of extended and eternal loyalty.

The deployment of the notion of patron–client ties, however, does not fully capture the full extent of the television/audience relationship. As with other commodified forms of patronage, while it allows television networks to attract anonymous masses through its circulation of 'false promises of salvation' (Coronel 2006; Gutierrez 2011), it also allows client-audiences to 'switch [to other] patrons' in the marketplace (Rafael 1990: 298). As such, client-audiences who are recipients of particular forms of symbolic recognition or material assistance may not always be expected to pay back the 'favor' if they would wish to confer loyalty to another TV channel. But, perhaps more significantly, audiences do not always seek to be clients and therefore do not actively seek offers for economic aid, but for more conventional needs to have a *libangan* (enjoyable activity; something with which to pass the time) in the context of hardship or poverty. In this light, the hospitality (albeit limited, generic, and conditional) granted to other poor people in spaces of television already address an ordinary yet profound need for social recognition among the economically marginalized, on whom oligarchic elites depend for economic, political, and moral legitimization.

Note

1 The broader socio-economic context behind these shifts in the media landscape is the expansion of the 'lower-class' or the bottom-of-the-pyramid category in the Philippine population. Market researchers and academics use lettered class categories of A (very rich), B (moderately rich), C (middle-class), D (moderately

160 *Jonathan Corpus Ong*

poor), and E (very poor), where the upper and middle classes are estimated to be between 7 percent and 11 percent of the population, class D between 58 percent and 73 percent, and class E between 18 percent and 32 percent (Schaffer 2002). This created a political situation where 'the mass (*masa*) vote' decides electoral outcomes, leading politicians to cultivate the poor vote. In economic terms, the Philippines is characterized as a 'sachet economy', driven by lower-class consumption of small-sized lower-cost 'sachets' of products such as shampoo and soap, as well as low-denomination prepaid phone cards used for texting and calling (Tolentino 2011). Television companies have adopted this business model employed by top advertisers Procter & Gamble, Unilever, and Smart Telecommunications after martial law. In the words of ABS-CBN owner Eugenio Lopez III: 'Under martial law, all of these stations were dominated by political concerns, not by economic or business concerns... [Now] we've also paid attention to local programming. We made a strategic decision... that we were going to be a mass-oriented TV station' (in Romualdez 1999: 55).

References

Abaya, H. (1968) 'Our vaunted press: a critique' in L. Teodoro, and M. De Jesus (eds.) *The Filipino Press and Media, Democracy and Development*, Quezon City: University of the Philippines Press.

ABS-CBN Broadcasting Corporation (1999) *Pinoy Television: The Story of ABS-CBN—the Medium of Our Lives*, Pasig City: ABS-CBN Publishing.

ABS-CBN Foundation Incorporated (2013) www.abs-cbnfoundation.com (accessed May 5, 2013).

Almario, M. (1972) 'The Philippine press as social critic' in L. Teodoro and M. De Jesus (eds.) *The Filipino Press and Media, Democracy and Development*, Quezon City: University of the Philippines Press.

Anderson, B. (1983) *Imagined Communities: Reflections on the Origins and Spread of Nationalism*, London: Verso.

Aquino, C. (1982) 'People, media and power' in L. Teodoro and M. De Jesus (eds.) *The Filipino Press and Media, Democracy and Development*, Quezon City: University of the Philippines Press.

Arceo, T. (2004) 'Big things come in small packages,' *Change/Agent*, http://www.synovate.com/changeagent/index.php/site/full_story/big_things_come_in_small_packages (accessed April 10, 2013).

Campos, P. (2011) 'The intersection of the Philippine and global film cultures,' *Plaridel: A Philippine Journal of Communication*, 8(11): 1–21.

Cannell, F. (1999) *Power and Intimacy in the Christian Philippines*, Cambridge: Cambridge University Press.

CMFR (2005) *Freedom of Expression and Press Freedom in the Philippines*, Manila: Center for Media Freedom and Responsibility.

CMFR (2007) *Philippine Press Freedom Report 2007*, Manila: Center for Media Freedom and Responsibility.

Cordova, J. (2011) 'Why the Filipino elite revile Willie Revillame,' *The Asian Correspondent*, http://asiancorrespondent.com/52569/why-the-filipino-elite-revile-willie-revillame (accessed April 25, 2013).

Coronel, S. (2006) 'Wowowee: television and the perils of peddling dreams,' *The Daily PCIJ*, www.pcij.org/blog/?p=593 (accessed April 10, 2013).

Couldry, N. (2003) *Media Rituals: A Critical Approach*, London: Routledge.

The television of intervention   161

De Jesus, M.Q. (2011) 'TV, *Willing Willie*, the public sphere,' *Rex Crisostomo's Blog*, http://rexcrisostomo.blogspot.com/2011/04/TV-willing-willie-public-sphere.html (accessed April 10, 2013).

del Mundo, C. (1989) 'Philippine television: a history of politics and commerce' in C. del Mundo (ed.) *Philippine Mass Media: A Book of Readings*, Old Sta. Mesa: Communication Foundation in Asia.

del Mundo, C. (2003) *Telebisyon: An Essay on Philippine Television*, Manila: Cultural Center of the Philippines.

De Quiros, C. (2009) 'Three,' *Inquirer.net*, http://opinion.inquirer.net/inquireropinion/columns/view/20090930-227605/Three (accessed April 10, 2013).

Donato, J. (2010) 'Kapwa ko mahal ko: a blessing to others,' *Philstar.com*, www.philstar.com/entertainment/642488/kapwa-ko-mahal-ko-blessing-others (accessed April 25, 2013).

Flores, P. (2001) 'The star also suffers: screening Nora Aunor,' *Kasarinlan: Philippine Journal of Third World Studies*, 16(1).

Garcia, C. (2013) 'For Pinoys, Church is "most trusted"; business "least trusted",' *ABS-CBNnews.com*, www.abs-cbnnews.com/focus/02/27/13/pinoys-church-most-trusted-business-least-trusted (accessed April 25, 2013).

Gimenez-Maceda, T. (1996) 'Modes of resistance in a globalizing popular culture industry,' *Kasarinlan: Philippine Journal of Third World Studies*, 12(2): 35–56.

GMA Kapuso Foundation (2013) www.gmanetwork.com/kapusofoundation (accessed May 5, 2013).

GMA Network (2001) *GMA Gold: 50 Years of Broadcast History*, Manila: GMA Network.

GMA Research Department (2004) *Cebu Audience Study*, Philippines: Quezon City.

Gutierrez, J. (2011) 'Philippine TV stations bring out trash,' *The Jakarta Globe*, April 14, http://jakartaglobe.beritasatu.com/archive/philippine-tv-stations-bring-out-the-trash (accessed March 25, 2015).

Hollnsteiner, M. (1973) 'Reciprocity in the lowland Philippines' in F. Lynch and A. De Guzman (eds.) *Four Readings in Philippine Values*, 3rd revised and enlarged edition, Quezon City: Ateneo de Manila University Press.

Ileto, R. (1979) *Pasyon and Revolution: Popular Movements in the Philippines, 1840–1910*, Quezon City: Ateneo de Manila University Press.

Kerkvliet, B. (1995) 'Toward a more comprehensive analysis of Philippine politics: beyond the patron–client, factional framework,' *Journal of Southeast Asian Studies*, 26: 401–19.

Kim, Y. (2007) 'The rising east Asian "wave": Korean media go global' in D. Thussu (ed.) *Media on the Move: Global Flow and Contra-Flow*, London and New York: Routledge.

Koh, E.L. (2006) 'The culture of poverty,' *Filipinojournal.com*, 20(5), www.filipinojournal.com/v2/index.php?pagetype=read&article_num=09182006014359&latest_issue=V20-N5 (accessed December 2, 2014).

Lapeña, C. (2010) '"Kapwa ko mahal ko" celebrates 35th anniversary,' *GMANews.TV*, www.gmanetwork.com/news/story/208912/showbiz/kapwa-ko-mahal-ko-celebrates-35th-anniversary (accessed April 25, 2013).

Lent, J. (1965) *Philippine Mass Communication*, Philippines: School of Journalism and Communications, Silliman University, Dumaguete City.

Livingstone, S. (2009) 'On the mediation of everything: ICA presidential address 2008,' *Journal of Communication*, 59(1): 1–18.

162 *Jonathan Corpus Ong*

Madianou, M. (2005) *Mediating the Nation: News, Audiences and the Politics of Identity*, London: UCL Press.

Maglipon, F. (1972) 'The press under siege' in L. Teodoro and M. De Jesus (eds.) *The Filipino Press and Media, Democracy and Development*, Quezon City: University of the Philippines Press.

Maslog, C. (1990) *Philippine Mass Communication: A Mini-History*, Quezon City: New Day Publishers.

McCann Erickson Philippines (2009) *2008 Philippine Media Landscape*, Makati City: McCann Erickson,

McCoy, A. (2009) 'Rent-seeking families and the Philippine state: a history of the Lopez family' in A. McCoy (ed.) *An Anarchy of Families: State and Family in the Philippines*, Madison, WI: University of Wisconsin Press.

Miller, D. and Madianou, M. (2012) 'Should you accept a friend request from your mother? And other Filipino dilemmas,' *International Review of Social Research*, 2(1): 9–28.

Nieva, A. (1983) 'The media under Marcos' in L. Teodoro and M. De Jesus (eds.) *The Filipino Press and Media, Democracy and Development*, Quezon City: University of the Philippines Press.

Ong, J.C. (2010) 'Essay on the Manila bus tragedy: the safety in the cliché,' *GMA News Online*, August 30, www.gmanews.TV/story/199737/essay-on-the-manila-bus-tragedy-the-safety-in-thecliche (accessed April 25, 2013).

Ong, J.C. (2012) '"Witnessing" or "mediating" distant suffering? Ethical questions across moments of text, production, and reception,' *Television & New Media*. Published online first August 22.

Ong, J.C. (2015) *The Mediation of Suffering: Classed Moralities of Television Audiences in the Philippines*, PhD thesis, University of Cambridge.

Ong, J.C. and Cabañes, J. (2011) 'Engaged, but not immersed: tracking the mediated public connection of Filipino elite migrants in London,' *South East Asia Research*, 19(2): 197–224.

Padilla, A. (2009) 'Analysis: beyond Ondoy and climate change, blame goes to Arroyo, Teodoro,' *Bulatlat.com*, October 2, http://bulatlat.com/main/2009/10/02/analysis-beyond-ondoy-and-climate-change-blame-goes-to-arroyo-teodoro/1 (accessed April 25, 2013).

Peters, J.D. (1999) *Speaking Into the Air: A History of the Idea of Communication*, Chicago: University of Chicago Press.

PIA (1987) *Mass Media Infrastructure in the Philippines*, Quezon City: Philippine Information Agency.

Rafael, V.L. (1990) 'Patronage and pornography: ideology and spectatorship in the early Marcos years', *Comparative Studies in Society and History*, 32(2): 282–304.

Rafael, V.L. (2000) *White Love and Other Events in Filipino History*, Quezon City: Ateneo de Manila University Press.

Reyes, J. (1986) 'Radio soap opera' in C. del Mundo (ed.) *Philippine Mass Media: A Book of Readings*, Old Sta. Mesa: Communication Foundation in Asia.

Rimban, L. (1999) 'The empire strikes back' in S. Coronel (ed.) *From Loren to Marimar: Philippine Media in the 1990s*, Quezon City: Philippine Center for Investigative Journalism.

Rodrigo, R. (2006) *Kapitan: Geny Lopez and the Making of ABS-CBN*, Quezon City: ABS-CBN Publishing.

Romualdez, E. (1999) 'Interview: Eugenio Gabriel Lopez III' in S. Coronel (ed.) *From Loren to Marimar*, Quezon City: Philippine Center for Investigative Journalism, pp. 54–7.

Sainath, P. (2009) 'No issues: a recession of the intellect', *The Hindu*, www.hindu.com/2009/04/20/stories/2009042051620800.htm (accessed April 20, 2013).

Schaffer, F.C. (2002) 'Disciplinary reactions: alienation and the reform of vote buying in the Philippines,' paper presented at the 2002 Annual Meeting of the American Political Science Association, Boston, August 29–September 1.

Scott, J. (1972) 'Patron–client politics and political change in Asia,' *American Political Science Association*, 66(1): 99–113.

Sidel, J. (1989) 'Beyond patron–client relations: warlordism and local politics in the Philippines,' *Kasarinlan*, 4(3): 19–30.

Silverstone, R. (1988) 'Television myth and culture' in J.W. Carey (ed.) *Media, Myths, and Narratives: Television and the Press*, London: Sage, pp. 20–47.

Silverstone, R. (2005) 'The sociology of mediation and communication' in C. Calhoun, C. Rojek, and B. Turner (eds.) *The SAGE Handbook of Sociology*, London: Sage.

Stuart Santiago, A. (2011) 'Social media as mosquito press,' *Stuart Santiago*, www.stuartsantiago.com/social-media-as-mosquito-press (accessed April 10, 2013).

Tadiar, N. (2004) *Fantasy Production: Sexual Economies and Other Philippine Consequences in the New World Order*, Quezon City: Ateneo de Manila Press.

Teodoro, L. (1998) 'Covering the elite game' in L. Teodoro and M. De Jesus (eds.) *The Filipino Press and Media, Democracy and Development*, Quezon City: University of the Philippines Press.

Teodoro, L. and Kabatay, R. (1998) *Mass Media Laws and Regulations in the Philippines*, Quezon City: Asian Media Information and Communication Centre.

Tolentino, R. (2011) 'Kabataang Katawan, mall, at Syudad: Gitnang Uring Karanasan at Neoliberalismo,' paper presented at Space, Empire, and the Postcolonial Imagination Conference, Ateneo de Manila University, Quezon City, Philippines.

Tovera, D. (1975) *A History of English Teaching in the Philippines: From Uniligualism to Bilingualism*, PhD dissertation, UMI Dissertation Services, Ann Arbor.

Valisno, J. and Marcelo, S. (2011) 'Game shows and the culture of dependency,' *Business World*, November 17, www.bworldonline.com/weekender/content.php?id=41808 (accessed March 25, 2015).

Yean, S.C. (2008) 'Politics from below: culture, religion and popular politics in Tanaun City, Batangas,' *Philippine Studies*, 56(4): 413–42.

10 Taiyu serial dramas in Taiwan

A history of problem-making

Fang-Chih Irene Yang

The construction of a problem, be it a crisis or a moral panic, is an attempt of policing and control, for the maintenance of hegemony and authority (Hall et al. 1978). A problem emerges as a problem only when it is out of its proper place, just like dirt becomes dirt only when it is not properly placed in the earth. The elimination of dirt is necessary in maintaining the cleanliness of the social order (Douglas 2002). In other words, it is the need for a particular social arrangement that constitutes the existence of a problem. Taiyu,[1] the lingua franca of the Taiwanese, became a problem of dialect (called Minnanyu) to be eliminated when the KMT colonial regime moved to Taiwan, building it as a Chinese nation and instituting Mandarin as the national language. Television is central to the building of the Chinese nation. Taiyu serial dramas were broadcast soon after the first network was established in 1962, but have been constructed as the most problematic and debased genre since the early 1970s when the second TV station, CTV (1969), and the third, CTS (1971), were established and used serial drama to compete for profit. Accusations directed at the poverty of its quality and the vulgarity of the audiences have characterized mainstream criticisms and constructions of Taiyu serial dramas as problems from the 1970s to the present. This chapter investigates not only the how and what but also the why of this problem-construction, as an attempt to understand the power mechanisms at work in struggling for hegemonic control. It charts two historical moments – the 1970s and from the 1990s to the present – when language has played a significant role in the articulations of serial dramas as problems and explores the changing political, economic and cultural forces that situate them as problems worthy of discussion. I argue that the history of this problem-making demonstrates the centrality of Chinese culture in political domination through cultural means, with ethnic/class politics playing a central role in the maintenance of a hierarchical social order. In the 1970s, Chinese culture was used to create ethnic/class divisions within Taiwan while simultaneously creating the illusion of a symbolic whole under the name of the Republic of China. However, since the 1990s, and intensifying after the 2000s, with the entanglement of democratization and neoliberalization in Taiwan and the rise of China, the ethnic/class tension is not just complicated by conflicted national identifications and Chinese culture

Taiyu serial dramas in Taiwan 165

promoted by both the KMT Party's Republic of China and the People's Republic of China, but also for unification purposes. While democratization, which involved the search for Taiwanese identity, led to the rise of Taiyu-based Hsiangtu drama, the neoliberal definition of culture as economic resource, which consecrates Chinese culture through capital investment, facilitates this unification process while creating further ethnic/class/national identity divisions within Taiwan. The result is a disparaging of Taiyu-based culture in general and, in particular, Taiyu serial drama as a problem to be reformed.

Mapping conjunctures: the 1970s

After World War II, the Kuomintang (KMT) Party took over Taiwan from Japan in 1945. In 1947, martial law was implemented as a result of Taiwanese resistance against KMT colonial rule. When the KMT lost China to the Communist Party, they moved the Republic of China to Taiwan in 1949 and built Taiwan as a military base from which to mount the campaign to reclaim China.

Culture plays a significant role in the KMT's nation-building project. Chun points out that

> the reality of the 'Republic of China' is a paradigmatic instance of the nation as semiotic invention. The invention of 'traditional Chinese culture' as Taiwan's national culture is a 'hegemonic presence whose fate is linked inextricably to the very mechanism of political domination that has served to perpetuate the domination of the state.
>
> (Chun 2000: 10)

In legitimizing its minority rule, the KMT state on the one hand used traditional Chinese culture to create ethnic divisions (between Waishengren, Mainlanders who came with Chiang Kai-shek to Taiwan, and Bengshengren, the early settlers) in order to suppress and subordinate existing local culture in maintaining the privilege of the Mainlanders. On the other hand, it also used this culture to construct an all-embracing vision of Chinese history and civilization that transcends primordial sentiments and, as such, to create shared values for a newfound community called 'Cultural China'. In the name of national survival, different social/cultural engineering projects were enforced, backed by martial law, to produce subjects/citizens of Chinese culture (Chun 2000; Yang 2008a).

Chun identifies three phases of cultural policy enforced by the KMT state in creating/politicizing Chinese culture as the national culture: cultural reunification (1945–67), cultural renaissance (1967–77) and cultural reconstruction (1977–2000). In the first phase, Mandarin was instituted as the only and official language (to purge Japanese influence and to subordinate the local Taiwanese), which in turn became the precondition for the extensive inculcation of Chinese culture. The second stage was marked by 'a systematic effort to redefine the content of these ideas and values [of Chinese culture], to cultivate a large scale societal consciousness through existing institutional means and to use the vehicle of social expression as the motor for national development in other domains, economic and political' (Chun 2000: 12). The third stage is characterized by the 'domestication' of ethnic culture and the 'sublimation' of Chinese culture into desirable objects of consumption, a process which coincides with the liberalization policy and the development of the culture industry (Chun 2000: 14).

This section focuses on the second stage, from the mid-1960s to the mid-1970s, when Chinese culture, implemented through the policy of 'Chinese Culture Renaissance Movement' (*zhonghua wenhua fuxing yundong*), was situated as a rhetorical weapon against the communist Cultural Revolution. But in practice it was used against the local people and culture through its large-scale inculcation as the hegemonic form of societal consciousness: 'Specifically, the movement worked to strengthen national spirit education, promote Mandarin Chinese and carry on Confucian traditions and culture' (Lin 2005: 75). The aim of this Cultural Renaissance movement was to uphold Chiang's leadership through defending Chinese culture. 'Chinese culture' meant a culture of adhering to the Three Principles of the People, supporting combat missions, denouncing Mao Zedong and opposing communism (Lin 2005).

The particular arrangement of the TV industry needs to be understood within this political juncture in which culture became the primary weapon that the KMT party-state used to fight against not only communist China but also the Taiwanese locals. Not only was the establishment of the first TV station a symbol of competition with communist China, it was also used as a political propaganda tool to build the Chinese nation in Taiwan and strengthen KMT rule. The missions propagated in the Cultural Renaissance movement were written into the goals of the three networks. For example, from 1962 to 1969, TTV stated that its goal was to:

- correct social consciousness, maintain national interests and national dignity;
- adhere to government policies and promote anti-communism ideologies;
- emphasize traditional ethics and morality and maintain free democracies;
- use Mandarin as the primary language (Su 1991: 125).

In 1976, the three networks all emphasized the same goals: to use Mandarin and to promote the Three Principles of the People and national policies, anticommunist ideals and Chinese culture and tradition (Su 1991: 125).

Despite the political imperative to use TV for propaganda, the government was unwilling to invest in the infrastructure for the TV industry. This resulted in the particular arrangement of the Taiwanese TV industry, generally characterized as 'clientelism' or 'patron–client dependency' between the government and private capital. The government gave favours to private capital in exchange for capitalists' loyalty so that it was possible to use TV for political control, while the capitalists used their support from the government to further their economic and political capital (Lin 2006). The three networks have slightly different industrial structures, each controlled by different factions of the government (Ministry of Defense, Ministry of Education and the KMT Party), which form the institutions for establishing TV policies as well as the main body of censorship boards, while private capital came from local capitalists, KMT members and foreign capital (Lin 2006; Su 1991). As a result, two contradictory goals emerge: the government's need to use TV as a propaganda tool and the capitalists' need to earn profit (Lin 2006). These two goals provide the epistemological conditions for the articulation of the problem of serial dramas.

Constructing Taiyu/Minnanyu serial drama as a problem

As serial dramas are seen as the most profitable genre among the three networks, commercialization was identified as the root cause of the problem in this period: in order to pursue profits, it has been argued that serial dramas sacrificed their goal of educating the people: 'In order to attract more advertisers, the three networks have succumbed to advertisers' demand for more cruel and violent content with fighting scenes, strange spirits, vulgar and dialect programs, especially in Primetime serial dramas' (*Central Daily News* 1972). The problem of commercialization involved two dimensions: content and audience. With regard to the content, serial dramas are seen as bad programmes that do not live up to the goal of Chinese nation-building; they contain too much violence, superstition and crying, and too little Chinese tradition, culture and positive thinking. Second, the criticism of commercialization always assumes a hierarchical relationship between the critic/the ideal audience and the uneducated and uncultured mass, as 'TV has direct impact on our consciousness and it is like a hypodermic needle... program content exerts absolute impact on audiences, especially those with low knowledge level and children who are easily infected/influenced' (*United Daily News* 1972). In this context, the low knowledge level audiences are marked by their ethnicity/language as the majority of the Taiwanese (Bengshengren) (about 80 per cent) who speak Taiyu, Hakka and Japanese. At the same time, children and teenagers, who are the future citizens, are constructed as potentially under threat from their vulgar parents and grandparents who know little or no Mandarin but mostly Taiyu and are hence in need of TV's education.

Here's a typical example of how the problem of serial dramas tends to be expressed:

> Families with television share a common concern: too much Minnanyu [Taiyu], superstition, and fighting scenes... Current programs are under

168　*Fang-Chih Irene Yang*

the control of advertisers... The purpose of business is to earn profit, not ethics and morality, hence, they believe that the more vulgar the programs are, the more money they can earn... TV's function is education, good programs can cultivate the culture of the society while bad programs will degenerate our morality... We have old and honorable history, we can get program ideas from our history... Serial dramas should find material from history, on the one hand, it helps us understand and re-live our history; on the other hand, history can teach us how to be a good Chinese. As for Minnanyu programs, there shouldn't be too many. Language plays an influential role in promoting national solidarity and uniting the nation. As we are promoting Mandarin, we should maintain the absolute privilege status of Mandarin.

(Hu 1972)

Similar criticisms abound (Jiang 1979: 149) that succumbing to advertiser's demands will ruin 'the government and education system's effort in promoting traditional ethics and morality, science, and Mandarin education' along with the mental health of children and teenagers (*Central Daily News* 1972). Many solutions were offered at the time, including eliminating serial dramas altogether from TV and replacing them with TV news. However, most discussions focus on two solutions: first, nationalize TV to eliminate commercial influence; second, enforce content control, especially with regard to Taiyu programmes. The patron–client dependency that upholds the industrial structure makes content control the easiest. As a result, network self-regulations in 1972 as well as Regulations for National Broadcasting in 1976 and 1977 were implemented to control TV content.

Here, I identify the essence of these regulations/solutions to illustrate how controlling content was designed to maintain the power of the KMT Mainlander elite. First, with regard to language, the three networks' self-regulation in 1972 stated that dialect programmes should not exceed 16 per cent of all the programmes; only one Minnanyu programme was allowed in prime-time for all the networks, thus restricting Minnanyu programmes to marginal, non-prime-time slots. In the same year, the Ministry of Education ruled that each network was allowed to broadcast Minnanyu programmes for no more than one hour each day (Jiang 1979: 66). In 1976, the Information Bureau implemented the first Broadcasting Law, demanding a gradual reduction of dialect programmes each year. Second, the promotion of Chinese culture, ethics and tradition was translated into policy terms by way of a number of restrictions on drama content: no more than a quarter of the content to describe the dark side of life; no depiction of the triumph of the villain over the hero and ethnic/racial tensions; no negative portrayal of the rich or the upper class as immoral or as using their power to exploit people; no positive portrayal of the lower class or ordinary people as possessing a better sense of justice; no description of anti-family ethics and no negative portrayal of the military or government officials; and no depiction of people as possessing superpowers (Jiang 1979: 67–8). These policies were meant to create the illusion of a harmonious, peaceful and prosperous society under KMT rule and to disempower ordinary people by depriving them of their sense of justice and their power to revolt, while maintaining the hierarchically structured society according to the required ethnic/language/class division.

Chinese culture is constructed as the national culture and norm, and along with it the power of the Mainlander elite is secured through the construction of Taiyu serial dramas as low quality for uneducated audiences. The vulgarizing of Taiyu serial dramas along with the banning of the language in education and public life created profound effects in the production of a language hierarchy as well as a hierarchy among ethnicities, such that people who speak Mandarin are considered better educated and more cultivated, while people who speak Taiyu are uncultured and uneducated.

Mapping conjunctures: from the 1990s to the present

The suppression of Taiyu led to the near extinction of Taiyu serial drama for two decades; however, democratization and neoliberal privatization fertilized the soil for the emergence of Hsiangtu drama in the 1990s and idol drama in the 2000s. Democratization demanded the KMT Party-state to withdraw their control of the TV industry, leading to a series of impacts: privatization and the legalization of cable in 1993, establishment of FTV (the fourth network) in 1997 and the privatization of TTV in 2000s. Moreover, the restriction on Japanese audio-visual products was lifted in 1993, as well as the ban on the use of dialects. These policies provided the conditions for the emergence of Hsiangtu drama and idol drama. The former literally means 'rural and earthly drama' and is referred to as indigenous (*bentu*) drama that uses Taiyu as its primary language in depicting the family affairs taking place in Taiwan, while the latter refers to Mandarin-speaking, idol-based urban love stories. Hsiangtu drama from the start has been constructed as a problem of value. Its valuelessness is legitimized through its counterpart, idol drama. This section maps out the political economic context, mainly the hegemony of the Chinese-language market, impacting on the devaluing and problemizing of Hsiangtu drama.

Processes of democratization began in the late 1970s; it led to the establishment of the second party, the Democratic Progressive Party (DPP), in 1986, the lifting of martial law in 1987, direct presidential elections in 1996 and the election of a DPP president from 2000 to 2008. What characterizes Taiwan's democratic process is its entanglement with neoliberal globalization, which is further complicated by the rise of China as an economic power. Culture is the primary battlefield where in the entanglements of democratization and neoliberalization are played out. This is the third stage that Chun identifies as characterized by the 'domestication' of ethnic culture and the 'sublimation' of Chinese culture into desirable objects of consumption. Democratization in the 1990s revolved around issues of ethnicity and language, in particular,

170   *Fang-Chih Irene Yang*

the search for Taiwanese consciousness through a (re)discovery of Taiwan's languages, cultures and traditions. Culture, defined as a traditional way of life rooted in the local communities, became the resource for the construction of Taiwanese identity (as opposed to Chinese identity) in Taiwan's democratic/ decolonizing cultural movements. However, this notion of culture is increasingly in tension with the dominance of the global discourse of creative industries, which sees culture as an economic resource, especially since the 2000s, when the 'invasion' of the Korean Wave in Taiwan and across Asia demonstrated the success of South Korea's cultural-economic policy. The neoliberal redefinition of culture domesticates the democratization of Taiwanese consciousness through the commodification of ethnic culture, exemplified by the state's implementation of a 'Culture Production Industry' (*Wenhua chanye*) in 1995. However, since 2000, the definition of culture that is central to the formation of Taiwanese consciousness, despite its entanglement with commodification, has shifted to Cultural Creative Industry (*wenhua chuangyi chanye*), which treats culture purely as an economic resource (Yang 2008b), as exemplified by the claim that 'culture creative industry uses small to win big... it is the route to money' (Pan 2001). In 2008 the newly elected KMT president vowed to develop creative industry, with his policy consultant claiming that, '[w]e need to change our ideas and think of culture as a form of capital and as a technology that brings about economic development. We have entered the new age of "The Fourth Wave"' (Hao 2009: 16).

The 'sublimation' of Chinese culture cannot be separated from the globalization process; however, this sublimation, rather than being defined through the consumption of China in the form of symbols as Chun identifies in the late 1990s, should be analysed through the hegemony of the 'Chinese-language market' in the 2000s. The shifting meanings of culture since the millennium as a result of neoliberal globalization facilitate the revival of Chinese culture in Taiwan. By essentializing culture as an economic resource, traditional Chinese culture, in particular Confucian tradition, is constructed as a means for generating profit and crystallized into the business lingo of the 'Chinese-language market' (*Huayu shichang*).

The hegemony of the Chinese language market, although constructed through economic terms, needs to be understood through the changing political situations in Taiwan. Two factors are essential to the formation of this hegemony: first, the entanglement of neoliberalization and democratization leads to democratization without corresponding transitional justice in Taiwan. In the realm of the TV industry, the domination of the KMT Waisheng elite was never addressed or reformed, but was now complicated by the privatization of the industry that led to the penetration of China's influences through capital investment, with these elites playing a major role in this process. Media industries which promote pro-China agendas are financially supported by the Chinese state (Hut 2012), leading to the formation of a new patron–client dependency between pro-China capitalists and the Chinese state. Second, with the loss of political office in 2000, the KMT

Party officially took up the strategy of allying with communist China to fight against the pro-independence DPP Party (*liangong zhi taidu*) in 2006. The support of China in winning presidential elections in 2008 and 2012 meant that the KMT's significant agenda became to promote economic and cultural integration with China, resulting in the re-visibility of 'traditional Chinese culture' in education, business and media, along with a polarization of wealth between the pro-China rich capitalists and the poor majority.

Culture plays a significant part in this process of neoliberalization through China for political ends. The Chinese state, KMT state and cross-strait capitalists promulgated a cultural-economic concept of the 'Chinese-language market' for political purposes. In this discourse, what binds together China and Taiwan through the Chinese-language market is Chinese culture, and Taiwan is best equipped to sell Chinese culture not only because it preserved Chinese culture but also because of its more sophisticated and advanced media industry: 'Taiwan's strength is its Chinese culture with Taiwanese characteristics. It is its best niche in the world, we should keep this position in the Chinese World... this is Taiwanese producers' strength' (Ma 2010: 95). Proponents of this view in Taiwan are mostly Mainlanders who occupy significant positions in the creative industries in Taiwan (such as Wang Wei-Zhong) as well as political positions (such as Long Ying-Tai, the minister of culture in Taiwan).

Across the Strait, both the Chinese state and Chinese entertainment businesses also undertake the mission to promote this view. For example, Liu Chang-le, the director for Phoenix Media Corporations in China, who is said to be 'a master who thinks from the perspective of all the Chinese around the world' claims that

> I think Taiwan has the great potential to be the dream factory for the Chinese in the world because of its rich experiences and great tradition. The best thing for Taiwan is to persist in promoting traditional Chinese culture... Taiwan should position itself as the foundation of traditional Chinese culture, using Chinese popular culture such as pop music and TV serial dramas as its modern expression.
>
> (Wu 2010: 110)

Ironically, the Chinese state, while silent on the impacts of the Cultural Revolution that destroyed traditional Chinese culture, now embraces Chinese culture as its combat strategy in uniting Taiwan. Chinese culture is constructed as shared by all Chinese because it is the greatest and longest civilization based on blood and morality. Zhou (2009) states that 'promoting Chinese culture is the shared project for scholars on both sides of the Strait' (Zhou 2009) and cites the Taiwanese scholar, Huang:

> it is the five thousand years of history that links our blood together and supports our shared values from both sides of the Strait. Chinese culture has been the bedrock for maintaining peace and harmony across the

Strait. To ground Chinese culture as our principle for cultural exchange is to intensify our sense of identity and belonging for the same culture, ancestors, and bloodline.

(Zhou 2009)

In 2008, China's president Hu Jintao announced 'Hu's six points' (*Hu liu-dian*) as policy guidelines, including promoting Chinese culture and emphasizing its spiritual connection with Taiwan (Zhou 2009). Similarly, president Xi Jinping, after assuming power in 2012, continued to use Chinese culture as a weapon for uniting Taiwan. As he claims, 'We hope people across the Strait can stay in solidarity and cooperate together in order to contribute to the recovery of Chinese culture and hence, the Chinese nation' (Zhou 2009). The minister of culture from China, Tsai Wu, further points out, 'we will continue to strengthen the cultural exchange across the Strait, endorse the development and promotion of Chinese culture, and fortify the cooperation between the culture creative industries on both sides of the Strait in order to increase their competitive edge in the world' (Tsuyoshi 2013).

From the 1990s, the older form of Chinese culture supported by the Waisheng elite persisted, even though it was challenged by the search for Taiwanese identity through a discovery of Taiwanese culture as a result of democratization. However, since the 2000s, neoliberalization, in particular, through China re-privileges Chinese culture through the economic rhetoric of the Chinese language market. The pro-China Waisheng elite benefit from being the dependent client of the patron Chinese state, along with the cross-straits capitalists, by promoting traditional Chinese culture for unification while simultaneously engaging in struggles to undermine Taiwanese culture/language. This constitutes the larger context in which Taiwan's TV industry has to work.

The TV drama industry in neoliberal times

Democratization through Bengtuhua (indigenization or Taiwanization) was the major factor contributing to the rise and popularity of Hsiangtu drama in the 1990s. First, the Bentuhua movement in the political sphere led to the search for Taiwanese consciousness and the construction of Taiwanese identity. Hsiangtu drama used Taiwan as the backdrop and addressed issues that were relevant to Taiwan's culture and society. Second, at the level of culture, Bengtuhua focused on the issue of ethnicity (divided through language). Third, democratic reform led to more open elections at the level of local government. The three networks, controlled by the KMT, used Taiyu as a gesture to promote 'the harmony of ethnicities' in order to get votes from the Taiwanese (Ko 1999). Hsiangtu drama was part of this political machine:

It suffices to say that 1995 and 1996 were the times when KMT power utilized, if not manipulated, the social meanings evoked by [Hsiangtu]

Taiyu serial dramas in Taiwan 173

dramas for its own political ends. The strategy was to re-formulate the raised anti-mainlander, anti-KMT hostility, to dissociate the KMT from the mainlander-complex, and to articulate the KMT with a more localized and grass-rooted image of President Lee Teng-Hui.

(Ko 1999: 47)

This is evidenced by the fact that Hsiangtu drama was banned from 1992 to 1994 when the KMT Party did not fare well in elections. It was only when the first directly elected president, Lee Teng-Hui, of Bengsheng ethnicity, assumed power in 1996 that Hsiangtu drama became a constant feature in Taiwan's television (Ko 1999).

Democratization as privatization also led to the constant presence of East Asia through TV dramas – mainly, Japanese and Korean dramas. The establishment of Japanese cable channels and the import of Japanese trendy dramas led to the Japan craze phenomenon in the 1990s. This, in turn, enabled the TV industry to copy Japanese scripts and formats and remake them as idol dramas in Taiwan. As opposed to Hsiangtu drama that targets older, working-class, Taiyu-speaking audiences who favour family-centred, mother- and daughter-in-law plots, idol dramas feature the love stories of young, Mandarin-speaking career-women in urban settings. As idol-driven placement ads fit the new lifestyle advertising, their ability to generate profit from the international market allows their cultural value to be elevated from being a symbol of re-colonization by Japan to becoming the driving force in the making of the Chinese Wave. This value shift is embedded in the hegemony of the Chinese-language market, which can only be understood through the 'China factor'.

As soon as Taiwan and China opened the door for exchange in the late 1980s and early 1990s, the Taiwan TV industry immediately caught 'Mainland Fever' (Lin 1991a). The TV industry, mostly controlled by Mainlander elites from the KMT Party, went to China to produce dramas that featured love stories taking place in the 'actual' China, replacing the constructed imaginary China that was the previous mainstream. As Bentuhua has given rise to the popularity of Hsiangtu drama, these Mainlander producers and directors began to ride on the trend of neoliberal globalization and use the notion of an overseas market (the Chinese market) to emphasize the value of these TV dramas shot in China. Since the 2000s, with the success of the Japanese-scripted, Taiwan-produced idol drama *Meteor Garden* in Asia, idol drama is touted as Taiwan's comparative advantage in the new cultural economy. Moreover, the popularity of idol dramas in China further heightened the significance of the concept of the Chinese-language market promoted by the Taiwanese industry and, later, by the Chinese state and Chinese capitalists.

In this discourse, China is described as the large market where the real profit lies while Taiwan is depicted as a small market that has no potential for generating profit. As Lihpao's editorial points out,

Taiwan's TV dramas need to leave Taiwan in order to reach the broader Chinese language audiences. The basic point is, we need to see China's large population as the market. If we position our dramas in the Chinese language world, even if they have low ratings, it also means a lot of people. The Chinese language market, of course, refers to Mainland China across the Strait.

(Lihpao 2011)

Caught in this entangled process of democratization, which views culture as a resource for Taiwanese identity construction, and neoliberalization, which treats culture as an economic resource, complicated by ethnic as well as political conflicts in Taiwan, Hsiangtu drama has become the placeholder for all these unresolved conflicts and anxieties being articulated as the problem of Taiwan's culture, and the Mainlander-controlled television industry in particular.

Hsiangtu drama as the problem

Two concepts are central to the construction of Hsiangtu drama as problematic: quality and commercialization (market). These two concepts, however, are intricately but contradictorily articulated. The terms of the debate were set when Hsiangtu dramas gained popularity in the 1990s, making the Mainlander producers, directors and managers, as well as actors and actresses, feel displaced (Ko 1999). When the first prime-time Taiyu Hsiangtu drama *Ai* (*Love*) was featured in 1990, the language had to be changed to Mandarin due to policy regulations; however, as more TV dramas began to use Taiyu as a result of the KMT's need to get votes from the Taiwanese (hence, looser regulations), criticisms focused on the use of Taiyu in dramas as the cause of ethnic tensions: 'It is inappropriate for Mandarin dramas to overuse Minnanyu... we need to trim down Minnanyu in order to "balance" language use so as to avoid the tensions caused by Mandarin-speaking actors and actresses' (Lin 1991b).

After 1993, when the language restrictions were relaxed, Hsiangtu drama reached its peak. However, at the same time, Hsiangtu drama is constructed as made for an elementary school-level audience (Chen 1997a) and, thus, is of low taste and low quality. The concepts of international audience, overseas audience or international perspective are constantly invoked to justify Hsiangtu drama's 'small feet', which limit the TV industry's becoming international (Chen 1997b: 12). The Mainlander producers and directors played a significant part in articulating the problem of Hsiangtu drama as too local, too small-minded. For example, the producer of the first Hsiangtu drama, *Ai* (*Love*), Kuo Jiang-hong, claimed he was not happy to see the 'overflooding' of Hsiangtu drama in prime-time: '[Hsiangtu drama] has good ratings but it does not have overseas markets.' He was disappointed at 'the short-sightedness of the networks' and advocated that the three networks should have their own principles and directions. Despite the good ratings generated from Hsiangtu drama, 'he will insist on having an "international perspective"' (*guoji guan*) (Lin 1994). Moreover, the chief manager of CTS in an internal policy meeting stated, 'television should lead the fashion, not be led by the audiences; media business should aim at more trendy topics and international markets, not to serve elementary-school level audiences' (Chen 1997b; Ko 1999: 64–5). Media celebrate these producers as having the vision to develop overseas markets and move forward in leaving Taiwan's small, local audience behind for the international world. 'New shows have begun to move forward to seriously consider the Chinese language market' (Chen 1997a).

Ethnic politics plays a significant part in determining the quality of the drama. If Hsiangtu drama's low quality is constructed through its articulation association with elementary school-level audiences, referring mainly to the Bengshengren who do not speak (standard) Mandarin, by implication the good-quality TV dramas are made by Mainlanders. Coexisting with the emergence of Hsiangtu drama is 'China Fever' in the TV industry. While the production of Hsiangtu drama causes concerns over the lowering of cultural taste, Mainlander TV producers such as Qiong Yao and Pei-pei Yang are praised for their insistence on quality by going to China to shoot dramas, despite the uncertainty of financial returns (Lin 1994). Moreover, the only quality Hsiangtu drama to be recognized is *The First Family* (*Diyi shijia*), a drama praised for its use of an all-Mainlander team as its base for production. It is constructed as 'a breakthrough in Hsiangtu drama genre' and represents 'Hsiangtu drama's conscience' because of its 'excellent skills in the well-managed dialogue, along with humour, humanity, and shared sentiments' (Chen 1996). Moreover, *China Times*' Center for Cultural News held a workshop called 'Debates on Artworks Under the Spotlight' (*jiaodian zuopin lunzhan*) and praised the show as 'our prospect for the future direction' of drama production (Chen 1996: 22).

Since the 2000s, ethnic politics has become a dirty concept in Taiwan, as it was seen to divide Taiwan and its association with electoral politics. These ethnic tensions became submerged in public discourse, despite their ghostly presence in everyday life. However, the entangled concepts of quality and market/audience that were used to denigrate Hsiangtu drama persist, albeit in a more complicated and contradictory manner.

In terms of quality, the notion of 'realism' is used in contradictory ways in order to situate Hsiangtu dramas as inferior to idol drama. On the one hand, Hsiangtu drama is criticized for not being real enough, for not reflecting the reality of the society (Chang 2013). Taiwan's Hsiangtu drama is very similar to American soap opera in terms of form and content. In terms of form, it follows the melodramatic mode, accentuating the binaries of right and wrong, hate and love in order to incite intense feelings and to eventually settle for the triumph of virtue over evil. Moreover, it follows the American 'neverending' format, which allows the drama to run for two or three years, depending on the ratings. In terms of content, it incorporates social events and timely issues, from graft and corruption in politics to topical references from Korean dramas. The plot is criticized for its diversion from reality as it is filled with 'perversion' and 'rotten tricks' including 'messy male/female relationships, life full of obstacles, tragic love, strange diseases, suicides and so on' (Zhu 2005: 13). American soap opera, ironically, is constructed as realistic: 'American soap operas are popular because they are realistic. They offer a real world for housewives to reflect on and learn how to solve their daily problems. This is what Taiwan's serial drama lacks' (Hsie 1999).

Realism is also used to elevate the quality of Korean idol dramas over Hsiangtu dramas. Korean dramas are considered more real through the concept of 'approximating everyday life' (*shenghuohua*), which facilitates women's identification (Yang 2008a). However, this principle of realism bends when applied to Hsiangtu drama. Hsiangtu drama is considered 'too real' to be love fantasies for women. Heiniao Lizi, a columnist on TV dramas in the *China Times*, claims,

> Are there any characters in Bentu [Hsiangtu] drama who can incite women's desire?... Who would dream about the kind of life that is full of schemes and dirty power struggles? Who would dream of competing for corporate ownership? You only have to ask the audiences whether they identify with the characters to understand how removed our TV industry is from our audiences.
>
> (Heiniao 2006)

The value of Korean drama or idol dramas in general lies in their escapist nature as love fantasies, something that the realistic Hsiangtu drama lacks.

The problem of Hsiangtu drama as either too unrealistic or too realistic is seen as the result of the TV industry's pursuit of ratings. Terms such as 'perversion' and 'exaggerated plot' are constantly invoked as examples of the problem of the commercialization of culture (Zhu 2005; TVBS News 2011: 13). Even Zheng Wen-hua, the scriptwriter of a very popular Hsiangtu drama, *Hurricane*, said the show was low-quality and vulgar and that, in order to survive, he has lost his principles and ideals (Yeh 2004). Implicit in these comments is the notion of vulgar audience and vulgarity is intertwined with gender, ethnicity and uneven geographic development, as demonstrated through the stereotypical image of the Hsiangtu drama audience, 'the rural obason' (Yang 2008a).

If Hsiangtu drama's low quality is attributed to excessive commercialization, it is also censured ironically for a lack of commercialization. Through the binary construction of the local versus the global/international and the privileging of the global over the local in terms of the size of the market, Hsiangtu drama is constructed as a problem because of its association with Bentu (local), meaning Taiyu language and culture. As value has 'no proper body of its own but can be expressed only in differential' (Anagnost 2004: 191), the derogation of Hsiangtu drama is made through the construction of idol drama as not only having the quality to 'open up people's mind and intellect' but as also 'accompanied by a huge consumer market' (Yeh 1999), offering 'business opportunities not just limited to idols'. Moreover, it also helps to sow the seeds to spread Taiwan's culture abroad and should be considered a 'good weapon to sell Taiwan overseas' and a form of soft power (*Commerce Time* 2012). Hsiangtu drama, despite its good ratings both in Taiwan and in South-East Asian countries such as Singapore and Malaysia, is constructed as having no market outside Taiwan (Lin 2003).

However, this international market is in effect defined as the China market. This is due to the fact that, in the 1990s, multinational corporations used Taiwan as a stepping stone to China's market, particularly in the domain of music. Many Mainlanders rode this wave to go to China and used the Chinese-language market as their leverage in the competitive field of the TV industry. Especially after 2008, with the support of the KMT state, the Chinese state and cross-strait capitalists, the Chinese-language market has become the unchallenged hegemony used to derogate the local as vulgar in cultural taste due to its small market size, be it Hsiangtu dramas or Taiyu-based movies and music. As the Taiwanese director Chen Kuo-chiang, who now works for a Chinese corporation, Huayi Brothers, says, 'any [cultural] commodity that appeals to the local audience can only reap profits from the local audience and that determines its significance... If we only engage with the audiences from the South [where Taiyu is still the lingua franca], we will never produce big international hits' (*TVBS News* 2013: 30). 'We need a mainstream market to nourish our own subjectivity and that market is China' (Lin 2003).

Within this context where culture becomes an economic resource and quality is measured in market terms, the local, embodied by Hsiangtu drama, becomes a dirty word, a problem to be solved. The solutions offered include: first, to 'target the middle class or elite market'; second, to 'walk out of Taiwan to embrace the broader Chinese language audiences' (Lihpao 2011). Despite the fact that Taiwan has a quite well-educated population and a strong middle class, these two solutions suggest that that the local audiences, the Taiwanese, are not middle-class or elite, and that the Chinese are the right audience. The association of cultivated taste with Chinese (Huaren) and vulgarity with Taiwanese (those who are from the south who speak Taiyu) through market terms cannot make sense unless analysed from the historical perspective of the KMT colonial period.

The dominance of the Chinese-language market led San-Li, the most significant TV station for idol drama and Hsiangtu drama production, to change its policy and produce a new genre of TV drama, Huaju (Chinese drama) in 2012. Huaju, according to San-Li, is made for Chinese people in general, and Chinese on the Mainland in particular, and is meant to bring out the Chinese Wave in Asia. However, to produce and sell Chinese dramas in China also means an emphasis on hierarchically structured family relations (in the name of Confucian tradition) and the elimination of anything offensive to the Chinese state, including San-Li's cancelling of the most popular political show in Taiwan, which advocated Taiwan's independence, in order to appease Beijing.

Conclusion

The construction of Taiyu serial TV dramas as problems can only make sense in the history of the implementation of TV to promote Chinese culture and Mandarin by the KMT state in the 1970s, the democratic movements in the 1990s and the hegemony of the Chinese-language market, supported by the Taiwanese state's policy to neoliberalize through China and the Chinese state's aim to unite Taiwan. Ethnic/language politics is central to this process. In the 1970s, within the patron–client based political-economic industrial structure, TV dramas carried the mission of inculcating Chinese culture through entertainment. Mandarin, imposed by the KMT state as the national language, was seen as the true expression of Chinese culture, which was used to unite the nation. However, the imposition of Mandarin worked not to unite the nation but to create and maintain ethnic division in order to subordinate the non-Mandarin-speaking people. Within this context, Taiyu serial dramas became a problem of quality caused by commercialization, with the state offering the legal solution to gradually eliminate the 'dialects'.

Democratization, which foregrounds issues of ethnicity/language, led to the rise of Taiwanese consciousness and, hence, the emergence and popularity of Hsiangtu drama. However, with the entanglement of democratization and neoliberal globalization, culture became an economic resource. Chinese culture, through the economic rhetoric of the Chinese language market, became leverage for the Mainlander elite, who have dominated the TV industry since its inception, to collaborate with Chinese capitalists, the KMT state and the Chinese state in maintaining their power. Hsiangtu drama, which uses Taiyu and addresses Taiwanese audiences, became a problem in need of reform. The concepts of realism and commercialization are contradictorily articulated to demonstrate Hisangtu drama's low quality as a way of increasing the value of Chinese-market-based, Mandarin-speaking dramas that promote Chinese culture.

Two counter-discourses are used to defend Hsiangtu dramas, but both fail to challenge the hegemony of Chinese culture, now transformed into the Chinese-language market. The first discourse is articulated by fan audiences: 'it's just entertainment, there is no need to be so serious about it' (Suzhu 2003). This discourse reinforces the dominant quality discourse that sees Hsiangtu drama as having no cultural value, but being a form of brainless entertainment; hence, not worthy of paying attention to. The second discourse adheres to the neoliberal definition of culture which values the quality of culture in terms of its economic value. It elevates the status of Hsiangtu drama by claiming South-East Asia as its overseas market, and emphasizes the profits it generates from placement ads and tourism (Huang et al. 2013). Instead of challenging the ethnic politics that undergird the political-economic process of value production, both these two counter-discourses unquestionably adopt the terms that are used to demean Taiyu serial drama. By using the master's tool, these limited and scattered resistances do not dismantle the master's house, but strengthen the hegemony of culture as economic resource and Mandarin/Chinese culture as quality.

The history of Taiyu-based serial drama as a problem demonstrates the centrality of Chinese culture in political domination through cultural means. It maintains the existing regime in order to benefit certain groups of people (based on ethnicity and class). However, the persistent popularity of Taiyu-based dramas speaks to people's need for local culture, for a sense of community, based on their everyday life experiences and the languages they speak. This is the domain of the social and Taiyu serial drama is the primary cultural form that undertakes the mediation of the social. If, as Bauman (2002) suggests, the social is the space where the political can be nourished then the celebration of Chinese culture through the logic of the economy by cross-strait capitalists, the KMT state and the Chinese state is an attempt to eliminate this political space for domination.

Note

1 Taiyu is the lingua franca of the people who lived in Taiwan before the KMT's language reform. The KMT party calls it Minnanyu to emphasize its provincial character, in order to legitimate the claim of a Republic of China that includes Taiwan. It is also called Hokklo because it originates from the Hokklo area. But I use the term Taiyu, not only because it has been called Taiyu since the Japanese colonial period among the Taiwanese population, but also to claim it as a language rather than a dialect.

References

Anagnost, A. (2004) 'The corporeal politics of quality', *Public Culture*, 16(2): 189–208.

Bauman, Z. (2002) *Society Under Siege*, Cambridge: Polity Press.

Central Daily News (1972) 'The impact of violent (dadou) TV programs on the young generation', *Central Daily News*, 14 January, p. 2.

Chang, C. (2013) 'Serial dramas do not reflect social reality', *United Daily News*, 9 April, p. D04.

Chen, N.T. (1991) 'The world view of the prime time', *Minsheng Daily*, 5 March, p. 21.

Chen, N.T. (1996) '*First Family* seeks the first in ranking: Mainlander production crew – a brand new picture for Hsiangtu drama', *Minsheng Daily*, 6 May.

Chen, N.T. (1997a) 'Small-feet Hsiangtu drama hardly takes international road', *Minsheng Daily*, 13 January, p. 12.

Chen, N.T. (1997b) 'The world view of the eight o'clock serial', *Minsheng Daily*, 15 January, p. 12.

China Times (1996) '*First Family*: leaving Hsiangtu drama's tragic feeling?', *China Times*, 24 June, p. 22.

China Times (2006) 'Give dreamers the right to dreams', *China Times*, 14 January, p. D4.

Chun, A. (2000) 'Democracy as hegemony, globalization as indigenization, or the "culture" in Taiwanese national politics' in Wei-Chin Lee (ed.) *Taiwan in Perspective*, Leiden: Brill Publications, pp. 7–27.

180   *Fang-Chih Irene Yang*

Commerce Time (2012) 'Idol dramas business opportunities are not just limited to idols', *Commerce Time*, 4 April, p. A4.

Douglas, M. (2002) *Purity and Danger: An Analysis of the Concepts of Pollution and Taboo*, New York: Routledge.

Hall, S., Critcher, C., Jefferson, T., Clarke, J. and Roberts, B. (1978) *Policing the Crisis: Mugging, the State, and Law and Order*, London: Macmillan.

Hao, M.Y. (2009) ' "Culture" activates the "fourth wave of the economy"', www. cw.com.tw/article/article.action?id=5005826 (accessed 10 July 2013).

Heniao, L. (2006) 'Give drama lovers the right to dream', *China Times*, 14 January.

Hsie, P.H. (1999) 'American soap operas', *Central Daily*, 14 June, p. 18.

Hu, Y.R. (1972) 'Chen, Li-fu talks about the improvement of TV programs', *Central Daily*, 4 April, p. 3.

Huang, R.P., You, Z.H. and Chen, Y.H. (2013) 'Studio opens up for tourism, creating Tailiu', *China Times*, 13 January, http://showbiz.chinatimes.com/showbiz/110511/112013011300002.html (accessed 10 June 2013).

Hut, K.K. (2012) 'The specter of China in Taiwan's media', http://clique2008.blogspot.fr/2013/09/by_24.html (accessed 20 October 2013).

Jiang, L.Z. (1976) *The Writing and Production of TV Dramas*, Taipei: Li-ming Publications.

Jiang, L.Z. (1979) *General Discussions on TV*, Minsheng: Daily Publications.

Ko, Y.F. (1999) *Nation, History, and Culture: A Case Study on Taiwanese Primetime Television*, PhD dissertation, University of Wisconsin-Madison.

Lihpao (2011) 'Media business and the topic of the third woman', 26 April, www. lihpao.com/?action-viewnews-itemid-106531 (accessed 12 March 2013).

Lin, G.S. (2005) *The Study of the Committee for the Promotion of Chinese Cultural Renaissance Movement (1966–1975): The Establishment and Transformation of Ruling Legitimacy*, Taipei: Daw Shiang Publishing.

Lin, L.H. (2006) 'Capital formation in Taiwan's television under the authoritarian rule', *Chinese Journal of Communication Research*, 9: 71–111.

Lin, M.S. (1991a) 'Mainland fever cannot be stopped', *China Times*, 5 March, p. 21.

Lin, M.S. (1991b) 'Inappropriate for Mandarin drama to overuse Minnan language', *China Times*, 22 October, p. 22.

Lin, M.S. (1994) 'Hsiangtu drama tastes sweetness, not afraid of audiences getting bored', *China Times*, 30 December, p. 22.

Lin, Z.Z. (2003) 'Special issue on globalizing or being globalized?', *China Times*, 7 February, p. 13.

Ma, Y.L. (2010) 'Claiming to be king in Taiwan: Wei-Zhong group seeks influence in media business', *Commonwealth Magazine*, 45: 94–7.

Pan, G. (2001) 'Special report: culture industry uses small to win big: knowledge economy creates money for the future', *China Times*, 22 June, p. 21.

Scott, D. (2004) *Conscripts of Modernity: The Tragedy of Colonial Enlightenment*, Durham, NC: Duke University Press.

Su, H. (1991) *The Study on the Cultural Implications of TV Programs in Taiwan: A Case Studies on Dialect Programs*, PhD Dissertation, National Cheng Chih University.

Suzhu (2003) 'Pilihuo is just entertainment, no need to be serious', *Minsheng Daily*, 5 July, p. C7.

Tsuyoshi, Nojima (2013) 'Both China and Taiwan embrace the flag of "Chinese culture"', 29 May, http://newtalk.tw/blog_read.php?oid=18569 (accessed 10 June 2013).

Taiyu serial dramas in Taiwan   181

TVBS News (2011) 'Hsiangtu dramas compete for ratings, using exaggerated plot such as revenge and blood cancer', 3 December, www.tvbs.com.tw/news/news_list.asp?no=betty0045520111203121704 (accessed 10 June 2013).

TVBS News (2013) 'National cinema comes back to compete for the market: it's hard for local films to enter into international market?', http://news.tvbs.com.tw/entry/202527 (accessed 30 March 2013).

United Daily News (1972) 'Our views toward the improvement of TV management and programs', *United Daily News*, 24 November, p 2.

United Daily News (1976) 'The three networks propose solutions to improve the content of TV programs', *United Daily News*, 7 September, p. 9.

Wang, J.H. (1993) 'The control of broadcast media' in *Deconstructing Broadcast and Electronic Media: Building New Media Order*, Taipei: Yun Chen Publications, pp. 77–128.

Wu, D.U. (1986) *Behind the Screen*, Taipei: Cultural Construction Committee, Ministry of Executive Yuan.

Wu, Y.Y. (2010) 'The breakthrough in culture creative industry is to embrace "pan-Chineseness"', *Commonwealth Magazine*, 440: 110–11.

Yang, I.F.-C. (2008a) 'The gentrification of "Korean dramas" in Taiwan', *China Information: A Journal on Contemporary China Studies*, 22(2): 277–304.

Yang, I.F.-C. (2008b) *'Rapping Korean Wave' East Asian Pop Culture: Analyzing the Korean Wave*, Hong Kong: Hong Kong University Press.

Yeh, J.J. (1999) 'Japan, idols, drama', *Central Daily*, 21 March, p. 19.

Yeh, Y.H. (2004) 'Zheng Wen-hua: Taiwan *Hurricane* is rough and vulgar', *United Daily News*, 28 September, p. D02.

Zhou, T.Z. (2009) 'Chinese culture, Taiwanese culture, and peaceful unification', *China Review*, 23 September, http://hk.crntt.com/doc/1010/8/4/4/101084434.html (accessed 10 June 2013).

Zhu, P.J. (2005) 'Primetime Hsiangtu drama uses perversion to fight for ratings', *Minsheng Daily*, 13 September, p. C3.

11 Shifts in Korean television music programmes

Democratization, transnationalization, digitalization

Sun Jung

Korea was the fifteenth country in the world to start television broadcasting when it first launched in Seoul in 1956. Since then, the structure, content and policies concerning Korean television have continuously transformed, due largely to changing contextual circumstances such as wide-ranging socio-political democratization and the rise of the neoliberal global economic system and digital technologies. Up until the 1980s, the oligopolistic structure of the two public broadcasting networks – Korean Broadcasting System (KBS) and Munhwa Broadcasting Corporation (MBC) – dominated the broadcasting market. However the landscape has dramatically changed since the early 1990s, with 11 newly launched commercial terrestrial broadcasting channels (including Seoul Broadcasting System (SBS) in December 1991) and 153 cable channels when the multichannel television era began (Jin 2005: 1). A digital satellite television system called Skylife was launched in March 2002, and airs 176 channels at the time of writing. Such changes stem from the shift in the domestic political climate where liberalization and privatization were promoted in assertively practiced neoliberal reform movement in the early 1980s, as well as changes in the global cultural industry environments based largely on globalization and the development of digital technologies. This chapter explores democratization, transnationalization and digitalization, three active factors within Korean television broadcasting by analysing changes and shifts in popular music programmes.

Although 'K-pop' widely refers today to Korean popular music, there was no such term during the early music show era. According to Furuya Masayuki (2010), K-pop is the Korean equivalent to J-pop (Japanese popular music), and was coined retrospectively after the initial idol boom at the end of the 1990s. K-pop does not therefore represent the entire Korean music industry, but rather refers only to the recently emerging popular phenomenon centred on idol music. Indeed, some fandoms outside Korea identify K-pop with idol pop music (D.Y. Lee 2011: 38). Korean popular music pre-K-pop was called *gayo* (가요) and its origins can be traced to the Japanese colonial period (1910–45). Before today's idol music-dominant K-pop market, the *gayo* market showcased various music genres including folk, rock and *trot*.[1] As public demand for more representative coverage of musical genres in the media increases, television networks have recently attempted to include more non-idol music in their programming. This article identifies key changes in music programmes from the pre-K-pop *gayo* era to the current DMB (digital multimedia broadcasting) era.

First, this chapter introduces the brief history of Korean television by focusing on the socio-political contexts from the 1960s to today, and key broadcasting policies across the period (e.g., mass media reorganization and 'general service' cable television channels policy). This section then considers the reformation of the broadcasting system and its content, and audience movements against politically biased policies. Second, it explores the ways contemporary Korean music programmes organize transculturally connected shows both in and outside Korea, embracing multinational audiences. Reflecting the recent success of K-pop internationally, this new trend demonstrates globalization and the transnationalization strategies of the Korean broadcasting sector in the neoliberal economic setting. Lastly, the chapter examines the newly emerging digital technology-empowered television broadcasting environment, focusing on cable television and the Internet. This section focuses on the ways in which many television audition programmes employ YouTube to recruit new foreign artists as well as to promote their programmes to the overseas market. In conclusion, the future of Korean television music programmes – driven as they are predominantly by the transnationalization and digitalization of the broadcasting environment – is predicted to attract an increase in both global capital and human resources within the neoliberal world order.

Birth and development of music programmes in the 1960s and 1970s

Television broadcasting in Korea began on 12 May 1956, when the Korea Office Radio Corporation of America Distributor (KORCAD) beamed television signals in Seoul (with the call sign HLKZ) where only 300 television sets were in the country (Shim and Jin 2007: 162). In 1961, army general Park Chung-Hee seized power through a military coup, and this authoritarian rule led the country into an era of state-controlled export-oriented industrialization based on tight cooperation between the state and the economic sector. As the Park regime saw the critical role of broadcasting in diffusing its new political order and economic ideologies, it launched the state-owned KBS in 1961 and began television broadcasts (Shim and Jin 2007). In addition to KBS, the Park regime allowed two commercial broadcasters – Tongyang Broadcasting Company (TBC) in 1964 and Munhwa Broadcasting Corporation (MBC) in 1969 – to engage in television broadcasting. Since its birth in the period from the early 1960s until the 1980s, the Korean television system thus constituted a mixture of state-owned and private-commercial networks (Kim 1997). During military regimes from Park Chung-Hee's to Chun Doo-Hwan's (1961–88), the three broadcasting networks KBS1, KBS2 (formerly TBC) and MBC came under tight state control and began to function as speakers of the illegitimate regime

184   *Sun Jung*

Table 11.1 Five periods in Korean television broadcasting

Period	Characteristics
December 1961–December 1964	Government network (KBS) monopoly
December 1964–August 1969	Duopolistic competition between government network (KBS) and commercial network (TBC)
August 1969–December 1980	Oligopolistic competition among the three networks (KBS, TBC and MBC); oligopolistic equilibrium among networks
December 1980–November 1987	Authoritative government control of broadcasting, virtually a KBS monopoly
November 1987–Present	Liberalization of broadcasting and rapid diffusion of new competitive media; competition between the three networks (KBS, MBC and SBS), [cable channels (particularly general-service cable channels) and online channels]

Source: Lee and Youn 1995: 59–60

(Kim 1997; Shim and Jin 2007). However, with the rise of democratization starting in the late 1980s and the rapid adoption of neoliberal economic and media policies in the 1990s, the Korean broadcasting environment has come to enjoy deregulation, liberalization and privatization (Kim 1997; Shim and Jin 2007). According to Lee Joon-Ho and Youn Sug-Min, the history of Korean television broadcasting can be divided into five periods according to the industrial structure changes (see Table 11.1). Furthermore, cable and satellite televisions emerged in the late 1980s as a new mode of broadcasting as well as viewing, expanding television viewership experiences.

In his analysis of Korea's music programmes during the 1960s and 1970s, Kim Jong-Jin remarked that music programmes were at the centre of the rivalry between KBS, TBC and MBC during the third phase of Korean television broadcasting from 1969 to 1980 (Kim 2010: 16). For example, entertainment shows made up a significant part of KBS programming, accounting for 61.9 per cent of total programme hours in 1969 (as opposed to 28 per cent in 1962) to compete with TBC and MBC (Jin 2005: 92). KBS's first music programme was called *TV Grand Show* and was launched on 31 December 1961 when KBS began. It later changed its name to *KBS Grand Show* and has since become the signature programme of KBS among others (see Table 11.2).

TV Grand Show was a weekly programme that aired every Monday from 8pm to 9pm and consisted of popular songs, gags, dancing and sketches (Kim 2010: 53). When it was reformatted as *KBS Grand Show* in 1962, it became mainly focused on popular music (Kim 2010). Since legendary music programme producer Hwang Jeong-Tae took over the show in 1963, it has become the top entertainment programme on KBS. According to Hwang,

Shifts in Korean television music programmes 185

Table 11.2 Major music programmes in KBS, 1961–4

Programme Title	PD	Style	Features
TV Grand Show	Hwang Jae-Mok	Variety show	KBS opening celebration show
KBS Grand Show	Hwang Jae-Mok, Song Young-Soo, Hwang Jeong-Tae	Variety show	KBS signature show programme
Weekly Variety	Hwang Jae-Mok	Variety show	Performance teams outside KBS
Sunday Carnival	Lee Pyeong-Je	Variety show	Musicals with storylines
Show Festival	Hwang Jae-Mok	Variety show	Jazz-style centred
Singers of Your Choice	Han Jeong-Jin, Lee Seong-Jae	Competition show	Audience participation
Hot Parade	Lee Nam-Seop		With live audiences
Golden Oldies	Hwang Jae-Mok	Genre show	Old songs

Source: Kim 2010: 52

to add more variety to the show they invited artists and performing teams working for the so-called *mipalgun-show* (*Eighth US Army Show*),[2] which was famous for its visual and audio qualities (quoted in Kim 2010: 53–4). By employing elements from the *mipalgun-show* and casting singers who were influenced by jazz, swing and American pop, Hwang brought a fresh, modern Western flavour to the show (Kim 2010: 55, 58). Along with this Western 'jazz-style' music, it simultaneously contained old-style *gayo* such as *trot* as well, targeting both young and old viewers.

Since TBC was launched in 1964, music programmes have become more established and refined through network rivalries and a spirit of competition. In particular, TBC's *Show Show Show* is a legendary music programme in Korean broadcasting history and aired for almost two decades (8 December 1964–26 December 1982). Hwang Jeong-Tae moved to TBC to produce the programme. Like *KBS Grand Show*, content was a combination of standard pop (influenced by American pop, jazz, chanson and canzone) and old-style *gayo* (mainly *trot*). According to Hwang, the programme aimed to be cosmopolitan and modern and targeted an urban middle-class demographic in their twenties and thirties (Kim 2010: 87). This reflects the socio-cultural climate during this period in Korea when a spirit of Westernization and modernization was sweeping the nation. One key feature of *Show Show Show* was the way it held a range of top singers under exclusive contracts with the station, such as Hyun Mi, Park Jae-Ran, Wicky Lee, Lee Geum-Hee and Nam Il-Hae (Kim 2010: 62, 86). This was possible because of the unbalanced power dynamics at a time when the broadcasting companies wielded much greater power than artists, a dynamic that has changed since the big entertainment companies appeared in the market during the mid-1990s and began managing

186   *Sun Jung*

Table 11.3 Broadcasting programming ratio of each station, 1970–1

Classifications	1970			1971		
	KBS	*MBC*	*TBC*	*KBS*	*MBC*	*TBC*
News	16	10.7	9.1	14.0	8.1	9.0
Education	32.0	24.6	23.4	39.6	21.7	24.2
Entertainment	52.0	52.4	55.9	42.6	56.7	57.6
Extra	1.0	10.0	11.6	3.8	12.3	8.3

Source: *1972 Korea Broadcasting Yearbook*, cited in Kim 2010

artists. Thanks to the success of many entertainment programmes including *Show Show Show*, TBC's advertising revenue increased 60–70 per cent every year between 1963 and 1969, becoming far higher than KBS's (Jin 2005: 93).

When MBC was launched in 1969, the three networks entered into fierce competition. This atmosphere influenced each network to rely heavily on this type of entertainment programme as they were uniquely positioned to influence television viewing numbers and ratings. During the 1970s, such strategies were continuously practiced in the broadcasting industry (see Table 11.3).

The euphoria surrounding the flourishing entertainment programme-dominated broadcasting industry during the early 1970s was interrupted by the 1972 *Yushin*. The early 1970s was a period of political turmoil as President Park Chung-Hee sought a third term by revising the Constitution. President Park declared a state of emergency – martial law – in October 1972 and announced a series of revitalizing reforms called *Yushin*. Under martial law, the press, speech and newscasts were strictly censored. In the process of establishing the *Yushin* system, the government was concerned that the mass media – heavily oriented as it was towards entertainment – might work against reforms such as modernization and peace talks between South and North Korea (Kim Kyu et al., cited in Jin 2005: 97). Accordingly, there were many rules and regulations controlling the content of television entertainment programmes, and television networks often exercised self-censorship. For example, on 4 February 1974, MBC announced they would ban foreign stage names and foreign programme titles (Kim 2010: 81–2). The broadcasting Ethics Commission officially enacted new regulations that August, whereby Westernized youth culture artifacts such as disco clubs, long-haired males and Japanese *enka*-style *trot* were banned (Kim 2010). Such tight control continued until the government abolished their guidelines in 1978 (Kim Kyu et al., cited in Jin 2005: 98).

In 1969, the nation was gripped by 'group sounds' or the rock music genre, which saw the launch of new types of music programmes.[3] TBS's *One Two Three Go* and MBC's *Youthful Rhythm* showcased various group sounds bands, on programmes where performers as well as their young audience danced to music (Park 2007: 17–19). The programmes were cancelled after four months due to government pressure, as authorities considered them decadent (Park 2007). With the folk music boom during the late 1960s and early 1970s, television stations introduced youth-targeted music programmes such as *Come Come Come* (TBC) and *March of Youth* (KBS). These music programmes reflected divisions in the domestic pop music market according to the different tastes of different age demographics. Youth began to be considered as a separate demographic, with an emphasis on rock and folk. Again, however, government pressure (along with a decrease in the popularity of folk music) meant these programmes were also soon cancelled. *Come Come Come* was cancelled only five months after its launch due to political pressure. The appearance of anti-government intellectual Kim Dong-Gil in particular has been considered the death knell of the programme, and its demise reflects the tyrannical media control of the military regime during the 1970s (Kim 2010).

Liberalization and idol-pop-dominant music programmes

In the early 1980s, the most influential music programme in Korean television history, *Gayo Top 10*, began; it lasted almost two decades (10 February 1981–11 February 1998). This was the first music chart programme, and the rankings provided in the show were a barometer of pop music trends in Korea. During the early 1980s, the Korean broadcasting system reached a significant turning point as it entered the age of public management and the introduction of colour television (Jin 2005: 103). Colour broadcasting played a key role in increasing demand for entertainment programmes, with their vivid colours and flash ornamentation. *Gayo Top 10* was not unique in this regard as the *mise-en-scène* of such programmes became more flamboyant. In the late 1980s, one of the most significant changes in the broadcasting industrial structure took place when the so-called mass media reorganization was enforced by Chun Doo-Hwan's military regime (Lee and Youn 1995: 58). It confiscated the until-then private broadcasting system and brought it under government control (Kim 1997: 69–70; Heuvel and Dennis, cited in Jin 2005: 104). It was in this climate that TBC was incorporated with KBS and became KBS2, while MBC remained as a separate station if, as the government requested, they turned over 70 per cent of their shares to KBS (Lee and Youn 1995: 58–9). Korean broadcasting was virtually a government monopoly until the Basic Press Law (which was the major policy tool for suppressing the press throughout the Chun regime) was abolished on 10 November 1987.

In the 1990s, the industry witnessed a growing liberalization of broadcasting through several remarkable changes. This included the launch of a new commercial network television service (SBS) in 1991, the steady development of the independent production industry, and the beginning of cable television and the satellite system (Lee and Youn 1995: 59–60). These changes reflect broader structural shifts in the global broadcasting industry, typified by the restructuring of the media sector through deregulation and privatization, and

188 *Sun Jung*

increases in transnational media flows and transnational competition that accompanied the rise of neoliberalism from the mid-1980s onwards.

It was in this pervasive mood of increased liberalization during the early 1990s that Seo Taiji and Boys, Hyeon Jin-Young and Wawa, and Deux launched the era of youth-oriented Korean pop music with mega-hits in the domestic pop market. They adopted and popularized African-American hip-hop culture and rap music in the mainstream Korean pop scene, which created a hip-hop dance music-centred youth pop culture that burgeoned in the 1990s. During the mid-1990s, major entertainment production companies – the so-called 'big three'; SM, YG and JYP – were established, and have since become the main driving force in the market leading the current K-pop boom. They produced a range of idol girl and boy groups that have significantly influenced music programme content. Along with the popular ballad genre, dance music-centred idol groups had often topped the *Gayo Top 10* chart during this period. *Gayo Top 10* was indisputably the top music programme until it finished in 1998. Right after the IMF crisis, KBS decided to cancel several entertainment programmes, including *Gayo Top 10*, because it was felt that laughter and comedy were inappropriate during a period when the nation was suffering through an economic crisis.

The cancellation of *Gayo Top 10* for this reason was met with public outrage, and in response KBS launched a new music programme called *Music Bank* in June 1998. Today, the three major music programmes are *Music Bank* (뮤직뱅크, KBS), *Show Music Core* (쇼! 음악중심, MBC) and *Popular Music* (인기가요, SBS). Their basic format is similar: MCs (mainly idol group members or young actors) introduce the weekly music charts, and artists ranked on the charts perform their songs accordingly. As idol pop has gained nation-wide popularity, these music programmes have come to be gradually dominated by idol band music, which often constitutes 80–90 per cent of programme content. While these shows are crucial platforms for showcasing new songs and promoting newly released albums, they also have often become the target of harsh criticism due to their unclear ranking process, suspicions of arrogation in the networks where unfair power dynamics between the stations and the artists are often pointed out, and for the dominant – and often monotonous – focus on idol music. Since the early 2000s, civil activist groups such as the Cultural Action Organisation and cultural critics have protested both on- and offline to abolish the ranking system of the television music programmes due to these reasons. Consequently, some programmes abolished the ranking system altogether while some still maintain it.

The rising cable television era, Mnet and audition programmes

Since 1995, cable television – as a subscription-based broadcasting business – has grown steadily and today the revenue of 94 cable television system operators contributes 17.9 per cent (US$1.88 billion) of the total broadcasting market revenue in Korea (KCC 2012). In 1999, a government task force was formed to promote digital cable broadcasting in Korea, and they announced that the technological standard selected for digital broadcasting would be ATSC, the same as the US. In November 2002, cable companies launched their digital cable television services; in 2004 a pilot service was offered by two companies (Curix and C&M), followed by a testing of MMS (Multimedia Service), IPTV and TPS (Triple Play Service) (Chung et al. 2010). According to the 2012 Korean broadcasting white paper, the number of businesses in cable broadcasting (including cable television system operators, relay operators and programme providers) was 369, and the total revenue was US$6.1 billion, almost double that of terrestrial broadcasting (KOCCA 2012). The cable era has indeed begun.

As observed earlier, these drastic shifts reflect how the Korean government quickly adapted to neoliberal globalization practices to meet the increased transnational competition in the changed global media broadcasting land-scape, demonstrated in the deregulation of national broadcasting systems as well as the creation of new commercial terrestrial and cable channels. Such shifts are also largely related to Kim Young-Sam government's *segyehwa* (globalization) movement, where Kim insisted on a borderless world econ-omy with transnational capital investment. The Kim government (1993–8) keenly enacted market-oriented media policies under neoliberal capitalism and *segyehwa*. Within such socio-political as well as economic climates in and outside Korea, *jaebeol* (or *chaebol*, family-owned conglomerates) had quickly become involved with commercial cable broadcasting beginning in the mid-1990s (Jin 2005: 212–15). While the *jaebeol* are prohibited to own ter-restrial broadcasting stations, mainly because the government are concerned with their expansion of political power, they instead became key players in the cable television industry. The media industry underwent a major shake-up in the post-1997 IMF crisis where by several conglomerates – such as first-tier *jaebeol* like Samsung, Hyundai and Daewoo – either left the media business or significantly decreased their involvement (Jin 2005: 220). While many left, CJ E&M remained and has now become a leading cable television enterprise.

In addition to the aforementioned music programmes on the three ter-restrial broadcasting stations, Mnet's *M! Countdown* has become a leading K-pop music programme inside and outside Korea. Mnet is a specialized music cable channel run by multimedia entertainment company CJ E&M, a subsidiary of the CJ Group, one of the top twenty *jaebeol*.[4] CJ E&M is one of the most influential media entertainment companies in Korea, if not the most dominant one.[5] Their business includes four divisions – music, media (broadcasting), games and pictures (cinema). According to the company's IR resource, the broadcasting sector (55 per cent) contributes the highest portion of the total revenue (US$1.25 billion) followed by cinema (16 per cent), games (15 per cent) and music (14 per cent) (CJ E&M 2013). The music division mainly deals with organizing live music events such as con-certs, musicals and music festivals (e.g., Jisan Valley Rock Festival) as well as online music downloading/subscription services and album distribution.

The company's mnet.com is the second largest online sound source provider in Korea after Melon, while the company occupies 30 per cent of the local album distribution market.[6] According to division director Ahn Seok-Joon, by collaborating with 86 entertainment companies they have released 400 albums and organized 170–200 concerts every year (quoted in Han 2013). CJ E&M's broadcasting division holds 15 cable television channels including Mnet. In K-pop in particular, its economic as well as cultural impact is unchallengeable as its music cable channel Mnet leads the current K-pop boom outside Korea along with three big K-pop companies, SM, YG and JYP. CJ E&M is also one of the major shareholders of YG Entertainment.

In early 2013, Mnet refurbished its website and the major changes were dominated by a focus on globalization and social media. By first targeting global pop consumers, it offers five different language services – English, Japanese, Chinese (both traditional and simplified) and Korean – and all song titles appear in English from the beginning. This means that even in Korean-language services they still appear in English. Second, almost every single K-pop act (as well as some popular actors) are listed on the first page of the website, where users can check the stars' social media activities at a glance (e.g., comments on their Twitter and Facebook pages and related YouTube videos). Their ardent use of social media is most visible on their official YouTube channel, which has more than 2.3 million subscribers and more than 1 billion channel views (accessed 20 April 2015). One can easily find most Mnet programmes through well-categorized play lists on the channel such as their signature music-ranking programme *M! Countdown* and audition programmes *Superstar K* and *The Voice of Korea*.

Superstar K began a new era of cable television broadcasting, attaining the viewership rate of 18.1 per cent at its peak, higher than programmes on terrestrial televisions airing in the same time slot (KISDI 2011). As soon as the show first aired on 24 July 2009, it became a national sensation and proved the competitiveness of cable television. In season 4 (17 August–23 November 2012), more than 500,000 contestants (1 per cent of the total population) participated in the competition (Kim 2012). Its popularity ignited audition fever across the nation and similarly formatted survival audition programmes were subsequently launched: *Star Audition Great Beginning* (MBC), *Top Band* (KBS), *K-pop Star* (SBS), *Korea's Got Talent* (tvN), *Miracle Audition* (SBS), *Master Chef Korea* (O'live), *Project Runway Korea* (On Style), *Super Rooky* (MBC), *The Voice of Korea* (Mnet), *Show Me the Money* (Mnet) and *Dancing9* (Mnet). This survival show phenomenon saw the singing competition programme *I Am a Singer* (MBC) launched on 6 March 2011, which also swept the nation. It showcased top singers from various genres who arrange and perform allocated songs. After these live performances, the audience vote and the lowest ranking competitor is eliminated. This programme largely affected the sound source market landscape where the songs performed at the show dominated all music charts and became bestsellers.

As the above list demonstrates, Mnet airs a variety of singing audition programmes such as *Superstar K, The Voice of Korea* and *Show Me the Money*. These shows attracted an enormous number of contestants as well as a large audience. The contestants are from all over the world; *Superstar K* held auditions in various cities such as New York, LA, Beijing, Tokyo, Osaka and Sendai. In season 3, it offered a '*Superstar K* World Super Tour UCC Audition' where contestants could upload their audition to UCC, while for season 4, they held a 'Global *Superstar K* 4 Cover Contest' on YouTube. For season 5, Mnet not only utilized YouTube but also employed Kakao Talk, a multi-platform texting application for their 'Audition Call for Global Applicants'. On Mnet's official YouTube channel, one can find three-language versions (English, Mandarin and Cantonese) of a video clip where potential audition contestants can obtain information for how to submit their audition videos to Mnet through Kakao Talk.

This Mnet channel is linked to YouTube's CJ E&M music channel as well as Mnet's other social media platforms. In addition to globally well-known social media platforms such as Google+, Twitter and Facebook, some also link to local Korean ones. Tvpot and Tvcast are video sharing websites operated by two leading Korean portals, Daum and Naver respectively. A local equivalent to Pinterest, interest.me is CJ E&M's 'social curation service' launched in July 2012, providing categorized and customized content that each user is interested in. It provides ten different language services and covers almost 1,000 topics from across the globe, and K-pop is one of the most frequently discussed topics. Mnet's recent website refurbishment and assertive use of social media and the multilingual service demonstrate how CJ E&M targets a global audience. As evident from the way Mnet includes a mobile social media application, Kakao Talk, in their audition process, their next move is towards mobile TV where they will continue to promote and distribute their programmes.

Online video sharing websites, IPTV and mobile TV

More and more television programmes are accessed and consumed through digital mobile media. In a news show on China Central Television (CCTV) in 2010, a Chinese journalist asked four guests which media they used to watch films and television. Three of the four interviewees answered 'the Internet', while the other chose 'DVDs and the Internet' (Zhao cited in Hu 2014). The show also pointed out that the post-1980s and 1990s generations in the PRC are no longer interested in sitting in front of a television or even buying DVDs; instead, they prefer online viewing and downloading material from the Internet (Hu 2014). Young generations today consume music primarily through digital media. Due to the increased use of high-speed Internet in Korea, with advances in mobile equipment such as MP3 players and PMPs (portable multimedia players), the local digital music market exceeded its offline counterpart in 2004 (Im 2012), and it was expected that the size of the former will be 38 times that of the latter by 2015 (Ha 2012: 9). In 2010,

192   *Sun Jung*

Korea's domestic music market was worth US$350million, and 83.3 per cent of that was the digital market (KOCCA 2011b).

This market shift is evident in the ways Mnet dynamically employs new media channels to expand their consumer market beyond Korea as discussed in the earlier section, which reflects the trend towards transnationalization and digitalization. Thanks to advanced Web 2.0 technologies, video sharing websites such as YouTube in particular have now become a main avenue for the Korean entertainment broadcasting industry to reach global audiences (Jung 2011b, 2014). For example, in October 2011, Google (the parent company of YouTube) and Korea's MBC television network signed an MOU that specifies the network will provide its broadcasting content to Google through its YouTube channel (Kim 2011). This is in line with how 'Big Content players – large media producers and rights holders such as the Warner and Universal Music Groups – have signed revenue sharing deals with YouTube' (Burgess and Green 2009: 5).

It is not only YouTube but also Chinese video sharing websites such as Youku, Tudou and Sohu that have emerged as the main distribution/consumption channels for Korean television programmes in China and, to a certain degree, to global audiences. Chinese video sharing websites emerged as early as 2005 and today have become large-scale businesses. Korean television drama series and game shows number amongst their highest selling content, and audiences with a range of ethnic and cultural backgrounds (including non-Chinese as well as Chinese) visit the site to access to the material. Youku even signed a strategic content partnership with SBS, Korea's commercial television station (CMM Intelligence, cited in Hu 2014). The above-mentioned Korean music programmes – both ranking and audition styled shows – are uploaded to these video sharing websites only minutes after their original broadcast. Due to the effectiveness of fan-subbing groups, often fan-subbed versions are uploaded online within a couple of hours after the initial broadcast (Jung 2013: 119).

IPTV and DMB are also used increasingly by audiences to watch television programmes. As is evident from Table 11.4, younger viewers in Korea are particularly keen to use these new methods.

Significant in Table 11.4 is the fact that the IPTV viewing rate is higher than that of satellite, and that the terrestrial DMB viewing rate is particularly high among those in their twenties and thirties. IPTV's popularity is due in part to the TPS (Triple Play Service) – the marketing term for the bundling of high-speed Internet access, Internet TV and telephone over a single broadband connection – and it has become popular because of its convenience and cost-effectiveness. It is also crucial to note how all three IPTV providers are the leading telecommunication enterprises either once-state-owned KT (OllehTV) or *jaebeol*, SK (Btv) and LG (U+). Along with the dramatic increase in mobile phone users, these companies offer a QPS (Quadruple Play Service) which includes their own smartphone service (KOCCA 2012: 235). As is evident from the figures in Table 11.4, DMB viewing is relatively high

Table 11.4 2011 audience behaviour in viewing methods

Divisions		Total	Gender		Age						
			M	F	10s	20s	30s	40s	50s	60s+
Number of respondents		6,669	3,288	3,381	769	1,049	1,259	1,317	1,051	1,224
Terrestrial Broadcasting		97.2	96.4	97.9	93.2	93.9	97.8	97.6	99.5	99.4
Cable Broadcasting		75.2	74.3	76.0	70.4	73.2	75.1	72.1	79.3	79.8
Satellite Broadcasting		7.3	7.4	7.2	8.5	6.0	6.0	7.7	8.5	7.8
IPTV	Real Time	13.8	14.2	13.5	14.6	18.8	19.2	15.4	11.6	3.8
	VOD	11.1	11.4	10.7	11.3	14.8	15.3	12.4	9.4	3.2
DMB	Terrestrial	22.2	26.8	17.8	25.0	37.5	30.4	25.5	13.9	2.5
	Satellite	2.1	2.3	2.0	2.2	2.9	3.6	2.4	1.4	0.2

Source: KOCCA 2012 (unit: per cent)

among users in their twenties (37.5 per cent) and thirties (30.4 per cent), and it is common to see young people watching DMB on their mobile phones on public transport today.

The most recent mode of consuming music programmes is through live-stream Internet television such as AfreecaTV, PopkonTV, Live Star and Wink TV. AfreecaTV (meaning 'A Free Casting' TV), launched in 2006, is a video streaming service based on P2P technology and operated by Nowcom in Korea.[7] There are two main functions of the website: while it retransmits mainstream broadcasting programmes, it also allows users to upload their own content, similar to YouTube's dedication to UGC distribution. However, it has a stronger live-stream feature than YouTube. Grassroots broadcasters, BJs (Broadcasting Jockeys), deliver live-streamed shows to viewers, and genres range from 'eating broadcasting' (먹방, *meokbang*, where the BJs are eating food and live chatting with other users online) to 'live dance lessons'. Each BJ has followers or fans and they form large online communities. The top BJ Beomprica, for example, has more than 300,000 fans. The key characteristics that distinguish AfreecaTV from other video sharing websites like YouTube are its live interactions and community-building.

Three dominant types of content in AfreecaTV are sports, online game playing and visible (or seeable) radio. While the first two are retransmitted materials, visible radio is UGC. In the visible radio section, many BJs run music programmes whose format is often similar to mainstream radio music programmes, and additionally audiences can see them BJing. Often BJs sing and dance live in front of the camera. One of the top three BJs is Singing Koteu and his show features Koteu singing popular K-pop songs live, and the show has more than 370,000 registered audience members. Each BJ's AfreecaTV page is called a 'station'. This demonstrates that a new mode of grassroots-centred Internet television has emerged where a grassroots

194 *Sun Jung*

community builds a one-person station and creates live-streamed video content that is consumed and shared by interactive users in online communities.

Live-streaming online television often gets criticized because of its uncensored, vulgar content, where sexual and violent material can be broadcast live to young audiences without any screening.[8] In April 2013, the Korea Communications Standards Commission held a meeting to promote 'Constructing a Healthy Internet Broadcasting Environment', where in it requested the industry to enact self-monitoring, to improve user reporting systems and to place restrictions on youth (Kang 2013). While Internet television has become a new mode of consuming television programmes today, it requires proper guidelines and regulations to operate the system optimally.

Conclusion

The 2012 broadcasting industry white paper identified seven key issues that arose in 2011: the launching of general-service cable television channels; the prolonged strike in the broadcasting industry; terrestrial–cable programme re-transmission; the popularity of podcasts; the improvement of the media broadcasting production environment; media broadcasting content in the *Hallyu* 2.0 era;[9] and the enactment of media representation policies. Among these, three items in particular – the launching of general service cable television channels, the broadcasting industry strike and the podcast boom – reflect the dark side of the broadcasting industry under the Lee Myung-Bak regime (2008–13).

For the first time since the arrival of democracy in 1987, reporters at MBC, KBS and YTN (a cable news channel), as well as journalists at popular newspapers, went on strike during 2011 and 2012. The main reason was government interference. According to Freedom House in the US, 'South Korea declined from Free to Partly Free to reflect an increase in official censorship, particularly of online content, as well as the government's attempt to influence media outlets' news and information content' (Freedom House 2011). The Lee government attempted to control the media through parachuting in presidential cronies to run the country's most prominent media outlets and to implement increased censorship (*The Economist* 2012). One of the most problematic actions Lee and his allies committed was enacting the 'general service cable television channel policy', which gave a right to launch integrated cable channels to four representative conservative newspaper companies: Chosun Ilbo, Joong-ang Ilbo, Dong-a Ilbo and Maeil Gyungje Shinmoon. Prior to this policy, all cable channels had to be specialized in certain categories such as comedy, drama, music, fashion and lifestyles.

On 1 December 2011, the four newspaper companies launched general-service cable television channels: TV Chosun (Chosun), JTBC (Joong-ang), Channel A (Dong-a) and MBN (Maeil Gyungje). The four channels immediately became mouthpieces of the Lee government and the ruling Saenuri Party (along with the existing state-controlled terrestrial stations KBS and MBC).

It is often stated that the four channels should be praised as being the reason behind the conservative Saenuri Party's return to power (Koh and Hong 2013). But this feels more like a regression to the days when all broadcasting stations were spokespersons for dictatorial regimes. This oppressed environment generated two movements in the domestic media landscape: a boom in alternative media and protests against oppression. As alternative media outlets, many podcasting services focusing on current affairs have begun while many media personnel participated in strikes, as mentioned earlier.

This changed media environment also affected music programmes not only in terms of the music itself but also in regard to the fact that dance and artists' appearances were all strictly censored under this strengthened censorship. The young post-democratization generations were dumbfounded by unclear censorship processes. Hyuna's 'Bubble Pop' was banned by network televisions because the dance was lascivious, while MC META and DJ WRECKX's album *MC and DJ* was banned due to the use of dialect in their rapping (D.-H. Lee 2011). On 22 August 2011, the Juvenile Protection Committee, part of the Ministry of Gender Equality and Family, released a list of 24 songs deemed 'harmful to youths' that included Hyuna's 'Bubble Pop,' 2PM's 'Hands Up,' 10cm's 'Americano' and B2ST's 'On Rainy Days'. Soon harsh criticism arose where in cultural critics, artists and music producers complained about the vagueness and unfairness of the standards. At the October Parliamentary Inspection, Jeon Byeong-Heon, a United Democratic Party lawmaker, insisted that the way KBS banned these songs was based largely on arbitrary decisions (cited in D.-H. Lee 2011). He stated 'after analysing the cases in recent three years, such a tendency has been increased since Kim In-Gyu (one of those who were parachuted in by the Lee government) took the office' (cited in D.-H. Lee 2011). This incident clearly demonstrates how media content can be easily controlled and challenged by an authoritarian government even in the so-called democratic society of Korea today. In early 2013, the new Park Geun-Hye government came to power and the new president made a point of saying that she will cherish the freedom of the press. We have yet to see how the media environment will shift under this new regime.

Notes

1 During the colonial period, *trot* began to gain popularity in Korea. It had its origins in translated *enka* songs combined with certain elements of a traditional Korean music genre called *minyo* (Zhang 2006: 117, 119). Given that *enka* was also originally influenced by Western musical elements (Zhang 2006: 118), *trot* has to be understood through the notion of cultural hybridization.
2 The Eighth United States Army (EUSA) is a field army, the commanding formation of all US Army forces in South Korea. The *Eighth US Army Show* refers to entertainment shows performed for the EUSA soldiers.
3 'Group sounds' are a localized genre of rock, the term originating in the Japanese rock scene.
4 The CJ Group was originally a branch of Samsung until the mid-1990s. Five subsidiaries of Samsung, including Cheil Jedang (a sugar and flour company), gained

196 *Sun Jung*

independent management in 1993, and CJ Group (formerly Cheil Jedang Group) was officially launched in 1996. The CEO of CJ Group, Lee Je-Hyeon is the eldest grandson of Samsung's founder Lee Byeong-Cheol.

5 In March 2011, CJ E&M was officially launched through the M&A of CJ's six subsidiaries – CJ E&M, CJ Entertainment, CJ Media, On Media, CJ Internet and Mnet Media.

6 Melon belongs to SK Telecom, which is a subsidiary of one of Korea's large family-owned conglomerates or *jaebeol* (aka *chaebol*), the SK Group. This wireless telecommunications operator has been the top mobile service provider for the past decade, with over 50 per cent market share (Choi 2013).

7 On 27 September 2012, AfreecaTV's English version was released through the Google Play store; http://en.afreeca.tv.

8 This is in part due to the 'star balloon' system; a star balloon is a present (or donation) that audiences give BJs to express appreciation and affection, which is exchangeable for cash. For this reason, some BJs intentionally provide viewers with provocative and sensational content to gain more star balloons.

9 *Hallyu* (aka the Korean Wave) refers to the ways in which Korean popular culture has gained popularity in the Asian region (later expanding to the global market). For further details see Chua and Iwabuchi (2008) and Jung (2011a).

References

Burgess, Jean and Green, Joshua (2009) *YouTube*, Cambridge and Malden: Polity.

Choi, Ik-Ho (2013) 'Clinging to 50 per cent of market share, SK Telecom', *MK News*, 1 February, http://news.mk.co.kr/newsRead.php?year=2013&no=82117.

Chua, Beng Huat and Iwabuchi, Koichi (eds.) (2008) *East Asian Pop Culture: Analysing The Korean Wave*, Hong Kong: Hong Kong University Press.

Chung, Joo Chung, Kim, Jang Hyun and Choi, Hong Gyu (2010) 'An analysis of media researchers' perceptions of the digitalization of broadcasting in Korea', *Global Media Journal*, 9(16).

CJ E&M (2013) '2012 Investor Relations Report', February.

The Economist (2012) 'No news is bad news', 3 March, www.economist.com/node/21549008.

Freedom House (2011) 'Freedom of the press: South Korea', www.freedomhouse.org/report/freedom-press/2011/south-korea.

Furuya, Masayuki (2010) *All About K-Pop*, Tokyo: Soft Bank Creative.

Ha, Yun-Geum (2012) 'Analysis of digital music market distribution and revenue model', *KOCCA Focus*, 27 December, www.kocca.kr/knowledge/publication/focus/1779780_4445.html.

Han, Oo-Ri (2013) 'Interview with An Seok-Joon', *Enjoy and Talk*, 21 March, http://blog.cjenm.com/1785.

Hu, Kelly (2014) 'Competition and collaboration: Chinese video websites, subtitle groups, state regulation and market', *International Journal of Cultural Studies*, 17(5).

Im, Gwang-Bok (2012) 'Debate over increase of sound source usage fee', *Financial News*, 1 April, www.fnnews.com/view?ra=Sent0901m_View&corp=fnnews&arcid=20120328010023769001 3860&cDateYear=2012&cDateMonth=04&cDateDay=01.

Jin, Dal-Yong (2005) *Political Economy of Communication Industry Reorganisation: Republic of Korea, 1987–2002*, PhD thesis, University of Illinois at Urbana-Champaign.

Jung, Sun (2011a) *Korean Masculinities and Transcultural Consumption*, Hong Kong: Hong Kong University Press.

Jung, Sun (2011b) 'K-pop, Indonesian fandom, and social media', *Transformative Works and Cultures*, 8, http://journal.transformativeworks.org/index.php/twc/article/view/289.

Jung, Sun (2013) 'K-pop beyond Asia: performing trans-nationality, trans-sexuality, and trans-textuality' in Lorna Fitzsimmons and John A. Lent (eds.) *Asian Popular Culture in Transition*, London and New York: Routledge.

Jung, Sun (2014) 'Youth, social media and transnational cultural distribution: the case of online K-pop circulation' in Andy Bennett and Brady Robards (eds.) *Mediated Youth Culture*, London: Palgrave.

Kang, Hyeon-Joo (2013) 'Internet TV industry will enact "restriction of the youth"', *inews24*, 17 April, http://news.inews24.com/php/news_view.php?g_serial=738875&g_menu=020310&rrf=nv.

KCC (2012) '2012 Broadcasting Industry Condition Report', www.kcc.go.kr.

Kim, Gyeong-Min (2012) 'Superstar K 4, more than 500k registered, leading new phenomenon', *OSEN*, http://osen.mt.co.kr/article/G1109375969.

Kim, Jong-Jin (2010) *Analysis of Korean TV Music Programs: 1961–1979*, MA thesis, Hanguk University of Foreign Studies.

Kim, Shin-Dong (1997) *The Politics of Economy of the Korean Television Industry: State, Capital and Media in Globalization*, PhD thesis, Department of Telecommunications, Indiana University.

Kim, Soo-Jin (2011) 'Google and MBC, signed the content distribution partnership', *Asia Gyungje*, 21 October, http://view.asiae.co.kr/news/view.htm?idxno=2011102113391758915&nvr=Y.

KISDI (2011) 'Media and communication outlook of Korea', www.kisdi.re.

KISDI (2012) 'Media and communication outlook of Korea', www.kisdi.re.

KOCCA (2011a) 'Creative industry white book annual report', www.kocca.kr.

KOCCA (2011b) 'Music industry white paper', www.kocca.kr.

KOCCA (2012) 'Broadcasting industry white paper', www.kocca.kr.

Koh, Jeong-Mi and Hong, Hyeon-Jin (2013) 'The less educated, working class, housewives, 50s and 60s were behind victory', *Ohmynews*, 22 April, http://bit.ly/11ZSndb.

Lee, Dae-Hee (2011) 'Hallyu, Nagasu, censorship debates', *Pressian*, 25 December, http://member.pressian.com/article/article.asp?Section=04&article_num=30111221191538.

Lee, Dong-Yeon (2011) 'What is idol pop? Reading the symptoms (*Aidol pabiran mueot-inga: Jinghujeok dokhae*)' in D. Y. Lee (ed.) *IDOL: From HOT to SNSD, Idol Culture Report (IDOL: H.O.T-eseo Sonyeoshidae-ggaji, Aidol munhwa bogoseo)*, Seoul: Imagine, pp. 14–48.

Lee, Joon-Ho and Youn, Sug-Min (1995) 'Industrial structure, government control, and network television programming: the case of South Korea', *Asian Journal of Communication* 5(1): 52–70.

Park, Yong-Gyu (2007) 'Television and popular music in the 1970s: focused on the youth popular music programs', *Journal of Korea Communication Association*, 51(2): 5–29.

Shim, Doobo and Jin, Dal Yong (2007) 'Transformations and development of the Korean broadcasting media' in Isaac A. Blankson and Patrick D. Murphy (eds.) *Negotiating Democracy: Media Transformations in Emerging Democracies*, Albany: State University of New York Press.

Zhang, Yoo-Jeong (2006) *Brother is a Musician (Oppaneun Punggakjaengiya)*, Seoul: Mineumin.

12 Cultural polysemy and vernacular cosmopolitanism in the theme songs of Hong Kong television dramas

Liew Kai Khiun

Introduction: torrential mixing of the tidal currents

In 1980, Hong Kong's commercial Television Broadcast Limited (TVB) television drama *The Bund* (上海灘) was popularly received in the city as well as in South-East Asia and the broader Chinese diaspora. Set in the cosmopolitan treaty port of Shanghai in the 1920s, *The Bund* revolves around the violent ascent of a coolie (Ray Lui) and a disillusioned student activist (Chow Yun-Fat) to become prominent mobsters. Not only were two sequels made within that year, but this historical gangster drama has been repeatedly resurrected in television dramas and films, including Chow's redux, *The Last Tycoon* (大上海), three decades later in 2012. From karaoke lounges to social media sites, theme songs of *The Bund* remain popular more than three decades after the dramas were screened. With music composed by Joseph Koo, lyrics by Wong Jim and sung by Frances Yip, the main and supplementary theme songs reflected the intimate role of the Hong Kong-based contemporary Cantonese popular music, or Canto-pop, in cultivating a more memorable and enduring televisual culture. With the smooth synchronization of Koo's classical music with the undulating pitch of Yip, the song articulates the unpredictable tribulations of the changing fortunes in the treaty-port of Shanghai in the interwar years. To a certain extent, it is also a narrative that reminds viewers in Hong Kong and beyond of similar socio-political and historical predicaments.

This chapter seeks to highlight the sonic presence of television soundtracks and theme songs in projecting and maintaining the reach of Hong Kong television dramas across the globe since the first productions were broadcasted in the 1970s. It will demonstrate from the wide array of theme songs the multiplicity of their roles in articulating and forging the cultural identities of both Hong Kong and the broader Chinese diaspora. What will be shown here, from the apparently messy cacophony of often linguistically and musicologically mixed genres of theme songs, underlines a more consistent process of the hybridization and stabilization of shifting global trends within more traditional and culturally local narratives. This chapter will attempt to conceptualize the theme songs of TVB drama productions against a televisual rhythmic spectrum that places the different music styles against the spatial-temporal narrative treatments of the various television genres that range from the abstracted historical times of premodern China to the nostalgic contemporary Hong Kong. Collectively, the changing and varying styles of the songs reflect both the continuous adaptation of compositions to new styles and the shifting moods arising from broader geopolitical changes in the city. Serving to amplify and entrench the affective dimensions of these televisual narratives, these theme songs are critical in marking the socio-cultural identities of the transnational audiences of TVB television dramas.

Under the Lion Rock: televisual soundscapes in the aftermath of the Maoist riots

The cultural evolution of Hong Kong television runs parallel to Hong Kong's historical position, as a former British colonial treaty port, as an intersection between the local, provincial, regional and diasporic. Unlike the narratives of nation-building associated with 'national television', Hong Kong television since its earliest inception has been distributed to and consumed by a multifaceted international audience. This audience pool has included not only Hong Kong residents, their immediate Mainland Chinese counterparts across the provinces and the transnational Chinese diaspora, but non-ethnic Chinese viewers in East and South-East Asia. Beneath the congested city of eight million lies a televisual culture that has projected the cosmopolitan imaginations of Hong Kong simultaneously as the complex urban metropolis as well as the homely harmonious family. Differing from trends of cultural decolonization in the region whereby emerging postwar popular culture has been associated with individualistic Westernization, the liberal-capitalist city of Hong Kong has had greater political space to define itself along more shifting trends. As such, not only are changing lifestyles and arrangements featured more frequently, but even historical fiction and events are given more contemporary, liberal interpretations, with changing worldviews and values also reflected in historical dramas that have also served in reshaping the understanding of the past and history according to the present.

Vernacularization of television

Hong Kong's beginnings in public broadcasting can be traced to the establishment of Radio Hong Kong (RHK) in 1928 which subsequently evolved to become semi-government Radio Television Hong Kong (RTHK) in 1976. Even as it was associated with critically acclaimed television documentaries and special themed projects, RTHK's presence has been dwarfed by the emergence of more popular commercial and vernacular radio stations. Currently, an approximate 6,000 hours of transmission devoted to mainly news and current affairs as well as cultural and educational programmes are televised through the main commercial television stations, capturing the attention of 956,000 through TVB and 229,000 viewers in the smaller rival Asia Television Station or ATV (RTHK 2012: 38). Television was initially associated with the English language, as the primary educational programmes for the expatriate and the more Anglicized classes in the British colony (Hampton 2011). Beginning in 1957 for ATV and a decade later for TVB, the two stations were instrumental in popularizing Chinese television culture in Hong Kong and the region as well as the Chinese diaspora worldwide.

Initially known as Rediffusion or RTV until it changed its name in 1982, ATV, which was broadcasted in Cantonese, served the domestic market with five channels alongside with a 24-hour satellite channel to subscribers in North America as well as the neighbouring Guangdong Television in China, to beam its programmes to the province. In general, ATV is associated with imports of regional and international entertainment programmes (ATV 2013). Its rival TVB, known in Chinese as 'Wireless Television Broadcast', has five local channels. With its two flagship channels, the English language Pearl Channel and the more popular Cantonese language Jade Channel, the station reportedly captures about 90 per cent of Hong Kong's 2.37 million households. With its productions translated and dubbed into local languages and distributed across 40 countries and 100 cities, the commercial broadcaster claims a global reach of 300 million households (TVB 2013). Overall, including ATV, TVB and RTHK, Hong Kong is home to about 270 pay and free-to-air local and international channels with more than 90 per cent of the population and their homes equipped with Internet Broadband and Digital Terrestrial Television (DTT) by 2011 (Digital TV 2011). In turn, it is this highly connected television network and industry developed over the past four decades that has enabled Hong Kong to project its cultural presence significantly in the global arena.

Situated within the multiplicity of stations and channels are the network of singers and composers of theme songs and television soundtracks for both local and imported televisual content. Differing from the educational emphasis of the pioneering English-language television, it was entertainment, song and dance that pushed the Cantonese-language-based TVB into prominence in the late 1960s with their signature variety show, *Enjoy Yourself Tonight* (歡樂今宵) (or *EYT* as it was popularly known), which ran nightly from 1967 to 1994. Another event hosted by the station that continues to grip public attention is the Miss Hong Kong Contest (香港小姐) that started in 1973. Many such programmes were crucial to the nurturing of artistes and singers in the city and beyond (Liew 2010).

Linked to the staged variety shows was the development of television dramas and theme songs that gave artistes further exposure on the small screen. In 1974, TVB produced the first theme song titled after its television drama, *The Story of Three Loves* (啼笑因缘). Popularly received, this composition has been recognized to have pioneered the trends including Cantonese-based theme songs in Hong Kong television dramas (Wong and Chu, 2011: 52–5). By legitimizing and elevating the status of otherwise vernacular Cantonese songs in the mainstream media, this move has also heralded the rise of popular Cantonese music or Canto-pop (To and Lau: 1995). From the 1970s, with immigration reforms that created the category of the 'Hong Kong belonger' (Ku 2004: 342–8), the colonial authorities sought to promote a greater sense of local identification with the colonial city instead of Mainland China after the upheavals of the post-Cultural Revolution a decade earlier. Once ideologically despised by leftist elements as part of the feudal and decadent 'Yellow Culture', vernacular Cantonese songs began to receive greater legitimacy as part of the city's sonic landscape. As the discussion will elaborate, a substantial part of the energies of artistes and singers have been channelled into producing theme songs for television dramas, in particular for TVB.

Typically television serials from TVB range from a minimum of 20 episodes, each 20 to 40 minutes long, to exceptionally long-running series that stretch for several years like *Seasons* (1984) or *Kindred Spirits* (1995). Aired during the weekday prime-time evening slots between 7pm to 11pm, family-friendly genres with light-hearted and humorous themes play during the earlier part of the evening while those dealing with more sophisticated adult themes slot in later at about 9:30pm. Underlying the multiple genres, from historical dramas to contemporary romantic comedies, are efforts to articulate and play out the otherwise repressed anxieties, fantasies and moral and social ideals of their viewers. As such, the scripts have also been tailored to be relevant to the changing values and lifestyles brought about by the increasingly rooted urban experience, as well as the shifting geocultural plates in Hong Kong responding to the rapid transformation of Mainland China. Complementing the dramas are theme songs complete with lyrics and compositions that match and set the tone for the historical settings, characterization and the narrative trajectory of the television serials.

The televisual rhythmic spectrum

In his critical formulation of textual paradigms in the television programming in Hong Kong, Eric Ma posits differences in television ideologies according to the concepts of 'choric' and 'lyric' dramas. Derived from the framework from Newcomb and Alley (1983) that sees the chorus or 'choric' as a type of collective expression, against the more individualistic and distinctive 'lyric', Ma classifies television using the ideological label of 'mainstream capitalism' as against programming with 'multiple layers of 'polysemic voices' (Ma 1999). In contrast to what he sees as the 'harmonious resonance' of the choric dramas, which tend to be more conservative and commercial, narratives of a polysemic nature tend to underline multiplicities and the negotiation of identities (Ma 1999). Even as he acknowledges the fluidity of the location of texts, Ma's assumption is based on the fixity of televisual identities along this perimeter. Along with growing discussions on the role of television in the formation and displacement of memoryscapes, television as a medium recalls, interweaves and collapses fragments of the past in real time, resulting

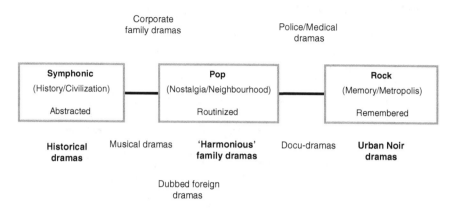

Figure 12.1 Televisual rhythmic spectrum of TVB's drama theme songs

in greater narrative complexities in the space-time modalities of television (Booth 2011; Mitchel 2006; Hoskins 2004: 110); a more dynamic theorizing of the interaction between the choric and lyric in different places and times would provide fresh insight into this field.

Figure 12.1 shows the attempt here to frame and locate these diverse genres and their related theme songs along a rhythmic marker ranging from 'symphonic' to 'pop' and 'rock'. Linked to these three main indicators are related temporal-spatial sub-markers that tends to fit with the musical genres of the theme songs. Theme songs from the symphonic category are those that tend to deal with a more abstracted, historical and mythically imagined notion of historical time in pre-modern Chinese civilization. At the far right of the spectrum is that of 'rock' or the emerging genre of urban noir television dramas that have been fronted by the more jarring, rock-based theme songs. In this category, the music becomes associated with a more disruptive and non-linear discourse on memory, amnesia and cultural and cognitive dissonance as characters try to recover and remember. Set around the desperate search for the presence of place and identity in the metropolis. The middle section of 'pop' is the mainstream category of the harmonious family dramas, where songs reinforce and foster the desire for a more routinized temporality of the domestic household placed within the familiarized neighbourhood with an intimacy that generates the ciphered and nostalgic elements of community and family.

As shown in Figure 12.1, there are some genres that are not as easily categorized into these three sections, although they may lean more towards one. Sharing the sensation of conflict and the struggle for control and power with historical dramas, in both narrative and music styles, are the corporate family dramas. While dubbed imported dramas have few references to the local in Hong Kong, their placement in this spectrum would be between the symphonic and pop. As for musical dramas, with the increasing trends of featuring the nostalgic with theme songs from the immediate postwar decades instead of the tragic themes of traditional Cantonese opera, this genre would be positioned nearer to the area of pop. At the right side of the spectrum are police/medical dramas and docu-dramas that strongly identify with the politics of place in Hong Kong. Even as they lack the stylized visual-dramaturgical treatment of urban noir dramas, docu-dramas share to some extent the focus on the issues of marginality, displacement, deviance and dissonance brewing under the metropolis. As a whole, the trajectory of the rhythmic spectrum reveals that the difference in the genre of TVB's dramas are not only manifested in the timing of the screenings and the 'maturity' of issues that are being treated. The concept of the symphonic-pop-rock reveals the multiple temporalities and spatialities that have drawn the imaginations of viewers not just in Hong Kong but in broader regional and transnational audiences as well.

Giving the past a beat: contemporizing historical dramas and literary classics

Popular especially with overseas audiences, one of the more outstanding genres of TVB's television drama serials has been that of the historical, *wuxia* or 'sword play' productions that are based either on classical literature and contemporary novels set in the past, or significant historical characters and events. It is in these fables that audiences can see historical re-enactments of epic battles, extraordinary martial arts duels, antiquated court rituals and inner chamber intrigues among competing concubines. In general, these historical period dramas give audiences the pleasure of seeing the screen affirmation of pre-modern idyllic values of chivalry, heroism, loyalty, justice and righteousness.

At the very end of the spectrum are light-hearted romantic comedies and modern family dramas revolving around the mundane dilemmas and everyday challenges of ordinary couples and households. Intermittent dramaturgical climaxes come in the unexpected romantic pairings of otherwise quarrelling individuals, and resolutions come in a united family pulling together in solidarity to manage a mini-crisis. Contrasting with the realist and at times solemn portrayals of the social pathologies of struggling households in RTHK's drama-documentaries, the families in these TVB dramas are portrayed to be generally humble but warm and endearing.

Increasingly located in older districts of Hong Kong, renowned for deeper neighbourly and community bonds where residents and shop-owners are well acquainted with one another, these dramas present a Hong Kong where the parents and siblings of the protagonists are still comfortably situated in the traditional nuclear family unit. Drama serials like *A Place of One's Own*

(大澳的天空, 1998), *Sky is the Limit* (緣份無邊界, 2000), *Watchdog Tale* (老友狗狗, 2010) and *Ghetto Justice 1 & 2* (怒火街頭 2009, 2012) have been specifically set in districts, namely the Tai-O, Sha Tau Kwok, and Hakka Villages in the New Territories and Sham Sui Po respectively. The serials feature screenplays that provide naturalized verbal interactions characterized by the use of the latest colloquial lexicons and phrases as well as witty and playfully sarcastic exchanges that are ratings pullers. Unlike the historical dramas, the emphasis of these productions lies in the screen celebration of the ordinary by featuring older housing estates, traditional businesses and trades that are considered to be of heritage value and a more colourful, vernacular and bustling street life that is associated with a more intimate sense of belonging. With a younger citizenry critical of the displacement caused by the demolition of old and iconic places by the property industry, postcolonial Hong Kong has been witnessing a resurgence in heritage and conservation politics (Lu 2009). This intensified sense of belonging and identification with the places in Hong Kong has also been picked up by TVB, keen to be part of the showcasing of such collective memories.

Studying the music of evening television dramas, Fairchild (2011) puts forward three points, namely, 'regularity', 'continuity' and 'payoff', to illustrate the role of music in framing the narrative on the small screen. While 'regularity' and 'continuity' serve to connect otherwise separate episodes to give audiences a sense of cognitive and aural consistency, the 'payoff' serves to link dramatic moments of the serial to its overall identity, one that will anchor the memories of the audience and generate commercial sales for its soundtrack. In this respect, the presentation of theme songs in TVB's Cantonese television dramas has followed an established pattern in preparing for the introduction, climaxes, and rolling of the end-credits in every episode.

Except for the genre of musicals, where in song and dance are being emphasized, usually three theme songs – the 'main theme' (主題曲), 'interlude'(插曲) and the 'tail end' (片尾曲) – complement most of TVB's television dramas. Played in the opening minute as part of a musical gloss-over of the highlights of the serial, the 'main theme song' (MTS) is crucial in defining the drama and announcing itself musically to prospective audiences. Whereas one would hear the instrumentalized version of the MTS during the programme itself, occasionally in the finale or dramatic climaxes the MTS gets replayed in parts. In some cases, the interlude tracks are used to suspend the development for characters in more intimate and endearing individual moments to be stretched out when the song gets inserted as a non-diegetic element. The supplementary tail end (TE) theme song, which is often slower and softer, gets aired along with the rolling of end credits and, in most cases, different singers are engaged for the MTS and supplementary songs. Nonetheless, the format has been modified occasionally in recent years, such that the artistes in the serials, several of them singers themselves, are screened in music-television styles singing the TE songs as the end credits scroll past. Usually meant for contemporary crime and corporate dramas with darker themes, under more

Theme songs of Hong Kong television dramas   205

depressive and melancholic settings, the camera will turn to more contemplative positions of the characters as they sing. Regardless of format, after repeated broadcast of the songs in at least 20 episodes, audiences are familiarized with these songs, which are also subtitled during the opening sequence.

Heroic and happy

A broad binary can be drawn among the ending songs of Hong Kong's TVB dramas, namely with the highly formalized songs prevalent in historical/ period dramas at one end and the informal counterparts associated with contemporary family dramas at the other. Table 12.1 shows the contrasting elements between these two ends of the 'heroic' (英雄) and 'happy' (喜劇) that can be used to frame the discussion to explore the multiplicity of these productions.

Based on the musical trends in theme songs that they have pioneered, two samples are used here, namely the MTS from 1976's *The Book and the Sword* by Adam Cheng and 1991's *The Family Squad*. Mainly defined along gender lines, these productions give more relevant and frequent emphasis to the highly fraternal and masculinistic notions of valour, honour, righteousness and courage that are often associated with *wuxia* and historical dramas (HD). In contrast, the category of 'harmonious' family dramas (FD) is associated with more feminized and domestic ideals of collegiality, compromise, sacrifice and sentimentality, love and affection. As such, the aesthetic structures of these theme songs are styled alongside the socio-cultural contours of these genres.

For historical dramas, especially those on significant wars and conflicts in Chinese history, the singer would commonly be the male lead in the drama, who both is highly skilled in the pugilistic arts and embodies the ideals of chivalry and patriotism in the *wuxia*'s world. Reflected in the formalized and tightly worded, honorific prose, the lyrics of these tracks demonstrate a sense of severity in the treatment of narratives that are placed in more significant macro-histories. In terms of composition style, the use of both solemn Chinese and Western classical music would be favoured, with rolling drums that bring the track to crescendos with the harmonizing of classical Western and Chinese traditional orchestras. Perhaps the closest composition that fits such a category comes from the MTS for *The Book and the Sword* (書劍恩仇錄), titled after TVB's 1976 regionally popular screen adaptation of one of Jin Yong's novels, which are frequently crafted along themes of modernity as well as Hong Kong's relations to communist China (Hamm 2005: 11–31). Sung by Adam Cheng, who was also the lead protagonist of the drama, set in the context of righteous groups resisting Manchu rule during the Qing Dynasty, with a strong patriotic lyrical flow, 'Book and the Sword' is a slow song with low and dense drums and solemn tones; the MTS relates directly to the synopsis of the drama. Singularly focused on historical reminders of the victimhood of Chinese civilization against foreign invaders, this song becomes a

206   *Liew Kai Khiun*

Table 12.1 'Heroic' and 'happy': characteristics of historical drama and contemporary 'harmonious' family drama theme songs

Historical (古裝) dramas theme songs *The Book and the Sword (書劍恩仇錄, 1976)*	Contemporary 'harmonious' (和谐) family dramas theme songs *The Family Squad (卡拉屋企)*
Singing tone: Masculine	Singing tone: Feminine
Lyrics: Formal literary	Lyrics: Informal, colloquial
Composition: Solemn, authoritative	Composition: Formal
Mood: Grandiosity	Mood: Casual, intimate
Discourse: Civilizational, nationalism	Discourse: Rootedness
Imagination: Historical-mythical	Imagination: Local

symbolic rallying cry for the restoration of national pride and loyalty. Unlike its counterparts in Mainland China and Taiwan, as a television station in the British colony, TVB's nationalistic soundtracks could only be linked to a more abstract civilizational appeal rather than the contemporary nation-state.

Nonetheless, it must be stated that many theme songs of historical dramas give greater emphasis to individual romance and angst, rather than extolling the glories of empire. One prominent set of theme songs has been those related to television adaptations of Jin Yong's historical novels, most of which conclude with the protagonist happily giving up his leadership position (that he is often compelled to assume) to walk off with his beau. Sung by Roman Tam and Jenny Tseng in the *Condor Heroes* (射鵰英雄傳) series between 1981 and 1983, in the lyrics the duo sing felicitously about finding romance over the vast plains and amid the geopolitical divides, which is characteristic of Jin Yong's utopianism (Song 2007: 121–54). With the quick tempo and the optimistically high-pitched tones of these singers, the messages of these songs suggest a modern and more liberal perspective of the otherwise feudal pre-modern era.

At another level echoing the painful restraint of history that separates characters from love and desire, theme songs for HDs would often amplify feelings of sadness and tragedy. Used often in historical dramas that portray the travails of otherwise ordinary characters like eunuchs, concubines and cooks, these songs reflect the helplessness of being caught not only within court intrigues, but also as victims of circumstance. Played principally with Chinese classical instruments, the haunting antiquity of these zithers and erhu stands in contrast with the more emancipatory hybrid of the modern popular music or even the symphonic versions. One prominent theme song that reflects on such historical angst comes from the 2010 production *Beyond the Realm of Conscience* (攻心計). This was sung by veteran singer Suzanna Kwan, whose voice is associated with dramas with more tragic themes. Underlying the characteristics of these MTSs is the role of Hong Kong's TVB in retuning and contextualizing classical Chinese music along the flows of HDs and fictions set within the modern context. Given the decades of intense disruption and suppression of Chinese cultural and classical traditions in Mao's China, Hong Kong's television dramas have played a critical role in preserving and adapting these texts both dramaturgically and musically for its domestic and overseas audiences.

In contrast, the orientations of the FDs are often cast in more feminine directions, with softer and more melodious tunes accompanied by usually gentler beats and smoother piano and guitar backups to complement the comfortable colours and watermarked images in the opening highlights. With the general portrait of the family in the centre followed by splashes of images of individual couples and relations, the highlights move into scenes depicting casual family moments as well as more eventful emotional resolutions and reconciliations. Through phrases celebrating enduring human relationships, the lyrical content moves towards the micro virtues of memory, affection, bonds and kinship.

Unlike the call to arms and the display of might in the more haughty HD theme songs, the songs in FDs direct the attention of audiences to reminiscence about the joys and simplicities of daily living. Juxtaposed with *mise-en-scènes* in the opening highlights that include not only actual footage from the action to come but often also unrelated, staged family activities set within dreamy and innocent crayonized children's art depicting houses and gardens, these theme songs assure audiences of the culturally mild nature of the serial. Such transitions can be seen from the earlier FDs like *Seasons* (季节) in the 1980s and *Kindred Spirit* (真情) in the 1990s to that of *Come Home, Love* (爱, 回家) in 2012. Increasingly, with the emphasis on distinctive districts and estates of heritage value, the highlights of the theme songs for these FDs feature the local landmarks and sceneries that these sentiments are being anchored within. Although the theme songs are principally associated with these FDs, the crafting of the lyrics without any direct references and dedication to larger family including parents gives these tracks some malleability to be marketed as individual romantic love songs on the singer's album.

One of the milestones for the use of vernacular Cantonese in theme songs was the MTS for the 1991 sitcom *The Family Squad* (卡拉屋企), which reflects one of the patterns of a FD that runs in direct contrast to the HD. Unlike the more abstracted themes of patriotism and civilization in the HD, the narrative of this theme song is more rooted in the local context of Hong Kong society, especially at this changing political juncture prior to the handover in the 1990s. Titled in Chinese as 卡拉屋企, which can be sounded out as 'karaoke' when read in Cantonese, the lyrics to the light-hearted sitcom are written in the more vernacular Cantonese script, appealing to the simplicity of urban living with the basic pleasures of smiling family members, home-cooked dishes and karaoke entertainment. Mixing the more formalized Chinese script that can be read in Putonghua with vernacular Cantonese and English allows audiences to readily identify such music with the contemporary family sitcoms where audiences expect workplace tensions to be defused playfully, wars of the sexes to end in relationships and marriages and where

208 *Liew Kai Khiun*

jokes can be played on anyone, regardless of domestic seniority. In turn, the emphasis on a more intimate and witty colloquialism in these FDs has also been sustained by the incorporation of more trendy music genres like rap and hip-hop that were once considered alternative in Hong Kong. The theme song of *Wars of the In-laws II*, for example, is a duet between veteran singer-actress Liza Wong – who is associated with theme songs of the 1980s – and then-emerging rapper Fama. Layering Wong's conventional and familiar tunes with Fama's carefully timed rapping suggests that there were efforts made to bridge the generation gap between the older viewers and post-1980s Hong Kongers who are more acquainted with the urban sounds of hip-hop. With the use of such colloquialisms and localized euphemisms, both FDs and their MTSs become representative of the discourse of the localized and enduring family that forms the pulse of the city amidst the influx of more Mainland Chinese since the 1980s.

Nostalgic musical to urban noir

The HD and FD represent the two extreme binary poles of TVB dramas, with their corresponding theme songs falling somewhere at the two opposite ends. In dramaturgical and musicological trends, these productions have never been rigidly boxed between the 'formal historical' and 'contemporary local'. In contrast, they have been subjected to significant and consistent lyrical and musical contemporization and hybridization. Observing the constant mixing of genres and their accompanying fluid intertextual relations, Mitchell (2001: 9) calls for a discursive and decentred framing of the boundaries of the music genre to map out as many articulations as possible. Rather than perfecting the classics, these dramas and theme songs are seen to be constantly appropriating new languages, styles and expressions. While some genres have not fundamentally changed, their treatments have gradually changed to address the changing socio-cultural trends that see audiences demanding, paradoxically, film noir visualization of urbanscapes and at the same time the desires of the happy family.

Table 12.2 represents the efforts to establish a more structured overview of the voluminous productions associated with TVB over close to half a century. It includes HD- and FD-representative films from genres such as corporate soap operas, police and medical dramas, contemporary urban, musical, docu-dramas and dubbed imported dramas. Although most theme songs can be generally categorized as modern popular music, variations go along with the severity of the topics that are featured in these dramas. One variation of the formal historical dramas has been the 'musical dramas' that are often concerned with nostalgic, innocent and endearing relationships. Aside from *wuxia* novels, TVB has also adapted some of its television dramas from traditional Cantonese opera as well as resurrecting the entertainment cultures of past decades. For audiences of what would seemed to be a more cynical and disenchanted fast-paced present, the interludes in these musicals when

Table 12.2 Classification of TVB dramas and theme songs

Genre	Genre	Lyrical content	TV dramas	Artiste
Historical dramas (pre-modern to Sino-Japanese War)	Chinese-Western classical symphonic mix	Nationalistic and tragic	Jin Yong adapted novels	Jenny Tsang, Roman Tam (singer)
			The Book and the Sword (書劍恩仇錄, 1976)	Adam Cheng, Liza Wong (artiste-singer)
			Beyond the Realm of Conscience (攻心計, 2010)	Suzanna Kwan (artiste-singer)
Family/romantic comedy (contemporary and contemporarized)	Rap, pop, easy listening	Endearing	*Seasons* (季節, 1987–8)	Gallen Lo (artiste-singer)
			The Family Squad (卡拉屋企, 1991–2)	Entire cast (artiste-singer)
			A Kindred Spirit (真情, 1995–9)	Joyce Lee (singer)
			Wars of the In-laws II (野蠻奶奶大戰戈師奶, 2008)	Liza Wong (artiste-singer) and Fama (singer)
			Come Home, Love (愛‧回家, 2012–13)	Linda Chung (singer)
Corporate soap operas	Symphonic	Struggle and triumph	*The Greed of Man* (1990)	Adam Cheng (artiste-singer)
			The Drive of Life (歲月風雲, 2007)	Hacken Lee and Steve Chou (singers)
Police and medical dramas	Contemporary pop	Motivational	*Police Cadet* (新紮師兄, 1984)	Tony Leung (artiste-singer)
			Armed Reaction (陀槍師姐 1998)	Sammi Cheng (singer)
			EU (學警狙擊, 2009)	Michael Tse, Ron Ng, Samuel Chan (artiste-singer)

Table 12.2 (cont.)

Genre	Genre	Lyrical content	TV dramas	Artiste
Urban noir	Rock-rap	Urban angst and alienation	When Heaven Burns (天與地, 2011)	Paul Wong (singer)
			Ghetto Justice (怒火街头, 2011)	MC Jin and Hanjin (singer-artiste)
Musical dramas	Traditional Cantonese opera	Tragic	Legend of the Purple Hairpin (紫釵記, 1975)	Liza Wang and Adam Cheng (singer-artiste)
	Rock 'n' roll, traditional pop, street music	Nostalgic, innocence	Old Time Buddies (難兄難弟, 1997)	Gallen Lo, Francis Ng, Jessica Hsuen and Cheung Hoi Yee (singer-artiste)
Docu-dramas	Folk	Belonging	Under the Lion Rock (獅子山下 1974–2006)	Roman Tam (singer for 1980s version)
				Eason Chan (2006 version)
Dubbed regional dramas and cartoons	Korean/Japanese	Transliterated	Legend of the Condor Hero (神鵰俠侶 コンドルヒーロー, 2001) jointly produced between TVB Jade Animation and Nippon Animation	Andy Lau (singer)
			Jewel in the Palace (大長今 Korean, 2005 in Hong Kong)	Kelly Chen (singer)

the storyline freezes for either a dance or a song seems to be more acceptable. With music rather than plot as the central focus, audiences expect these televisual musical dramas to bring back the popular theme songs of either Cantonese dramas like *The Purple Hairpin* (紫釵記, 1975) or the forgotten Cantonese rock 'n' roll songs of the 1960s, as in *Old Time Buddies* (難兄難弟 1996). Here, departing from what would be a more sophisticated and urbane electronic-based pop music, these tunes from musical dramas would project nostalgia for a more innocent imagined past.

In sharp distinction to the 'contemporary harmonious dramas' that are filled with humour and warmth for the viewers, the corporate family dramas are often large-scale productions with factions of family members and their corporate partners feuding over stock markets, company positions and inheritances. Filmed often in grandiose mansions, luxury yachts, golf courses, prominent landmarks (when part of the production is overseas) and huge studio reconstructions of offices and boardrooms, the MTSs of this particular genre are often heavy and symphonic in nature. Among the singers associated with this genre is Adam Cheng, whose song and acting in *The Greed of Man* (大时代, 1991) have made the production one that defines the genre of corporate family drama. The grandiose and triumphant natures of these corporate family dramas can perhaps be seen most recently in the opening theme song for *The Ride of Life* (歲月風雲, 2007), which details how two estranged brothers overcame the separation of history between Hong Kong and China as well as corporate and family rivalries to build an automobile industry in Mainland China. Set against a symphony orchestral background and footages of highways and automobile factories, Hacken Lee of Hong Kong sings the Cantonese version while his Chinese counterpart Steve Chou covers the rest of the song in Putonghua. Titled 'The Sky is Always Blue' (天这么蓝), the theme song becomes part of the serial's reignition of the nationalist mission that Hong Kong can participate in the same capitalist ethos to develop post-Mao China. Although these songs here share the same themes, associated with the public and masculinistic values of righteousness, loyalty and perseverance in the face of challenges, the nationalistic discourses of civilization and Chineseness seem absent from the contemporary corporate family dramas.

Attempts at finding more contemporary and modern notions of chivalry and gallantry in the medieval battlefront lie in the frontline of Hong Kong's uniformed services, particularly the security, rescue and medical services. Usually involving the moulding of young men and women into disciplined and professional uniformed officers, the appeal of these dramas lies in the excitement of seeing the process of training in boot camps as well as the subduing of criminals and rescuing of victims. With multiple purposes, these serve as promotional materials for recruitment and public education as well as providing dramatic car chases and shootouts and harrowing rescue and life-saving operations. Reinforcing sonically the pace of these dramas are soundtracks and theme songs with usually more youthful voices singing over

212   Liew Kai Khiun

faster drum and electronic synthesizer beats, to suggest the elements of speed, decisiveness and efficiency.

One such song that set the template was the 1984 version of *Police Cadet* (新紮師兄), which starred and was sung by the young Tony Leung. A decade later, the theme songs of four instalments of *Armed Reaction* (陀槍師姐) focused on the role of female officers were sung by one of Hong Kong's more prominent singers, Sammi Cheng. Containing messages about women's liberation and independence, the songs emphasize the ascendency of women officers in more prominent and active positions in the police force as indicators of the more professional and progressive outlook of the Hong Kong state. Following the spate of films dealing with the conflicting loyalties of undercover cops, in the third instalment of *Emergency Unit* (學警狙擊, 2009) the main theme song expresses the angst of putting up with multiple identities in the grey areas between law and ethics in an increasingly complicated city facing identity issues as Hong Kong was being handed from British to Chinese control.

Linked to the issues of crime and other related social problems is an emerging genre of film noir-related themes concerned with the repressed and violently pathologized urban society. In contrast to the cardboard villains and victims in police action dramas, the productions of what would be called urban noir here deal with the more disruptive spatial-temporal landscape of one of the most congested and densely populated cities in the world. Presented usually in dramas centring on criminal forensic scientists, psychiatrists and social workers and legal activists, these dramas dredge the hidden memories and forgotten injustices of the underbelly of society in the darkest corners of the city. In episodes dealing with flashbacks, delusionary and amnestic tendencies coupled with social injustices and inequalities, the urban noir television dramas have tended to take more critical perspectives on the framing of the city.

Whereas one sees the incorporation of additional languages and musical styles into the mainstream, as discussed earlier, it is in such urban noir dramas that more leeway seems to be given in experimenting with new noises and lyrics. One such example would be the musicological and linguistic mix in the opening theme song of *Ghetto Justice* (怒火街头, 2011), which features the role of a renegade lawyer providing legal support to the poor in the Sum Sui Bo neighbourhood against social injustices. Known as 'No Time to Regret' (沒時間後悔), the Putonghua version is sung in the pattern of freestyle rock by the Singaporean singer MC Hanjin, while the Chinese-American MC Jin provides Cantonese rapping along the way. With a messier tone structure, the song is supposed to be able to highlight the jarring complications of urban society.

When Heaven Burns (天與地, 2011), however, received significantly greater controversy as its production was banned by the highly sensitive Mainland Chinese authorities for its political references to the Tiananmen massacre. Arising from the repressed memories of four members of a rock band who were forced to eat one of their friends in desperation when they were lost on a hiking trip in Tibet almost two decades earlier the drama places viewers in a discontinuous timeframe as it oscillates frequently between the past and the present without any indications of visual transitions. Alongside split screens and shaky and blurred images in the opening theme song, either hard rock or the more moody and melancholic pop tunes are deployed to add more jarring and haunting sonic elements to the production.

Heavy riffs and intensive drumming gives a sense of displacement and abandonment not caused by the temporalities of history, as seen in historical dramas, but the claustrophobic pressure of the changing urban environment that constantly acts to erase and repress memories. Produced two decades after the Tiananmen massacre, this production and the accompanying theme song have become part of the struggles of Hong Kong society to keep the memories of the event alive even as the city is part of Beijing's jurisdiction.

A less dramatized look at the urban underbelly of Hong Kong society comes within the docu-drama productions of *Under the Lion Rock*, a reference to the peak of the Eagle's Hill that resembles the shape of a lion head overlooking the city. While more progressive documentaries are often associated with RTHK, including the series of *Under the Lion Rock* that has run in several instalments since its first season in 1974, TVB's appropriation of the genre is noteworthy here for its process of appropriating different genres. However, although it has been subsequently sung by different singers, the original lyrics are still reverently retained as the de facto anthem for Hong Kong residents.

Aside from its docu-dramas, TVB also uses Cantonese-language theme songs and dubbing of dialogue particularly for the Japanese and Korean language serials and cartoons that it broadcasts, to help local Hong Kong viewers understand. More significantly, with the change in theme songs, it partakes in the transliterization of foreign programmes by interpreting the narrative according to its own geo-linguistic rhythmic texture. Two examples of such a process of transliteration include *The Legend of the Condor Heroes*, jointly produced by TVB's Jade Animation and Nippon Animation in 2001, and the Korean-based MBC *Jewel in the Palace*. In the former case, one of the 'Four Heavenly Kings', Andy Lau, sang the Cantonese version of the theme song 'The Bitterness of True Love' (真愛是苦味). Differing from the lighter and more childlike sounds of the Japanese version, Lau's tone for this song was solemn and deep. A similar reversal could also be seen in Kelly Chen's rendition of the original theme song of *Jewel in the Palace*, which details the tribulations faced by a court chambermaid in the early modern Josen Dynasty who rose to become a court physician of the king. Even as the distinctive ethnic cultural composition and tunes of the traditional pansori style were kept, Chen's version, 'Hope' (希望), seems more like a song celebrating the struggle of the heroine rather than the more restraintive version 'Onara' (오나라). Collectively, the transliterization of the theme songs of these TVB imported dramas has served to connect them more seamlessly with their mainstream local counterparts

214 *Liew Kai Khiun*

to enable more seamless programming for the station. This process of localization and hybridization of foreign content has been described by Chu and Leung (2013) as the key to the Canto-pop industry's success in the cultural negotiation and translation of non-Chinese productions for the Hong Kong market, which in turn becomes one crucial indicator of the city's cosmopolitan projections.

Conclusion

Often treated as peripheral in both public attention and scholarly discourses, theme songs and soundtracks are, however, critical in layering the televisual soundscapes, amplifying the emotional flow of the narrative and anchoring audience memories of the events. In the case of the television dramas of TVB, it is the musical aspect of its productions that has been instrumental in extending and maintaining its popularity in Hong Kong and the larger Asia-Pacific region for the four decades since the station's first broadcast. Along with a mixed bag of dramas are theme songs and soundtracks tailored as closely to the serials as possible. Even as templates have already been established to define different genres, the inclusion of Putonghua and English into a repertoire of predominantly Cantonese-based theme songs, the appropriation of less mainstream rock and rap music, the use of different combinations of veteran and new as well as local and foreign singers, and the localization of imported programmes all reflect on the malleability and evolution of the television culture in Hong Kong along with changing socio-cultural undercurrents.

References

ATV (2013) 'About us', www.hkatv.com/zhhk/about/atv/en (accessed 24 June 2013).

Booth, Paul (2011) 'Contemporary television memories, temporalities, fictions: temporal displacement in contemporary television', *Television & New Media*, 12(4): 370–88.

Chu, Yiu-Wai and Leung, Eve (2013) 'Remapping Hong Kong popular music: covers, localization and the waning hybridity of Cantopop', *Popular Music*, 32(1): 65–78.

Digital Television (2011) 'Digital TV coverage further extended to 90% of the population', 3 January, www.digitaltv.gov.hk/general/news_03012011.htm (accessed 24 June 2013).

Fairchild, Charles (2011) 'Flow amid flux: the evolving uses of music in evening television drama', *Television & New Media*, 12(6): 491–512.

Hamm, John (2005) *Paper Swordsmen: Jin Yong and the Modern Chinese Martial Arts Novel*, Honolulu: University of Hawaii Press.

Hampton, Mark (2011) 'Early Hong Kong television, 1950s–1970s', *Media History*, 17(3): 305–22.

Hoskins, Andrew (2004) 'Time and the collapse of memory', *Time & Society*, 13(1): 109–27.

Ku, Agnes (2004) 'Immigration policies, discourses, and the politics of local belonging in Hong Kong (1950–1980)', *Modern China*, 30(3): 326–60.

Liew, Kai Khiun (2010) 'Symbolic migrant workers: Southeast Asian artistes in the East Asian entertainment industry' in D. Shim and A. Heryanto (eds.) *Pop Culture Formations across East Asia*, Seoul: Jimoodang, pp. 181–208.

Lu, Tracey (2009) 'Heritage conservation in post-colonial Hong Kong', *International Journal of Heritage Studies*, 15(2–3): 258–72.

Ma, Eric Kit-wai (1999) *Culture, Politics and Television in Hong Kong*, London: Routledge.

Mitchell, Jason (2001) 'A cultural approach to television genre theory', *Cinema Journal*, 40(3): 1–24.

Mitchell, Jason (2006) 'Narrative complexity in American television', *The Velvet Light Trap*, 56: 29–40.

Newcomb, Horace and Alley, Robert (1983) *The Producer's Medium: Conversations with Creators of American TV*, New York: Oxford University Press.

RTHK (2012) 'Corporate brochure', http://rthk.hk/about/pdf/corporate_brochure_ 2012.pdf (accessed: 24 June 2013).

Song Weijie (2007) 'Space, swordsmen and utopia: the dualistic imagination in Jin Yong's novels', in Ann Huss and Jianmei Liu (eds.) *The Jin Yong Phenomenon: Chinese martial arts fiction and Modern Chinese Literary History*, Youngstown, New York: Cambria Press, pp. 155–77.

TVB (2013) 'Corporate profile', www.tvb.com/affairs/faq/tvbgroup/tvb_e.html (accessed: 24 June 2013).

To Yiu Ming and Lau Tuen-Yu (1995) 'Global export of Hong Kong television: Television Broadcast Limited', *Asian Journal of Communication*, 5(2): 108–22.

Wong Chi Hwa and Chu Yu Wai (2011) *Discussing the Lyrics of 80 Hong Kong Songs*, Hong Kong: Wise Publications.

Appendix
Television data across countries

Bhutan (Bunty Avieson)

Date of first TV broadcast: 2 June 1999.

Total number of FTA television channels available in the market: Two.

Number of publicly funded broadcast channels: Two.

Number of commercial broadcast channels: None.

Number of cable/pay TV channels: 45 channels on cable, via India; 200+ via satellite television stations from outside the country, mainly India, known locally as DTH (dish to home), which is illegal. The government estimates illegal satellite subscribers are in the 'thousands' (Bhutan Information and Media Impact Study 2013).

Number of pay TV providers: 57 licensed cable operators (BICMA Annual report 2012), across 19 of 20 dzongkhags (regional government areas).

Penetration of cable and FTA as a percentage of the television market: Survey data shows that 88 per cent of the urban households paid local cable operators while only 25 per cent of rural households paid local cable operators; 2 per cent of urban households paid agents in India, while 13 per cent of rural households paid agents in India. This indicates proliferation of DTH TV in rural areas as compared to urban areas, making up for the limited cable TV coverage in rural areas (15 per cent of rural households and 3 per cent of urban households watch TV but did not pay anyone, which refers to households with 'informal' TV connections and/or access to free-to-air channels only).

Languages used in the market: Bhutanese TV broadcasts in English and Dzongkha. Cable and satellite TV is predominantly in Indian languages, such as Hindi, Telugu, Bengali, etc., but also Nepali, Korean, etc.

References

Bhutan Information and Media Impact Study (2013) *Final Draft, Department of Information and Media, Ministry of Information and Communications,* Thimphu: Royal Government of Bhutan.

Appendix 217

BICMA (2012) *Annual Report*, Thimphu: Bhutan Infocomm and Media Authority.

China (Wanning Sun and Lauren Gorfinkel)

Date of first TV broadcast: 1 May 1958.

Total number of FTA television channels available in the market: There are more than 1,000 channels (Sun 2012). At the end of May 2012, there were 197 television stations, 43 'educational television stations' (*jiaoyu dianshi tai*) as well as county-level TV stations (Pang 2012: 41). By paying a basic maintenance fee for cable (in areas serviced by cable – most areas) audiences can freely access CCTV's main channels, provincial satellite TV channels from other provinces, other local provincial, city-level and county-level stations, and other selected stations (Zhu 2006: 1891).

Number of publicly funded vs commercial broadcast channels: All TV channels are operating independently of government management. Advertising revenue is the main source of income. Cable TV networks are the second largest source of income (Pang 2012: 58).

Number of cable/pay TV channels: As of 2009, there were 142 pay TV channels, with 112 broadcast nationally and 30 broadcast provincially. This figure includes 13 CCTV pay TV channels. Digital pay TV channels usually transfer on satellite and are picked up by local Internet service providers who then transfer the channels to users' homes via local digital Cable TV networks (Zeng and Heng 2013). In 2011 there were 36 satellite uplink stations, transferring 373 television programmes and 362 radio programmes (Pang 2012: 40). Chinasat-9, launched on 9 June 2008, has a capacity for up to 200 standard-definition and high-definition radio and TV channels and can transmit to users in China, Hong Kong, Macau and Taiwan (Zhou 2008). Since September 26, 2011, Sichuan-based Kham (康巴) Tibetan-language TV satellite programmes have been transmitted via the Star B6 satellite, expanding Kham Tibetan TV satellite coverage in the Asia-Pacific region (Pang 2012: 40). From April 2011, the Central Propaganda Department and the State Administration of Radio, Film and Television (SARFT) embarked on a process of establishing direct broadcast satellite to broadcast basic channels to rural households not served by cable networks. More than 37 million users in 150,000 villages in areas including Ningxia, Inner Mongolia and Hebei have been provided with access to direct broadcast satellite services (Pang 2012: 40). International satellite channels are available in restricted contexts; for example, to foreigners in hotels and workers involved in research, journalism, trade.

Number of pay TV providers: 39 central-level media, provincial-level media and central bodies (e.g., the China Meteorological Administration) run 112 national digital pay TV channels; 19 units sponsor 30 provincial-level digital pay channels (Zeng and Heng 2013: 38).

Penetration rate of cable: 45 per cent of all TV households (174.6 million out of 388 million TV households) had cable TV at the end of 2009 (Wang et al. 2010).

218 *Appendix*

Penetration rate of FTA: This depends on the definition of FTA. Most households where cable is available pay a small maintenance fee for their television service. This fee is separate to the pay TV option, which has limited appeal due to the availability of a wide range of freely accessible programmes (Wang et al. 2010). There is suggestion that some migrant workers purchase 'illegal' satellite dishes for use in cities to avoid paying the maintenance fee. Satellite TV available in rural and remote areas is FTA.

Languages used in the market: Specific number is unknown. CCTV has domestic, international broadcast and online channels (via CNTV) in English, Spanish, French, Arabic, Russian, Korean, Mongolian, Tibetan, Uyghur and Kazakh. Some local stations broadcast programmes in ethnic languages and local dialects; for example, there is a Kunming dialect programme on Kunming Television. Tibet television offers Chinese and Tibetan bilingual programmes. Xinjiang television offers programmes in six languages including Chinese, Uighur, Kazakh, Mongolian, Ke language and Xibe language (Pang 2012: 51–2).

References

Pang, Jingjun (ed.) (2012) *Annual Report on Development of China's Radio, Film and Television (Zhongguo Guangbo Dianying Dianshi Fazhan Baogao)*, Beijing: Social Sciences Academic Press.

Sun, Wusan (2012) 'Top-down policies versus grassroots resistance: the management of illegal satellites in the Chinese village' in Wanning Sun and Jenny Chio (eds.) *Mapping Media in China: Region, Province and Locality*, London: Routledge.

Wang, Wenbo, Bisson, Guy and Aguete, Maria Rua (2010) *China Cable Television Market Assessment and Forecast to 2014*, www.screendigest.com/reports/2010920a/10_10_china_cable_television/view.html (accessed 25 November 2011).

Zeng, Fanbin and Heng, Wu (2013) 'Development of pay television channels in China', *Asian Culture and History*, 5(1): 34–50.

Zhou, Hao (2008) 'China's first direct broadcast satellite to enter service', *China Daily*, www.chinadaily.com.cn/bizchina/2008-05/20/content_6698467.htm (accessed 15 March 2015).

Zhu, Xia (2006) 'Analyze the changes of Chinese television – from free to charge', *China Digital Cable TV*, 19–20: 1890–2.

Hong Kong (Jinna Tay and Liew Kai Khiun)

Date of first TV broadcast: 19 November 1967 (TVB)

Total number of FTA television channels available in the market: Four analogue channels each owned by ATV (World and Home) and TVB (Pearl and Jade) broadcasting networks; the 11 digital channels incorporate these four channels.

Number of publicly funded broadcast channels: One (Radio Television Hong Kong broadcaster feeds programmes to the FTA networks and pay television; it does not carry a broadcast licence).

Appendix 219

Number of commercial broadcast channels: 11. This includes the cross-border broadcast of CCTV 1 and CCTV 9 as well as simulcast of ShenZhen TV. Technically CCTV is not included under commercial channels but is reflected here in the overall number of FTA channels available in Hong Kong.

Number of cable/pay TV providers and number of channels: Three cable providers: PCCW, Wharf's i-Cable and HK Broadband. Together they provide about 360 channels. Due to the 'Open Sky' policy, satellite antenna television sets can receive any unencrypted satellite television programme channels.

Penetration of cable and FTA as a percentage of the television market: The proportion rate of subscription penetration is estimated to be around 85 per cent of the total population. Currently FTA has around 31 per cent of the market, translating to more than 1.9 million viewers.

Languages used in the market: English, Cantonese and Mandarin.

References

Communications and Technology Branch, Commerce and Economic Development Bureau, www.cedb.gov.hk/ctb/eng/broad/tv.htm.
CASBAA, Hong Kong (2012) www.casbaa.com/advertising/countries/hong-kong.
Nip, A. (2013) 'Slide in ratings is no drama', *South China Morning Post*, www.scmp.com/news/hong-kong/article/1295323/tvb-says-its-slide-ratings-no-drama.

India (Divya McMillin)

Date of first TV broadcast: 1959.

Total of number of FTA television channels available in the market: 825 channels.

Number of publicly funded broadcast channels: One: Prasar Bharati, which comprises the Doordarshan television network and All India Radio.

Number of commercial broadcast channels: 821 (licensed) and 660 (operational), as of 2012, with about 40 of them in HD; 1,220 (licensed) and 985 (operational) expected by 2015.

Number of cable/pay TV providers: Nine: Arasu Cable TV, Asianet Digital, DEN Networks, Hathway, InCablenet, Siti Cable, Sun Cable Vision, Tamil Nadu Arasu Cable TV Corporation Limited and You Scod18.

Number of pay channels: 163.

Penetration of cable and FTA as a percentage of the television market: Penetration rates in 2012 are as follows:

- 44 million digital homes
- 126 million cable and satellite homes
- 148 million television households
- 231 million combined television households

220 *Appendix*

The number of pay-television households in India was 127 million in 2012.

Languages used in the market: All official languages.

- Hindi
- English
- Gujarati – language of Gujarat and Union Territories of Dadar and Nagar Haveli
- Punjabi – the official language of Punjab
- Bengali – the state language of West Bengal
- Assamese – official language of Assam
- Dogri, Urdu – the language of Jammu and Kashmir
- Oriya – the state language of Orissa
- Marathi – language of Maharashtra
- Kannada – the official language of Karnataka
- Tamil – the state language of Tamil Nadu
- Telugu – the official language of Andhra Pradesh.
- Malayalam – the official language of Kerala
- Sindhi
- Konkani – the state language of Goa
- Manipuri – the official language of Manipur
- Khasi – the official language of Meghalaya
- Mizo – the official language of Mizoram
- Lotha – the official language of Nagaland

References

India Entertainment and Media Outlook 2013, PriceWaterhouseCooper.
Maps of India, www.mapsofindia.com/culture/indian-languages.html (accessed 8 August 2014).
IndianTelevision.com, www.indiantelevision.com/headlines/y2k12/apr/apr129.php (accessed 8 August 2014).

Japan (Alisa Freedman)

Date of first TV broadcast: First successful public TV broadcast 13 May 1939. Regular broadcast began on 1 February 1953 (2pm to 8:45pm on NHK).

Total number of FTA television channels available in the market: Japan does not have FTA television. In general, the Japanese broadcast system combines that of Great Britain and the United States. Under the Broadcast Law of Japan (1950), television primarily consists of NHK (Nippon Hoso Kyokai) public broadcasting system, modelled in part on Great Britain's BBC, along with five major commercial networks, which rely on advertising revenues as American commercial networks do. There are several regional affiliates and local channels. Under Article 64 of the Broadcast Law of Japan, television owners must pay receiver fees (*Jushinryo*) to NHK in order to have reception. Radio listeners have been exempt from fees since 1968.

Appendix 221

Number of publicly funded broadcast channels: NHK has two major networks: NHK General TV (NHK Sogo Terebijon) and NHK Educational TV (NHK Kyoiku terebijon). Broadcasting began in 1960. Programmes carry the 'NHK E' mark in the corner.)

Number of commercial broadcast channels: Five: Nihon Television (NTV), Tokyo Broadcast System Television (TBS), Fuji Television Network (Fuji TV), TV Asahi and TV Tokyo. The five commercial networks are affiliated with major newspapers: NTV (Yomiuri shimbun), TBS (Mainichi shimbun), Fuji (Sankei shimbun), TV Asahi (Asahi shimbun) and TV Tokyo (Nihon keizai shimbun).

Number of cable/pay TV providers and number of channels: Broadcast Satellite TV (BS) became a chargeable service in 1989. Around 11 BS channels available in high-definition:

- NHK BS1, NHK BS 2 (BS Premium) – NHK Broadcast Satellite was established in 1989
- BS Nittele (operated by NTV)
- BS Asahi (operated by Asahi TV)
- BS-TBS (operated by TBS)
- BS Japan (operated by TV Tokyo)
- BS Fuji (operated by Fuji TV)
- WOWOW – established in 1984, first private satellite and pay TV station in Japan; three channels: WOWOW Prime (general entertainment), WOWOW Live (sports and live performances) and WOWOW Cinema
- Star Channel HV – three movie channels (Star Channel 1, Star Channel 2 and Star Channel 3)
- BS 11 – established in 1999, private satellite broadcast channel owned by Bic Camera, Inc.
- World Hi-Vision Channel – owned by Mitsui and Company, Ltd., features programming from Disney, National Geographic Channel, MTV, Takarazuka female theatre revue, Fox and QVC shopping network

Commercial direct broadcast satellite providers include Sky PerfecTV!, JCOM and Hikari TV.

Penetration of cable and FTA as a percentage of the television market: In March 2012, 26.6 million households, or 49.6 percent of all households nationwide, subscribed to cable television services (self-originating broadcasting using licensed facilities).

Languages used in the market: All stations air in Japanese but have historically included programmes in other languages. For example, NHK educational network has featured language-learning programmes since the 1960s; weekly in 1977, 50 hours of lessons in the five official languages of the United Nations – English, Spanish, Chinese, Russian and French – along with German were offered (Blair 1997: 4). Foreign drama series (first

222 *Appendix*

primarily English and now Korean) have aired for decades on NHK general network on Saturday nights. Commercial networks regularly broadcast Hollywood movies and other foreign films (available in bilingual format since around 1995).

References

Blair, R. J. (1997) 'The role of English and other foreign languages in Japanese society', *The Internet TESL Journal*, 3(7): 74–86.

Statistics Bureau (2012) *Statistical Handbook of Japan*, www.stat.go.jp/english/data/handbook/c16cont.htm (accessed 29 May 2014).

South Korea (Sun Jung)

Date of first TV broadcast: 12 May 1956.

Total number of FTA television channels available in the market: Five: KBS1, KBS2, EBS, MBC and SBS.

Number of publicly funded broadcast channels: Three: KBS1, KBS2 and EBS.

Number of commercial broadcast channels: Two: MBC and SBS.

Number of cable/pay TV channels: 205 (excludes satellite).

Number of pay TV providers: 98. IPTV providers include KT's OllehTV, SK's Btv and LG's U+. Digital satellite broadcasters include KT's Skylife. Cable television system operators include C&M, CMB, JCN, t-broad, CJ's Hello Vision and Hyundai's HCN.

Penetration of cable and FTA as a percentage of the television market: FTA 2.4 per cent, cable 97.6 per cent (cable's revenue is double that of FTA).

Languages used in the market: Mainly Korean with various foreign programmes in English, Chinese, Japanese, Spanish, etc.

Malaysia (Umi Khattab)

Date of first TV broadcast: 28 December 1963.

Total number of FTA television channels available in the market: Eight.

Number of publicly funded broadcast channels: Three.

Number of commercial broadcast channels: Five (four owned indirectly by UMNO through Media Prima).

Number of cable/pay TV channels:

- One cable pay TV
- One digital satellite pay TV

Appendix 223

- One digital satellite free TV
- Mobile TV service: MITV with about 40 channels (pay TV)
- IPTV: Fine TV unlimited channel with Internet access (pay TV)

Number of pay TV providers: Four.

Penetration of cable and FTA as a percentage of the television market: FTA: 59.9 per cent, pay TV 40.1 per cent.

Languages used in the market: Bahasa Malaysia (Malay language), English, Chinese and Tamil.

Philippines (Jonathan Corpus Ong)

Date of first broadcast: 23 October 1953.

Total number of free-to-air TV channels: 12 major national stations plus 73 local TV stations.

Number of publicly funded broadcast channels: One.

Number of commercial broadcast channels: 11 at a national level.

Number of cable/pay TV channels: 130+ (including satellite).

Number of cable/pay TV providers: 386 nationwide.

Penetration of cable and FTA as a percentage of the television market: Cable 17 per cent, free-to-air 83 per cent.

Languages used in the market: Predominantly English and Filipino, with at least five local languages in provincial television programming.

Singapore (Jinna Tay)

Date of first TV broadcast: 15 February 1963.

Total number of FTA television channels available in the market: Seven.

Number of publicly funded broadcast channels: Seven.

Number of commercial broadcast channels: Seven. Mediacorp holds the television monopoly and it is both a commercialized outfit and a government-owned corporation, as it is fully owned by Temasek Holdings, the investment arm of the government.

Number of cable/pay TV providers and number of channels: There is currently one cable and one IPTV provider, Starhub and Mio TV respectively. Starhub offers around 170 channels and Mio offers 120 channels.

Penetration of cable and FTA as a percentage of the television market: The penetration rate of pay television ranges between 67 per cent and 70 per cent

224 *Appendix*

of the market, or about 900,000 homes. The free-to-air (terrestrial) market is reported to have a 'reach of 91.7% of the market' (MDA 2013), or 4.5 million viewers. The 'reach' is 'the total percentage (or number) of unduplicated individuals who tune into a TV program over a given time period (based on the Kantar Media "Television Audience Measurement" system)' (MDA 2013).

Languages used in the market: English, Mandarin, Malay and Tamil. The predominant language for business use in Singapore is English, as seen on Channel 5 and Channel News Asia (CNA, 24/7 news channel). Some feature documentaries on CNA are produced and broadcasted in Mandarin. Channel 8 and Channel U are Mandarin-language channels and Suria is in Malay language. Vasantham is a dedicated Indian Tamil-language channel but offers some non-Tamil programmes such as Bollywood films in Hindi.

References

CASBAA, Singapore (2012) www.casbaa.com/advertising/countries/singapore (accessed 20 July 2014).
Mediacorp (2008) 'MediaCorp to launch Indian and children's TV channels in major programming refresh', 29 February, www.mediacorp.sg/en/media/mediacorp-to-launch/1106028.html (accessed 20 July 2014).
MDA (2013) *Annual Report: Media Convergence, Media Development Authority of Singapore*, www.mda.gov.sg/Documents/AnnualReport/2013/media/MDA_AR_All.pdf (accessed 31 July 2014).
Singtel (n.d.) 'Your channel TV guide to a brand new mio TV experience!' http://mio.singtel.com/miotv/channels-on-demand_channels.asp (accessed 20 July 2014).

Taiwan (Fang-Chih Irene Yang)

Date of first TV broadcast: 10 October 1962 (the date when TTV was formally broadcast).

Total number of FTA television channels available in the market: 20.

Number of publicly funded broadcast channels: Eight.

Number of commercial broadcast channels: Three networks, 12 channels.

Number of cable/pay TV channels: Cable (domestic): 157 channels; foreign: 111 channels, a total of 268 channels (including satellite).

Number of pay TV providers: Domestic, 78 providers; foreign, 29 providers.

Penetration of cable and FTA as a percentage of the television market: Cable TV accounts for 93 per cent and FTA accounts for 7 per cent of the market.

Languages used in the market: Mandarin, Taiwanese, Hakka (one public broadcasting channel), indigenous languages (public broadcasting channel), English and Japanese.

Appendix 225

References

Association of Terrestrial Television Networks (2012) September, Taiwan, ROC.

Thailand (Brett Farmer)*

Date of first TV broadcast: 24 June 1955, called Thai Thorathat (TV4, later TV9 or Mondern9 TV). Colour telecasts (PAL, system B 625 lines) in 1969, full-time colour transmissions in 1975. Digital switchover expected to be completed in 2015 (subject to change to 2020).

Total number of FTA television channels available in the market: Six channels.

Table A.1 List of television stations in Thailand

Operator	6 FTA channels
MCOT (Mass Communication Organization of Thailand Plc.)	Modernine TV
	TV3
Royal Thai Army	TV 5
	BBTV 7
NBT (National Broadcasting Services of Thailand)	NBT
Public TV	Thai PBS
Defunct	ITV, TVT-11, TCTV-9

Number of publicly funded broadcast channels: Two channels.

- NBT (formerly TVT-11); fully owned by the government (Public Relations Department, and Office of the Prime Minister).
- Thai Public Broadcasting Service (Thai PBS) endorsed by the Thai Public Broadcasting Service Act, BE 2551 (2008). Under this Act, the TPBS holds the status of state agency with legal personality, but not being a government agency or state enterprise.

Number of commercial broadcast channels: Three channels (TV3, BBTV 7 and Modernine TV).

- Modernine TV is a state-owned free-to-air television network operated by MCOT.
- Thailand Colour Television Channel 3 (TV3) operated by BEC-TERO under MCOT concession.
- Bangkok Broadcasting & TV Co. Ltd. (BBTV 7) under the concession and management by Royal Thai Army.

Note: Channel 5 is fully operated by Royal Thai Army Radio and Television. However, the National Broadcasting Telecommunications Commission of

226 *Appendix*

Thailand (NBTC), a single converged regulator for telecoms and broadcasting sectors, is set up to manage TV and telecoms businesses. One of its major missions is to have the government return the frequencies and reassign the spectrum for fair use.

Number of cable/pay TV channels: Including satellites, 465 channels; excluding satellites, 240 channels (mainly local cable TV providers): 41 channels already granted licences, while 199 channels are waiting for a licence from NBTC.

Number of pay TV providers: Approximately 250 including radio.

Table A.2 Structure of television provision in Thailand

Provider	Free or pay	No. broadcast channels	Transmission
Analogue terrestrial	Free	6 (switch off in 2015)	Analogue terrestrial
Digital terrestrial	Free (mainly experimental)	48	Digital terrestrial television
TrueVisions	Pay TV	Around 250 (TV and radio)	Digital satellite
STAT.or.th	Free and subscription	Around 20	IPTV

Penetration of cable and FTA as a percentage of the television market: FTA 9.1 per cent, cable 90.9% (normally includes six FTA channels as per a must-carry regulation).

Languages used in the market: In keeping with hegemonic Thai statist ideology, central Thai – or, as its colloquially known, Bangkok Thai – is the dominant language used in almost all Thai TV programming, whether government or commercial. Occasionally, some of the de facto regional languages of Thailand such as Isan (North-Eastern Thai) or Kam Meuang (Northern Thai) will be heard in the context of soap operas or music variety shows. There is also some limited educational programming in English. In 2013, the then ruling Pheua Thai government signalled a significant relaxation of the former official policy of central Thai monolingualism in national media when it announced plans to launch a 24-hour Malay-language satellite television channel to broadcast across the deep south of Thailand where Malay is widely spoken. However, as of the time of writing, this proposal has not been realized.

References

NBTC as of June 1, 2013.
* Information was compiled by Alongkorn Parivudhiphongs, lecturer in Communication Studies at Chulalongkorn University.

Index

Abaya, H. 144
Adams, D. 71n
Allen, R.C. 87n
Almario, M. 145
Amporn, J. 80
Anagnost, A. 176
Anderson, B. 23, 61, 133, 144
Anholt, S. 8
Annuar, M.K. 134
Apichart, J. 83
Appadurai, A. 133
Aquino, C. 151
Ashcroft, W. 39
Asian Idol 12
Askew, M. 84
Athique, A.M. 13
Atiya, A. 82, 83, 87n
Avieson, B. 11
Awakening, The 93, 100, 101, 105

Bandurski, D. 26
Barme, S. 87n
Batabyal, S. 52, 53
Bauman, Z. 179
Beijing TV 20–21
Bennett, T. 76
Bhutan Broadcasting Service (BBS TV) 58–62
Billig, M. 108, 133
Blandford, S., Lacey, S., McElroy, R. and Williams, R. 92, 93
Bly, R. 63
BMIS 59, 60, 61
Bonner, F. 5
Book and the Sword, The 205–6
Boonrak, B. 75
Booth, P. 202
Brooten, L. and Klangnarong, S. 75
Buckingham, D. 87n

Bund, The 198
Burgess, J. and Green, J. 192

Campos, P., 149
Cannell, F. 147, 155, 158
CCTV (China Central Television) 7, 24–25, 28–29
Chachavalpongpun, P. 83
Chairat, C. 85
Chakravarty, S. 42
Challenge, The 136
Chan, B. 92, 93
Chang, C. 175
Chang, T.-K. 19, 20, 22, 23, 24, 25, 30, 31
Chatterji, P.C. 42
Chavarong, L. and Leveau, M. 74
Cheah, B.K. 129
Chen, M. 33
Chen, N.T. 174, 175
Chin, C.B.N. 130
Chin, Y.C. 25, 26
China Media Project 28
Choi, I.-H. 196n
Chowdhury, K. 55
Chu, G.C. 22
Chu, W.-Y. and Leung, E. 214
Chua, B.H. 13, 93, 94
Chua, B.H. and Iwabuchi, K. 196n
Chun, A. 165, 166
Chung, J.C., Kim, J.H. and Choi, H.G. 189
Clayton, S. 69
commercial (private) networks; in India 46–53; in Korea 182–3, in the Philippines 146–7, 150–2, in Singapore, 98–99, in Taiwan 167, in Thailand 80–82
Connors, M. 83
Connors M. and Hewison, K. 74

228   *Index*

Cordova, J. 146
Coronel, S. 152, 159
Couldry, N. 77, 146, 152, 156
Croteau, D. and Hoynes, W. 63
cultural effects of television 62–64,
  myths about the 64–70
Curran, J. and Park, K. 2
Curtin, M. 14, 19, 24

Dahlgren, P. 78
Damayan (*Empathy for Each Other*) 150
Darian-Smith, K. and Turnbull, S. 5
De Jesus, M.Q. 153
del Mundo, C. 145, 147, 148
Dendup, T. 70n
De Quiros, C. 146, 153, 154
De Vogli, R. 71n
digitization: in India 53–4
Dignity of the Temp, 118
Ding, X.J. 30
Discovery of India, The 42
Dok Som Si Tong 82
Donald, S. H., Keane, M. and
  Yin, H. 19
Donato, J. 150
Doordarshan 13, 39, 41–51 , 54
Doordarshan Audience Research
  Unit 42, 43
dorama 112, 115–8, 123–4; working
  women in 115–119, 123–4
Douglas, M. 164

Fairchild, C. 204
Family Squad, The 206–7
Ferrara, F. 84
Fischer, T. and Tashi, T. 59, 60, 65
Fleet van, S. 81, 86, 87n
Fletcher, O. 27
Flores, P. 146, 149
Freedman, A. 8, 124n
Freedman, A. and Iwata-Weikgenannt,
  K. 117, 118
Fung, A. 15, 24
Fursich, E. and Shrikhande, S. 38
Furuya, M. 182

Garcia, C. 158
Gauntlett, D. 64
Ghandi, R. 43–4
Gimenez-Maceda, T. 148, 151
Giroux, H. 77
global formats 14–15
Gopalan, K. 53
Gorfinkel, L. 28

Grisprud, J., Hallvard, M., Molander, A.
  and Eide, M. 77
Guitierrez, J. 159
Guo, Z.Z. 20
Gupta, A. 47

Ha, Y.-G. 191
Habermas, J. 134
Hajkowski, T. 6
Hall, S. 130, 138
Hall, S., Critcher, C., Jefferson, T.,
  Clarke, J. and Roberts, B. 164
Hallin, D. and Mancini, P. 16
Hamilton, A. 78–79
Hamm, J. 205
Hampton, M. 200
Hao, M.Y. 170
Harada, N. 115
Hartley, J. 6, 77, 133
Haynes, A. 134
Heniao, L. 176
Hershock, P. 62
Hesse-Swain, C. 86
Hi-S Tales 79–80
Hng, H.Y. 130
Hobsbawm, E. 133
Hollnsteiner, M. 155
Hong, J.H. 20, 23, 24, 25, 30, 31
Hong, Z., 40
Hong Kong television drama 5
Hookway, J. 87n
Hoskins, A. 202
Hsiangtu drama 169, 172–6
Hsie, P.H. 176
Hu, K.[2014] 192
Hu, Y.R. 168, 191
Huang, R.P,, You, Z.H., and Chen,
  Y.H. 178
Hunan TV 29–30
Hut, K.K. 170

Ileto, R. 148
Im, G.-B. 191
Ishida, Y. 121
Ito, M. 113, 116, 120, 121
Iwabuchi, K. 15, 116

Jackson, P.A. 81
Jiang, L.Z. 168, 169
Jin, D.-Y. 182, 184, 186, 187, 189
Jung, S. 4, 192, 196n

Kang, H.-J. 194
Kanokporn, C. 80, 82

Karthegisu, R. 127
Kaur, A. 130
Keane, M. 19
Keane, M., Fung, A. and Moran, A.
    2, 3, 19
Kerkveleit, V. 147, 154, 155
Khattab, U. 1, 9, 130, 136
Khiun, L.K. 5
Khoo, B.K. 135, Kim, J.J. 184, 185,
    186, 187
Kim, S.-D. 183, 184, 187
Kim, S.-J. 192
Kim, Y. 146
Kitazumi, T. 117
Ko, Y.F. 172, 173, 174, 175
Koh, E.L. 158, Koh, J.-M. and Hong,
    H.-J. 195
Kong, R. 82
K-pop, 182–3
Kraidy, M. 2
Krishaswamy, R. 39
Ku, A. 201
Kultida, S. 81
Kumar, K.J. 38
Kust, M.J. 42

lakhon (Thai soap opera) 80–86
Langley, W. 68–9
Lapena, C. 150
Lazarus, N. 55
Lee, D.-H., 124n, 195
Lee, D.-Y. [2011] 182
Lee, K.H. 130
Lee, J.H. and Youn, S.M. 187
Lee, P.S.N. 20, 22
Lent, J.A. 132, 148
Leo, A. 87n
Leong, W.K. 93, 100
Lessing, D. 63, 101
Levo-Henrikssen, R. 64
Lewis, G. 74, 75
Lewis, T., Martin, F. and Sun, W. 19
Li, X.P. 20, 22, 23, 24
Lieu, K.K. 200
Lim, K. 93
Lim, K.S. 98
Ling, S. 135
Lin, G.S. [2005] 166
Lin, L.H. [2006] 177
Lin, M.S. [1991, 1994] 173, 174, 175
Liphao 174, 177
Livingstone, S. 146
Loh, K.S. 94
Loomba, A. 55

Lu, T. 204
Lull, M. 20, 22
Lumby, C. and Fine, D. 64

Ma, E. 6, 10, 201
Ma, Y.L. 171
McCargo, D. 74, 75
McCoy, A. 145, 150
McDonald, R. 62
McGuigan, J. 77, 80
Mackay, H. 64
McMillin D. 1, 7, 11, 43, 51
McQuail, D. 64, 66–67
Madaniou, M. 146
Maglipon, F. 144
Mahathir, M. 127–8, 135, 136
Making it National 9
Malay Dilemma, The 128, 135, 136
Manchanda, U. 44
Mankekar, P. 38, 43
Martial law and Filipino television
    149–150
Maslog, C. 149
Matusomoto, Y. et al, 124n
Maya, Y. 82
Means, G.P. 127
Media Impact Study (Bhutan) 2003 59,
    65, 66, 67
Media Impact Study (Bhutan) 2008 62, 64
MediaCorp Singapore, 98, 99
Miller, D. and Madaniou, M. 154
Mitchell, J. 202, 208
Mitra, A. 38
modernity/modernization and television
    9–12, 47, 96, 102, 127, 135–6
Mohd Sani, M.A. 131
Moores, S. 77
Morley, D. and Robins, K. 133
Morris. M. 76, 134
Montesano, M., Chachavalpongpun, P.
    and Chongvilaivan, A. 83, 84
Moten, A.R. and Mokhtar, T.M. 127
Mullen, R.D. and Ganguly, S. 38
music programming in Korea: on
    broadcast television 183–8; on
    cable and internet 188–91; on
    digital 191–4
music soundtracks for television,
    202–210; music themes 204–6

Nain, Z. 136
nation-building/national identities 6–9,
    92–93, 95–7, 102–3, 104–8, 112, 114,
    128–130, 133–7, 139, 165–7

230 *Index*

Namgyal, G. 69
Nattapong, S. 82, 85
Nehru, J. 42
Newcombe, H.and Alley, R. 201
Newman, J. 103
news television: in India 43–4, 46, 51–3;
  in Korea 194–5; in Malaysia 131–3; in
  Thailand 75–6
Nieva, A. 149
Norris P. and Inglehart, R. 64

Oakes, T. 29
Ong, J. 4, 8, 146, 151, 152, 156, 158
Ong, J. and Cabanes, J. 153
Ongmo, S. 65, 71
Ordinary people, representation on
  Filipino TV 146–7
Oren, T. and Shahaf, S. 14
Ota, T. 121

Padilla, A. 153
Pan, G. 170
Park, Y.-G. 186
Penjore, D. 58, 71n
Perfect Woman 117
Pertierra A.C. and Turner, G. 2, 9, 10
Peters, J.D. 156
Pieterse, J.N. 39
Poole, R.M. and Takaya, R. 115
Poowin, B. 85
popular entertainment genres: political
  function 79–81, 86; on Thai television
  77–9, 80–84
Powdyel, T. 58
Prakash, G. 42
Putnam. R.D. 63

Raeng Ngao 82, 85
Rafael, D.L. 147, 148, 154, 157, 159
Rajagopal, A. 38, 43
Remembering Television 5
RemSg, 103
Reyes, J. 148
Ride of Life, The 211
Rimban, L. 144, 153
Rodrigo, R. 144, 147, 148
Romauldez, E. 160n
Roth, L. 63
Roy, A. 42, 45
Rubens, J. 71n

SAFRT (State Administration of
  Film Radio and Television) 25
  passim, 29, 32

Saimon, F. 120
Sainath, P. 146
Sankaran, C. and Pillai, S. 3
Sata, M. and Hirahara, H. 114, 115
Scannell, P. 133
Schaffer, F.C. 160
Schilling, M. 113
Schurmann, F. 22
Scott-Clark C. and Levy, A. 65, 67, 69
Sen, B. 13
Servaes, J., Malikhao, P. and
  Pinprayong, T. 75, 87n
Shamsul, A.B. 129, 130, 140
Shashidhar, A. 41
Shields, P. and Muppidi, S. 44
Shim, D. and Jin, D.Y. 183, 184
Sidel, J. 147, 154, 155
Silk, M. 137
Silverstone, R. 152
Singapore historical dramas 92–3,
  100–102
Singapore model, the 13
Sirinya, W. 80, 81
Somkiat, T. 75
Son of Pulau Tekong 101
Song, W. 206
Star TV 44, 45, 47–9
state-controlled broadcasting 6–7,
  in Bhutan 60–61; in China 7; in
  Hong Kong 199–200; in India 7, 13,
  42–45; in Korea 183–4, in Malaysia
  131–2, 134–5; in the Philippines
  149–150; in Singapore 97–99; in
  Thailand, 74–5
Streckfuss, D. 79, 84
Stuart Santiago, A. 151
Su, H. 166
Sugg, C. and Power, G. 92
Sukamar, R. 38
Sun, W. 19, 22, 24, 33
Sun, W. and Chio, J. 29, 33
Sun, W. and Gorfinkel, L. 7, 11, 92
Sun, W. and Zhao, Y. 3, 19
Sun TV 49–5
Suzhu, 178

Tadiar, N. 149
Taiyu serial drama 167–9
Tan, K.P. 92
Tashi, T. 71n
Tay, J. 1, 4, 9, 13, 24
Teo, P. 103
Teodoro. L. 144
Teodoro L. and Kabatay, R. 149

Teoh, A. 130
Thai soap opera (*lakhon*) 80–85
Tipton, E. 112
To, Y.M. and Lau, T-Y 201
Tokyo Love Story 112, 119–122, 123
Tolentino, R. 148, 154, 160n
Tong, J.R. 26
Tovera, D. 148
Tsuyoshi, N. 172
Turner, G. 9, 62
Turner G. and Tay, J. 1–2, 14

Ubonrat, S. 74, 75
Udaya TV 49–50
Under the Lion Rock 213

Valisno, J. and Marcelo, S. 155
Van de Veer, P. 38
Van Driem, G. 71n
Venn, C. 47
Vogel, B., Grabow, K., Korte, K.-R. and Weissenbach, K. 75

Walker, A. 79, 85
Wang, F.I. 1, 8
Wang, J. 19
Wang, L.K. 134, 135
Wang, W.B., Bisson, G. and Aguete, M.R. 23
Wangdi, T. 62
Washburn, K. and Thornton, J. 63

When Heaven Burns 212–13
Williams, R. 76
Winn, M. 63
Woodier, J. 75
Woman Workaholic 122–3
Wong, C.H. and Chu, Y.W. 200
Wu, Y.Y. 171

Yang, I.F.-C. 165, 170, 176
Yean, S.C. 147, 155
Yeh, J.J. [1999] 177
Yeh, Y.H. 176, Yeshi, S. 59
Yomiuri, S. 115
Youngsamart, D. and Fisher, G. 87n
Yu, F.T. 22, 24

Zakaria, F. 38, 40
Zellen, B.
Zhang, X.L. 19, 24
Zhang, Y.-J. 195n
Zhao, Y.Z. 19, 25, 33
Zhao, Y.Z. and Guo, Z.Z. 19
Zhaung, W.R. and Fang, M.Q. 23
Zee TV 47, 49, 51
Zhou, H. 23
Zhou, T.Z. 171, 172
Zhou, Y. 27
Zhu, P.J. 176
Zhu, Y. 19
Zhu, Y. and Berry, C. 19
Zhu, Y., Keane, M. and Bai, R. 19

eBooks
from Taylor & Francis

Helping you to choose the right eBooks for your Library

Add to your library's digital collection today with Taylor & Francis eBooks. We have over 50,000 eBooks in the Humanities, Social Sciences, Behavioural Sciences, Built Environment and Law, from leading imprints, including Routledge, Focal Press and Psychology Press.

Choose from a range of subject packages or create your own!

Benefits for you
- Free MARC records
- COUNTER-compliant usage statistics
- Flexible purchase and pricing options
- All titles DRM-free.

Benefits for your user
- Off-site, anytime access via Athens or referring URL
- Print or copy pages or chapters
- Full content search
- Bookmark, highlight and annotate text
- Access to thousands of pages of quality research at the click of a button.

Free Trials Available
We offer free trials to qualifying academic, corporate and government customers.

eCollections

Choose from over 30 subject eCollections, including:

Archaeology	Language Learning
Architecture	Law
Asian Studies	Literature
Business & Management	Media & Communication
Classical Studies	Middle East Studies
Construction	Music
Creative & Media Arts	Philosophy
Criminology & Criminal Justice	Planning
Economics	Politics
Education	Psychology & Mental Health
Energy	Religion
Engineering	Security
English Language & Linguistics	Social Work
Environment & Sustainability	Sociology
Geography	Sport
Health Studies	Theatre & Performance
History	Tourism, Hospitality & Events

For more information, pricing enquiries or to order a free trial, please contact your local sales team:
www.tandfebooks.com/page/sales

www.tandfebooks.com